WHAT'S YOUR MARRIAGE LIKE?

How deep is communication in your marriage? Can you talk together about things that really matter?

Can you tell him how you feel when he comes home two hours late for dinner without using it as a springboard for argument about a hundred other dissatisfactions?

When was the last time you made love someplace other than your bed? Do you want to? Does your mate want to? How do you know?

Can you tell her how you feel when she comes home with a provocative new dress? Even if it means admitting that you feel threatened by a display of her sexuality?

Can you say to each other, "I'm afraid"?

LOVING FREE

is the story of one couple who asked themselves, and each other these questions, who
took the answers and built a strong, beautiful
relationship, from what they learned.

It shows how any couples can do the same,
just by trying—and caring—a little more.

"A real self-actualized couple. This book is a laboratory manual about experiencing and expressing what I call the *Freedom to Be*."

—Everett Shostrum, Ph.D.
author of *Between Man and Woman*

LOVING
FREE

Paula and Dick McDonald

BALLANTINE BOOKS • NEW YORK

Library of Congress Catalog Card Number: 72-90838

ISBN 0-345-25649-2-195

This edition published by arrangement with
Grosset & Dunlap, Inc.

Manufactured in the United States of America

First Ballantine Books Edition: August 1974
Eighth Printing: September 1976

To all those who helped—we wish them good things. And to one above all, Tom Gard, who lives the spirit of this book.

Contents

Preface

IS THIS BOOK NECESSARY? To anyone standing in front
of a bookcounter, today, it would certainly seem ques-
tionable. The market is flooded with books on sex
written by doctors, swingers, wife-swappers, and hook-
ers; and with books in which marriages are compared,
analyzed, and categorized by psychologists and psychiatrists. The question, "Is there anything left to be
said?" certainly seems valid.

We think there is a lot left to be said. The current
wave of literature designed to liven up your sex life
does a masterful job of guiding you through the bedroom, assuming you are completely comfortable saying
to your partner, "Our sex life is dull. I'm left unsatisfied. Let's change things." Many of us do not have
such total and open communication; many of us are not
at ease discussing that most delicate of subjects—our
own sexual needs and fears.

The psychologically oriented marriage manuals
tackle the part of the relationship that takes place outside the bedroom: communication, human needs, how
to fight, and how to love. But very often the approach
is clinical. A doctor tells us what we already know:
People need to be open and honest with each other.
People want to be close and trust someone with their
inner feelings. People crave love and understanding
in their intimate relationships. But the psychologists
don't tell us how to take that first awesome step. They
don't tell us how to overcome the agony and hurt of,
"He never talks to me." "She doesn't understand me."
"I don't know who I am." They don't tell us how to

begin from the point we are at today. Often psychologists offer a theoretical approach. They don't seem to be hurting the way the rest of us hurt. That first step is past for them. They ask us to join them on a mountaintop, which is where we would like to be. But for many of us, the foothills are obscure and frightening.

This book is not a marriage manual, nor a sex manual, nor a how-to manual. Rather, it is a how-it-was story, written by two ordinary people who started at the bottom. We came to marriage with many of the hangups, fears, and biases that other couples have. We found ourselves mired in the same dull ruts, the routine sex life, and the occasional feelings of misunderstanding and aloneness. We often went through hell just trying to tell each other our needs and fears. There was love, but there was pain and uncertainty too. We, like our friends, got bogged down with children and diapers, conformity and in-laws, suburbia, TV, lack of privacy, fights, and, of course, sex. Sex was a big hang-up. We're no different from others of our generation. We had been given a license to practice sixteen years ago without the ability to fully and joyfully use it. Sex was only part of the picture, however. At times, we lost track of where we were going, of who we were, and what we wanted to be to each other. And yet, we believed that what we had was good. But by risking those first steps, could we help each other make it better? We cared enough to try no matter what the price. And we finally broke free!

This book is the story of how and why. It was conceived after years of watching many of our friends struggle with the same problems: sex, boredom with each other, lack of understanding, lack of communication. It was born after watching the agonies of divorce within our families and among our friends and after seeing people painfully hanging onto a relationship after the love had gone.

This is the story of how it was for us, how we made it work and recaptured the excitement that can exist between two people. There's no moralizing here, no rights or wrongs for anyone except us. We have few axes to grind. We're not professionals nor are we psychologists. We're two people who love each other and believe there is something worth fighting for in marriage. Our only qualifications are honesty and the realization that it's tough to create an intimate, enduring relationship in today's world. We've been there. We can't solve your problems, but we can share with you, step-by-step, the way we've worked out our own. After sixteen years of marriage, we still believe that love is the best shot we've got. We're still willing to put our all into it, and are more enthusiastic than ever about our life together—in or out of bed.

Uniting Through Sex

1.

Starting Down the Road

ONCE UPON A TIME there was a man and woman who got married and started practicing rhythm. He was a bright commmunications executive. She had once gotten an A in calculus and thought she could count. Three years later they had three children. She was almost hysterical, becoming indifferent toward sex and convinced she couldn't count worth a damn. He was frustrated, masturbating from time to time, buried financially by baby shoes, and convinced she had lied about the A in calculus. Does that little story sound familiar to any of you? We're being flip because we almost have to. After sixteen years of marriage, the agony of that period is still so real in our minds that we have to laugh about it or I think we'd both cry.

We came to marriage, we thought, with open eyes and a healthy attitude toward sex. We loved each other and were eager to share our bodies. Three years later we were both so hung up on sex that we were pecking each other on the cheek after work instead of giving each other bear hugs. At bedtime, I undressed quietly in the bathroom so Dick wouldn't see me, and instead of sleeping in each other's arms, we were sleeping about as far apart as two people could sleep in a double bed without falling out. We hardly touched each other for fear of starting something we couldn't finish or weren't prepared to take the consequences of finishing.

In addition to being the most fertile female that ever walked, I was also the most irregular. And we were caught up in a moral bind of being Catholic and having to use rhythm as our only means of birth control.

Unless you've lived by the rhythm system it's almost impossible to convey the frustration and fear that this can cause in your sex life—your whole life. We are both, by nature, affectionate people who love to snuggle, sometimes with really no other thought in mind that being close. But during those rhythm years, sex was on our minds so much, so negatively that very little snuggling was done around our house. Our failure rate at rhythm had dramatically convinced us that the only way to beat this thing was to repress our natural impulses toward one another so tightly that there would be no slips till the calendar said go. For us the calendar said go very rarely. We had honestly tried every known means to figure out my fertile periods, yet nothing seemed to work except longer and longer periods of abstinence. By the time our third child was conceived, we had worked up to seventeen block-out days a month. This was followed by a few safe days before my period began, then we started the whole miserable cycle again.

Dick's father is an obstetrician and gave all the help possible. When we say we tried everything, we're not exaggerating. There were little litmus-paper test tapes that I inserted in my vagina every day with a syringe-like apparatus. When the tapes turned pink to blue, you knew you were fertile. Mine never turned blue, ever! I stuck those darn tapes into me every day for so many years that I felt like a recorder. Push my button and I'll play my tape for you—but always in pink. Dick never really had much confidence in them from the beginning, which proved right since they showed that I never ovulated and yet I managed to get pregnant twice while using them.

For the first time in our marriage we were having a communications breakdown. It was becoming awkward for us to discuss sex and birth control simply because it wasn't working. We were both frustrated and unhappy, and the procedures were degrading. I preferred to do the tape test when Dick was at work. However, since it entailed getting undressed and lying in bed with the syringe inserted vaginally for five minutes, mornings or evenings were better. Dick would pretend he was asleep if he rolled over and saw me in the morning, or I'd wait till I thought he was sleeping at night. Here was a problem we were trying to work out together, but since it was a humiliating experience each time, Dick was trying to give me the privacy that I needed to maintain some semblance of dignity. A wall of silence began to close around the subject. He didn't want to ask constantly, "Did it turn blue today?" That would have made me look like a failure because all I could ever produce were pink tapes. So it simply evolved into a silent way of life, as did temperature charts.

Supposedly a woman's temperature is six-tenths of a degree below normal during ovulation. If you take your temperature faithfully every day at the same time of day, you can determine the fertile period. The best time to do this is before you get out of bed each morning, because you should be relaxed and probably have had no outside stimulant or excitement to cause your temperature to vary abnormally. Unfortunately, a cold or tension or almost anything can cause a 1/10-degree variance so the method isn't too reliable. And certainly waking to the sight of your two toddlers feeding the baby peanuts in the shell can make that temp soar. Besides, how do you scream with a thermometer in your mouth?

The most frustrating aspect of our early years of marriage was the calendar calculations. We both lived with the month's calendar indelibly imprinted on our brains. At any given moment we could tell you the date of the Tuesday after next—that was the next time we could make love. That was the day I could throw my arms around Dick when he came home from work and say, "Hey, I love you." We could snuggle in his chair at night and just be close with no fear of where it might lead. Month after month we lived this way, afraid to get too close, always with the fear hanging over our heads that my menstrual period would be late because somewhere we had goofed again.

It's incredible how two people could become so tense three days before a menstrual period started, but it happened in our home every month. By the time the red-letter day rolled around, we were both so nervous that we were snapping at the children and at each other. If I was a day late, and I often was, we silently began to pray, curse or despair, as the mood struck us. Two or three days late and Dick was calculating the obstetrics fee and hospital bill in his head, and I had all the symptoms of pregnancy—morning sickness, backaches, tiredness, labor pains. I'd run to the bathroom one hundred times a day to check the tampax that I'd inserted each morning, looking for any sign that would have eased my mind. At least I was helping to keep the tampon industry solvent—I'd use several boxes before my period ever started. When, if, that first little spot appeared, we'd both feel like getting drunk. We had been given a reprieve for another thirty days.

The unnaturalness of a life such as this was very effectively putting a wedge into our closeness. There are times when two people need to comfort each other—when things go wrong for a man and he needs a woman to put her arms around him and just hold him and say, "Honey, it's going to be alright." But we couldn't always do that. It was almost a relief for us when I did get pregnant each time because at least we could be ourselves for nine months.

During this period our attitudes toward sex began to frighten both of us. Rationally, we believed we were

4

doing the "right" thing because of our religious beliefs, but how do you intellectualize with your heart and body? Realistically, we were regressing in our sexual outlook.

Dick could never keep track of exactly where we were on the calendar. That was my job, but it was becoming uncomfortable for both of us to talk about. I couldn't bear the thought of getting into bed at night, with him hoping that the "dry-dock" days were over for the month, and hearing that sigh in the dark when I said that they weren't. It finally got to the point where I could no longer say no in words so I devised a signal system with flags. He had a planter on his dresser and I made two small flags to stick into the dirt—red for "no" days—white for "yes" days. The first thing he did when he came home each night was to empty his pockets onto the dresser top so that he couldn't miss the flag. After several months of that system, I made sure I wasn't in the bedroom when he changed. The look on his face when he saw that he would have to hold back his yearnings was almost worse than the sigh in the dark.

I was terrified when he had to go on a business trip during the no-sex periods. Instinctively I knew this was no way to send a man out-of-town for a week. Sure, he loved me but he was also very human and needed arms around him, warmth, and a shoulder to cry on once in a while.

I knew he understood that the restraint was a mutual decision, but I always deeply felt that it was my fault (while he felt it was his) and that this was my problem with which we were confronted. How can two people live with any kind of spontaneity when they spend the month waiting to see if the woman is going to menstruate? The worst frustration was the futility of living from one month to the next, knowing that next month was going to be just as bleak.

I remember the night our third child was conceived. It was on the seventeenth day. The next day was safe but Dick was coming home from a business trip that night. I rationalized that the chances had to be one in a million of getting pregnant, so we cut a tiny corner and made love. Immediately after intercourse, while Dick was still in me, the consequence hit me, "Paula, you blew it!" My God, what a terrible thought to have! Love is supposed to be beautiful. Procreation is supposed to be beautiful. But we had reduced this aspect of our lives to "you blew it."

The effect the rhythm method was having on sex and on our whole marriage was tragic. Dick was masturbating occasionally, which I didn't know at the time. How could you blame him? I was so afraid of getting pregnant again that intercourse was filled with dread. Even when it was supposed to be a safe day, worry and doubt hung over us. We couldn't throw ourselves joyfully and wantonly into lovemaking when visions of calendars were swirling through our minds. We found ourselves enjoying it less and less. At one point we calculated that at our current rate of reproduction, we'd have seventeen children by the time I reached menopause. That thought alone is enough to make anyone run shrieking from the room.

The aspect of sex by calendar that was driving the biggest wedge into our lives was the loss of spontaneity. Picture two people in love who already know on Monday that they can't make love on Friday. We began to devise all kinds of fillers just to avoid getting into bed at the same time. That damn double bed seemed to be mocking us. Dick started watching the late-late show. He also found a bachelor friend who would come to our house to play gin with him until the wee hours of the morning, a few times a week. We filled our social calendar to overflowing because it was just too difficult to stay home together and not want to make love.

The turning point came while I was still in the hospital after the birth of our third child. After nine months of relative freedom, it was time to return to gut-level frustration. Nothing had changed. I in the hospital, and Dick at home, were both agonizing over the same question: "Where do we go from here?" Total celibacy or our old game, which made it just a matter of time again? I'll share something with you which I only had the courage to tell Dick recently. I laid in the hospital bed wishing for a mild form of cancer of the cervix to develop so that I could have a hysterectomy. At twenty-four, I was that desperate.

A few weeks later we went back to the rhythm method again, but we knew we couldn't live that way any longer. At least not if we wanted to have any type of deep relationship together. We desperately wanted to use artificial birth control but each was afraid to mention the subject for fear of treading on the other's religious beliefs. Eventually, little by little, we began to talk about our feelings and our frustrations. For the first time we shared what we *wanted* to do, not what we felt we *should* do. Dick was worried about the pill, which was new and controversial. My obstetrician was not enthusiastic about the I.U.D., which was also new. And we weren't home free in our own attitudes yet; we were still very hung up on the teachings of the Church. We talked ourselves blue, tried rationalizing, and swung back and forth like a seesaw. Then one night we decided that we had to live as two human beings, regardless of the consequences.

We chose rubbers, and it was like giving a dying man water. It was about eleven at night and Dick went running out to find an all-night drugstore, ran back in, kissed me, and ran out again. We were so excited. We had a new lease on life, we thought, but only part of life as it turned out.

Bucking the Church was traumatic for us, and the condoms were slow to unravel the web of fear we had built around sex for almost four years. We had made a decision but we weren't really ready to live with it yet. I worried that a rubber would leak and therefore rushed to get Dick out of me immediately after intercourse before he lost his erection and the sperm ran out. He'd have to hurry to the bathroom and flush it down the toilet. There has to be some psychological hang-up for a man, seeing his sperm literally go down the drain.

We both still wondered if what we were doing was

wrong. Now sex began to take on the furtive implications of making love in the back seat of a car. We really didn't look at the condoms in broad daylight because of our guilt feelings. If we thought we might be making love that night, one of us would sneak it under the pillow beforehand, so we didn't have to get up to find it. There we were, trying to find a happy sex life and quietly unwrapping rubbers in the dark. That is, when we could find them. Half the time they had slipped onto the floor. You can imagine the scene if you haven't been through it yourself. Passionate sex play, climax approaching, hand fumbling frantically under the pillow, gruff voice: "Where the hell is it?" Meek voice: "I don't know; I put it under your pillow." Turn on the lights and crawl around the floor on all fours looking for it. "Aha, you rascal, there you are." By this time, Dick has usually lost half his erection, and we had to start again, making one-handed love while clutching the rubber in the other hot little hand.

Even worse, if we didn't make love that night for some reason, I'd flip back the pillow in the morning while making the bed and there would be that damn thing staring at me.

I'll never forget the time Marion, our cleaning lady, found an escapee under the bed and calmly handed it to me saying, "Did you want me to vacuum this?" I wanted to sink through the floor. Besides, I had convinced myself prior to this that Marion had the hottest sex life in town, and, furthermore, that she could read my mind. She could certainly read my red face. Marion wasn't the only one to find them. The children found them once, thought they were balloons, and asked me to blow them up. "No, darling, you can't take that outside and play catch with Billy."

Occasionally we'd run out and I'd have to buy them because Dick wasn't aware that we'd used the last one. It would have been easier for me to make a public confession of beating up old ladies than walk into a drugstore and ask for a box of rubbers. I tried to find a drugstore that did the least amount of business, with

8

the prescription counter in the back. Now for the approach. Is it best to just march in with a sophisticated swagger and say, "Gimme a box of rubbers," or slink in and whisper in the pharmacist's ear, "Prophylactics, please"? I remember just marching in there, clearing my throat twenty times, and asking for a package of condoms. "What size?" Panic—I never measured Dick; I didn't know I was supposed to. The druggist, taking pity on me, repeated, "What size box?" (Panic again. Mine?) No, of course not, the condom box. Give me the biggest box you've got—500, 5,000, a million (so I won't have to come back till my menopause). Does he think we screw that much? Oh, let me out of here!

Another approach that I'd pondered was struggling in, carrying all three babies, and gasping "condoms." Hopefully, this would evoke sympathy and put the druggist immediately on our side. In my fantasy the look that crossed his face said more than sympathy. It seemed more like, "Look, lady, there aren't any directions with these, but I'll be glad to explain what to do. You don't seem to have the idea."

Five or six years into our marriage, after agonizing over our religious beliefs, I began taking the pill. We had spent countless hours discussing it, reading books, talking with clergy, and friends. But it always came back to the same answer: "This is a matter of conscience and if you choose to do this, you must be at peace with your conscience." How can your conscience be clear when you are fighting a lifetime of teaching contrary to what your heart is telling you must be right? We both wanted to scream, "Somebody, anybody, just tell us that it's alright—that we can be free." But of course no one would, and they were right. We were looking for a scapegoat to whom we could shift the responsibility. We finally had to come to the realization that the responsibility was ours alone. We had to face ourselves, our relationship with our God, and with each other. Facing ourselves was hard. But we did it and concluded we were going to live in the way God wants all people to live; freely, with love and joy.

Your hang-ups don't disappear overnight, however. It took all my courage to walk into the obstetrician's office and ask for that first prescription. He was an old family friend and a Catholic. I was sure he'd condemn us in his mind for going against the Church's stand, or worse, try to talk me out of it. He probably could have, but he never batted an eye.

In retrospect, it may seem rather silly and childish to have worried so about what he would think of us. But nine years ago, the pill was at the height of controversy in the Church. It was what young Catholic married couples discussed most in those days. I belonged to an eight-woman bridge group affiliated with our church, and for years the pill dominated every discussion. The women were more prolific than I—most had at least four children already, spaced about a year apart. Listening to them talk about their lives and their fears each month, convinced me that the future was really bleak. We were all in the same boat and no one could seem to keep it from sinking.

As we struggled more deeply with the problem at home, a tremendous anger was building inside both of us at the injustice there seemed to be in life. We would rage at times over the idea that we would suffer the torments of the damned here on earth and probably be damned anyway for doing the same things our non-Catholic friends could do with no guilt, no hang-ups. We hated them at times for being born Episcopal or Jewish, and we envied them for being able to express their love for each other with freedom, joy, and spontaneity while we were forced to feel guilty for that same love expression.

Probably I was well on my way to becoming a frigid woman at that point, even though I loved my husband and thought we communicated as well as two people could. But sex the way we were being forced to play it was just not fun—not joyful. I could feel myself withdrawing from the physical side of love simply because I was too hung up on pregnancy, and on the teachings of the Church; I was afraid to really let myself go and enjoy it. Once Dick aroused me and we made love, there was no question of the pleasure I received. But many nights when he would approach me I would have to fake an enthusiasm to match his. Perhaps this is the point when those excuses start that are bantered around in so many jokes—I have a headache, I'm too tired, I have a hangnail on my big toe.

Fortunately, it never got to that point or he might have been turned off forever. I was always conscious of never saying no to him—never playing games. Although most men have fragile egos, my husband in particular has great sensitivity. He just didn't deserve games and excuses. Nor should he have to feel that he was the cause of this, that he hadn't turned me on, that he had failed me sexually in some way, because that wasn't the case. But knowing him well, that's the way he would have reacted or felt deep down. I also knew his needs, any man's needs, and had been around enough to realize that if he was hurt or felt rejected, those needs could or would eventually be filled by someone other than me. A few years of traveling before marriage were responsible for a great deal of exposure to the realities of life in this world, and the habits of many married men on the road. Dick had always shared himself and his needs with me. I was able to know instinctively at that point that he could be hurt so deeply by a sexual rejection that the wound between us might never heal. There we were after six years of marriage, turned-off wife, turned-down husband. A thousand paperback novels tell you what the next chapter will be. He has an affair, or they get a divorce, or they just go on surface living for twenty years for the sake of the kids. But that didn't happen to us.

What did happen? Did a miracle come into our lives in the form of a little pink pill that instantly solved all our problems? Not quite! Getting from that point to black satin bedsheets (which I'm still embarrassed to give the laundryman—so you see I'm not truly sexually liberated yet) was not an overnight phenomenon. The pill was the turning point certainly, but it took a great deal to erase the hang-ups of six years in the other direction. Just to be able to make love without looking at the calendar, without breaking the mood and racing for the john to flush or douche, to be able to lie in bed as long as we liked, talking afterward, was enough to satisfy us for quite a while. To feel that we could show our love, without fear, whenever we wanted was such a dramatic change that we noticed nothing else missing. But when the novelty of that began to fade in six months or a year (we can't remember exactly), both of us began to get the vague, gnawing feeling that something was still missing from our sex lives.

It's sad that we didn't talk about it. Why is it that sex is the hardest thing in the world to discuss on a personal level? We can all sit around, pretending we're broadminded, and discuss techniques and attitudes objectively as long as we don't have to apply it directly to ourselves. I just couldn't say to Dick, "I don't think what we're doing is too exciting." He couldn't say to me, "We're in a rut." It was too personal. We know that love is the key. If you love the other person, you don't want to hurt him. To say that your sex life is not what it could be is a reflection on your mate's ability to perform.

Broaching the subject outright was obviously more than either of us could handle at that point, so we suffered along in silence for a time. Suffer is a bad word; we don't mean to imply that there was anything repulsive or distasteful about sex to either of us at the time. It just wasn't that great—firecrackers didn't go off in the sky and the earth didn't shake, and we didn't find ourselves crumpled in a heap of exhausted passions after a five-hour session of incredibly wild lovemaking. The movies and *Portnoy's Complaint* were telling us that that was happening in all those other dark bedrooms on our block. All we did was get into bed and make love. I guess we suspected that if we had X-ray eyes, all the other homes but ours would be rated X.

Before starting on the pill I'd never had an orgasm. Now I had experienced several. Not every time but enough to make me realize that sex could be fun and not an accommodation. Having one orgasm seemed to open up a whole new world for both of us. It was so fantastic that naturally I wanted to try for one every time instead of just occasionally and was eager to make love more often. Dick was delighted seeing me able to climax and pleased he could make it happen for me. About this time, he brought home a few marriage manuals that he had picked up and read on a business trip. For the next few days he'd ask off and on, "Have you read *Dr. Wham Bamm's Ideal Marriage* yet?" I was devouring them but playing it cool. Women probably read dozens of these "How to" books in a lifetime but never have the nerve or chance to put the suggestions into practice. Result: They probably get as frustrated as I was, wondering why all the couples we knew had great sex orgies and we didn't. Looking back, we're convinced that most have a sex life far worse than ours was in our "rut" period, and quite a few are living in absolute hell, thinking they are alone with their problems. Let's face it, premature ejaculation, frigidity, or lack of understanding of your partner's sex needs aren't topics that come up too frequently at the bridge table. You have to be able to break the ice at home yourselves.

Slowly, tentatively, we began to discuss the books we'd read. It was slow going, however. I can remember absolutely dying to say, "Why don't you spend more time on my breasts—I'd love that," but something still held me back. Being very small busted I was embarrassed that they wouldn't turn Dick on as much as if I were a size 38D. It was easier not to mention it. But I wanted him to maybe just to make me feel that they were important to him even if they were small.

We kept talking and getting new books. As the talk loosened up bit by bit we loosened up. Both of

13

us were very conscious of each other's reactions and it was like tossing a hot potato back and forth. Every time it got a little easier because each knew that the other was trying too. Until this point we had been very formal in our language, calling everything by its proper name—a penis was a penis, never a prick; breasts were breasts, never boobs. The only exception was the nickname I had for Dick's penis, given in a silly mood one night. I remember laughing and calling it MacArthur because it always came back.

It's funny that we were so proper in language because both of us knew all the four-letter words and used them mentally when thinking about sex. But we were afraid that if we spoke the terms we thought, the other person would think it was crude or shocking. The two of us regarded sex as a beautiful thing, something almost sacred and not to be sullied or mocked. Don't get me wrong—that's a fantastic viewpoint and we still believe that. But sex, like love, encompasses many moods. It is beautiful, but it should also be fun, silliness, tenderness—whatever two people can share together. And that was the part which was missing for us. Because of our upbringing, we had always treated our sex life with reverence and respect. We had put it on such a pedestal that it was as solemn as a cathedral. Like children in church, we never laughed while making love, we never talked, we never fooled around. And like youngsters, there were times when we both wanted so badly to giggle.

There were times when I had a wild desire to just bite Dick on the butt as he rolled over. (Doesn't everybody once in a while?) Of course you could never do that in a cathedral, could you? We couldn't then but since that time we've moved out and together built a home for ourselves—a place that encompasses the solemnity of a cathedral, the delights of a geisha house, and the intimacy of a retreat.

In order to break the ice sometimes, you have to use a sledge hammer. Thank God, my husband isn't a subtle man. One day he simply said, "Hey, why is it we never talk while we're making love? Why are we so damn serious about it?" So we had a serious discussion and decided that both of us would like to lighten it up and proceeded to try. Well, what followed was like a scene from a bad movie. We had talked about talking but we didn't know what to talk about because the naturalness wasn't there. We were trying so hard that we literally couldn't think of a thing to say. We both took a couple of swipes at "I love you," "I really love you," "I really love you, too"— and then collapsed in embarrassed silence. Meanwhile, we were both thinking, "Oh, shit, this is ridiculous," when we should have been saying just that aloud. But the ice was broken and we found it getting easier every time.

We began talking about terminology at this time and agreed on what was comfortable for us. That was easier because we were honest and could say, "I've never liked the term *pussy* because some creep making obscene phone calls used to say it to me all the time." So we'd run through the possible alternatives for pussy—cunt, snatch, box, muff—and chose those which came most naturally. The next thing I knew, Dick was saying in bed one night, "Hey, your boobs are starting to grow!" A double triumph! Not only boobs, but they were growing, too. A few small strides, but what a long way we had come from our early days. All of a sudden, sex was fun.

This was a rather belated discovery in our marriage, but we have worked hard over the past few years to make up for lost time. There are so many books and manuals on the market that tell you what to do but none seem to tell you how it feels, how to get there, what's good or bad, or what simply doesn't work. We've struggled laughingly through most of the impossible feats and stumbled across a few things guaranteed to liven up any bedroom. We'd like to share them with you.

2.

Attitudes and Bedside Manners

WHILE YOU WERE GROWING up was your sex education as bad as ours? We were taught only the bare necessities and then filled with dire warnings to help preserve our purity. As a result, some great stock lines emerged from that era: "Don't wear patent leather shoes because boys can see the reflection of your underpants!" "Don't stand next to puddles on sunny days for the same reason." "Boys, always put a telephone book down first if you're going to have a girl sit on your lap." If you had an erection, it could thud against three pounds of paper and she'd never know. "Don't wear red, girls. It excites men." Incredible as it seems, these little goodies were rather universal. We've laughed about them with friends who grew up in all parts of the country; most had heard variations of these regardless of their backgrounds. Dick went to public schools and I attended private schools a thousand miles away, but each of us had these warnings instilled in us as part of our growing-up process.

The formal sex education each of us received from our respective parents was totally different. His consisted of a long car ride with his father who beautifully and clearly explained the facts of life, from a physical viewpoint only. For me, in the eighth grade, my mother handed me a book entitled *What Every Young Girl Should Know*. That was it! No conversation before or after, and it has never come up again to this day. That book, however, will always remain indelibly imprinted in my mind because it caused one of the most traumatic experiences of my life. Its *total* explanation of intercourse was, "pregnancy occurs from a long

16

and loving embrace." If you're thirteen and naive, what does that tell you? I had started going to parties at which postoffice and other necking games were played and, of course, I immediately thought I was pregnant. The next two weeks until my period started were the longest single unit of time in my life. Who could I tell? Certainly not my mother! Fortunately a girl friend straightened me out a short time later.

The reason we mention such ancient history is that both approaches to sex education were fairly typical of our era, and both have had a direct relationship to our marriage. Most of our friends today, and then, learned in one of those two ways; a few were told nothing at all. So why is that important in our marriage? Because the attitudes that were formed for us by our parents, our church, our schools and teachers, our friends, and society in general have had a negative effect on our sex life for the past twelve years. If someone sent us a dime for every hour we've logged in trying to un-tangle the web of misunderstanding, lack of knowl-edge and fears, we could probably retire to some island in the Caribbean. And we don't seem to be that unusual. Most of our friends entered marriage exposed to similar teachings. When sex is presented throughout childhood as either dirty, nonexistent (if we don't talk about it, it will disappear), or physical only (insert penis A into vagina B to produce baby C), it's not easy to make the transition on your wed-ding day to a totally free relationship. "O.K., for three years I've been told to fight you off in the back seat of the car but starting today, sweetie, anything goes." Our minds were unable to make that kind of a switch but we didn't even realize it for years.

Lack of information has caused almost as many problems. Did anyone ever tell you about a clitoris when you were growing up? Or that if it's stroked gently it feels great and that's how most women have an orgasm? Of course not! I had never heard of a clito-ris and no one had told Dick, either. Then why are we surprised today at the number of wives who are frigid or turned off due to an innocent lack of knowledge on

17

their husband's part? Why shouldn't intercourse become strictly an accommodation for a woman who's never had her body excited? Without stimulation, screwing is about as much fun as brushing your teeth. Some couples discover purely by accident that the clitoris exists, and that the underside of the penis head has the most sensation. They stumble across the fact that kissing or sucking nipples or the insides of thighs feels great for both partners. Some never do though. The women innocently, or in jest, drop remarks at the bridge table or over the morning coffee with a neighbor about their sex lives. "Well, I suppose I have to give Bob some tonight," or "I wish he'd keep that thing in his pants, or find somewhere else to put it and leave me alone." Keep that last line going and he will.

Dick hears the male version of the comments far more often, and it is always done jokingly when the subject of sex comes up at lunch, or in the office, or when he is out with the guys. "My wife? She forgot how!" or "Tonight is my night for this month." A fellow recently gave Dick a copy of a man's marital calendar for the month with the appropriate wifely excuse marked in for each day. "I'm tired. I have a headache. It's my period. It's my fertile time. The children will hear us. Again? You just got some last week!" The last entry was "Oh, alright, but get it over with quick."

Naturally, it's always the negative comments you hear. Couples who have a good sex life usually don't say anything, or they just sit looking bewildered by what they hear. For the most part, people seem to be unaware that their other half is talking about them. Women talk with women, and men talk with men, and both groups would probably be horrified if they knew the snide swipes at their sex life that were being dropped in their social or business set.

We tried an interesting experiment for ourselves once. Dick sat through a poker game one night trying to hear the comments being made through a woman's ears, and I tried to listen to what the gals were saying at a coffee klatch as if I were he. For both of us it was a ghastly revelation, but it shouldn't have been a shock. After we talked about what was really being said, we realized that it was the vocal surfacing of many of the same problems and anxieties we had had —natural outgrowths of our upbringing, our lack of sex education, our attitudes. The only difference was that when sex was mediocre for us, we never made cracks about it because we didn't want to hurt each other. We just kept quiet during the years it took us to pull the spider web apart.

Our parents honestly tried to do a good job. Our teachers, church, school system, society all were doing what they sincerely felt was best for us. It was the proper approach for that era, and who can you really condemn? Each of us is a product of our generation, our parents' generation, and their parents' generation. In our case, we had to muddy an awful lot of water wading out of our hang-ups to get to shore. Every once in a while Dick gets angry thinking back to the times during which we grew up. "Damn," he'll say. "Think of all the years we stumbled around in the dark. Do you realize how unprepared we were for marriage?" I don't get mad—only sad.

Now it seems so simple to put two and two together and see why I didn't have an orgasm for several years after we were married. Dick had been taught, and taught well, the anatomical side of sex—how a baby was made, grew, and was delivered. No one thought to tell him how to make love passionately to his future wife (namely me). No one told him how to turn me on, and let me enjoy sex the ninety-nine times out of one hundred when we were not trying to produce a child. And, of course, who was going to tell me how to make love to a man? Where to kiss him, where to hold him, where to stroke him, how to make it exciting for him after hundreds of nights. Picture some poor biology teacher trying to include that in his 10th-grade course and immediately being thrown in the clink!

Your parents certainly couldn't teach you because they were trying to keep you from thinking about sex, period. They didn't want you to get pregnant, or get someone pregnant before marriage, so after struggling through the birds and bees, the subject was dropped. "Now you know, but don't think about it any more till you're older and married and can handle it." If they gave you an inkling that sex was neat or pleasant or natural, how were they going to stop you from doing it before marriage?

The most natural result for many married women today would be total lack of interest in sex. They were taught to "fight 'em off" at any price, and men were never taught how to turn on their loves. The poor male was never told that he was supposed to. After marriage he went along for years inserting penis into vagina as he was taught, and that still felt good for him. Not exciting maybe, but it felt good. What he didn't know is that for his wife it just didn't feel like anything special. It was just another household duty to perform whenever his glands got too full. It reinforced all her old concepts: Men really are animals, sex isn't much fun for women, and let's get by with as little as possible. As a result, her husband gets angry at the lack of enthusiasm and commiserates with the other men at the office who make the same wisecracks and seem to have the same problem. This leads to the assumption that most women must be like that after a few years of marriage, so what can you do?

Before the two of us could feel totally free and at ease with deriving pleasure from each other's body we had to dynamite one basic concept: Sex is dirty. Dick believes the blame for that belongs on the doorstep of the churches and he's right, for they had the strongest hand in developing the concept. Shaking off that idea after marriage was harder for me than for Dick because it was drummed into girls harder and longer. We were the keepers of the flame—purity. It was our job to come out of the backseat wrestling matches every Saturday night unviolated. It was our job to say no to everything through five or six years of dating because the guy was always going to try to get in your pants, right? With tongue in cheek, Dick says that the boys in his hometown were never like that. Ha! Boys were the aggressors, we were told—they had the animal drive. All we had to do was keep our legs crossed and our pants on until we got to the altar and everything would suddenly be O.K. I'm not quite sure what was meant by O.K. because it certainly seems that you'd go on fighting them off mentally after marriage, just from sheer habit.

The teachers at my school coined a great word to cover every situation without really talking about sex. We were to remain "Marylike" (acting like the Virgin Mary would) in our relationships with boys. The term could be stretched to cover a multitude of things—Marylike conduct, Marylike ways of dressing, Marylike language, Marylike thoughts, and Marylike posture. (In case you can't figure that last one out, it's not sitting with your legs apart or throwing out your chest.) You have to admit that Marylike was a graphic image. You could apply it to any part of your life and know immediately where you stood as far as purity was concerned. Whatever it was, Mary wouldn't do it! At the same time, the boys were operating on a purely natural level. Nobody was telling them to be Josephlike. When they found themselves in the back seat with a hard-on, their instincts said, "Go ahead and see what happens." This only helped to reinforce the idea that "men are animals, right?" (This is a concept that infuriates Dick and most men who have heard it. I occasionally still hear friends say, "Men are such animals when it comes to sex." It always startles me because I thought it was an exclusive secret shared by the faculty and all-girl student body at my school.)

Fortunately, I never really bought that concept because I always thought that boys were great however they were made. Getting out from under the Marylike and "sex is dirty" concepts was a little harder. Although being Marylike was a sensible guide within the world in which I was growing up, it never seemed totally realistic. Mary hadn't had much fun in her life by my reckoning, and I wasn't sure that I was up to seventy years of adhering to those standards. I thought

21

I had totally rejected the whole idea by late high school, but years later it would come popping back into my mind when certain references to sex were made. Anything in sex that was fun or exciting couldn't possibly be Marylike. Would Mary have let Joseph kiss her breasts or would she have stroked his penis? Oh, God! You feel like you're going to be struck by lightning just thinking about it, right? Maybe it's easier to understand why women with my upbringing had a hard time handling something like oral sex in marriage. It might feel fantastic but it almost has to be a sin or something equally deadly.

"Sex is dirty" came across in many subtle ways for boys and girls. "Don't touch yourself THERE! It's not nice!" Everybody has heard that line as a small child. It's usually shrieked or whispered (nothing in between) by a mother or a teacher. "Don't scratch yourself in public." It was assumed that you knew all the various places that couldn't be scratched once you were outside of the bathroom. As young children we begin to believe that there's something wrong with those parts of the body if we're supposed to pretend that they're not there. What happens if you tried hard to be good for twenty years and not touch yourself THERE, no matter how it might itch? Then you got married and that night your husband wanted to touch you THERE. Lotsa luck!

"Don't look" was another early no-no and as a result, it made nudity a problem for many of us in marriage. Boys run around naked in the locker room, sometimes swim nude, and eventually become pretty comfortable with the idea of exposing and seeing their bodies. Not girls—no communal showers for us. We always had separate stalls with flowered curtains in the locker room. Boys and men have considered the female body beautiful. And it's been available for them to look at, dream or lust over, and get used to, even if it had to be done behind closed doors or under the blankets at night with a flashlight.

This has not been so for women. Who had pictures of male nudes to pass around at the slumber party twenty years ago? Who sculpted a male nude with an erection and put it in the museum for girls to look at? Instead of being taught that the male body is equally beautiful, we got the impression that it must be something gross from comments such as, "Make sure he keeps that *thing* in his pants." What thing? The first time I saw a man with an erection I couldn't believe it! No one prepared me for the fact that it was that big and stuck out so far. I was shocked but fascinated. The reaction could just as easily have been revulsion and fear. "My God! It'll never fit."

Many of us who didn't have a chance to learn to be comfortable with our bodies expected that in marriage we would automatically feel at ease with another person's body. Of course this didn't happen. So the problems were carried to our marriages and handled in the same way that we had seen our parents handle them. Never undress in front of each other. Don't let the children see us naked. Make love wearing our nightclothes. We know about an all-girl family in which the mother will not allow the father to leave the toilet seat up because this is embarrassing for her and for her daughters. Another friend recalls that as a small child it was a rare and fun treat to be able to take a bath with Daddy. However, Daddy always kept his underpants on. What goes on in a child's mind? "If you have to wear underpants and I don't, then you must have something bad that you want to hide." No wonder we can calmly sit at a dinner party and discuss our pet's breeding habits but we can't go home and look at our husband's penis in the light.

It isn't our fault; it isn't anyone's fault. We were never taught to handle our own sexuality, to regard sex as a natural, healthy part of our makeup. Because we can't handle it ourselves, it causes problems for our children, too. We continue perpetuating the *What Every Young Girl Should Know* approach.

Here is a sad story about an inherited hang-up that Dick heard on a business trip several years ago. He was talking to a salesman who worked for one of the large manufacturers of sanitary napkins. Over several

23

drinks in a bar, the salesman told him how a letter from an irate mother had caused his company to expand the directions included in their packages. Evidently the woman's daughter had reached adolescence without much preparation concerning sex or her approaching womanhood. Naturally, she was upset when she began to menstruate for the first time. When she went to her mother, worried about the bleeding, the woman calmed her down by saying that this was something that happened to all girls at a certain age. Mama handed her a box of sanitary napkins and told her to go into the bathroom and read the directions as to how to put one on. Nothing more was said until four days later when the little girl asked why the napkin was hurting her, and how long she had to leave it on. The directions in the box hadn't said anything about changing and so she hadn't. While our friend may have saved herself some embarrassing moments by not helping her daughter through that first menstrual cycle, I doubt that any mother could help but cringe thinking of the impression left on that child. Instead of casting the blame on herself, this woman wrote a stinging letter to the company, saying that the directions were inadequate. Learning to live with such a hang-up isn't always easy, but passing it on is tragic.

Several months ago, we had a nun as an overnight guest in our home. As she was walking upstairs in the afternoon, I handed her my purse and asked if she'd put it on my bed. She looked startled for a minute and then said, "I couldn't go in there. The Holy of Holies, the Sanctum Sanctorum, your bed." No kidding, those were her exact words. At first I thought she was joking, but she was dead serious, and would not go into our room. I didn't want to embarrass her or myself any further so it was just dropped, but the phrase she used stayed with me for a long time. It frightened and saddened me that there was a class of grade-school children who would absorb some of her thinking during that school year. And another class the next year, and another after that. She may barely influence them, but her inability to accept any human sexuality will leave its mark. It may take the form of Marylike pleas for good conduct, or it may be in the form of that old line "That's dirty!"

Fortunately, the next generation is learning to handle their sexuality better than we did. Recently we heard something that, in the context of our upbringing, is really shocking and yet so very beautiful. A young engaged couple told us that when they talk on the phone, he gets an erection often just from thinking about her and how much he loves her. This is not unusual—you men might remember back to your high-school or college days and smile. What is unusual is that he tells her so. Instead of being shocked, horrified, or disgusted, she's pleased. She knows that his love is strong, it's normal, and that that erection is for her alone. Now Dick and I can do that in our marriage today but we could never have done it eighteen years ago. To reach that point of free and natural regard for our sexual natures, we had to grow out of our old thoughts and into new ones.

Wouldn't it be great if someone would start adult sex education courses today for the married men and women who grew up as we did. Courses which you could attend without embarrassment and at which you could ask freely all the questions that you could never ask your spouse. We can think of no better "someone" to help accomplish this than our churches. In the past they had a part in the formation of our negative attitudes toward sex. In the future, they could provide us and our children a beautiful vehicle for learning new and positive attitudes. Many people would accept church-initiated programs of sex education more readily than they would those sponsored by the schools or the government. The churches have a strong enough influence, probably the only influence, to prevent the perpetuation of our negative attitudes. If they would only use it, they could provide the means for us to face our own sexuality and, above all, learn to be comfortable with ourselves and each other.

Being comfortable with each other has probably

been the single greatest achievement of our marriage. It's knowing that Dick can suggest something new in lovemaking and that I won't label him sick or perverted because it went through his mind. We tend to automatically categorize anyone who is more sexually free than we are as a pervert. They point up our own insecurities, and we feel better if they are the ones who are sick. Dick and I feel that there is no such thing as perversion between two people who *love each other*. For us, that excludes whips, chains, and torture, because hurting one that you love doesn't mesh with our concept of love. Other couples may be able to handle things that we can't and still be comfortable within their concept of love. Still others may want less adventure in their sex lives and be happy with that. Hooray for them! And hooray for us!

Equally important in our feelings of comfort is the ability to say No. Two people at any point in marriage may not necessarily have the same degree of freedom. Remember the different backgrounds we brought to this joint life. Thus, the ability to say No honestly, is vital to any relationship that's going to grow. Make him feel like some slimy thing for his thoughts, or make her feel unMarylike again, and it will probably be the last thoughts you hear on sex. Retreat behind the veil of headaches or tired blood, and the message will come through. Eventually someone else will fulfill your mate's needs. Lack of growth people can live with; lack of honesty they cannot.

In our marriage, if Dick suggests something new that I'm not ready for, I've got to be able to tell him freely. I also must tell him honestly where I am right now and why this isn't comfortable for me. How else can he understand me? For example, one night about a year ago we were talking about masturbation—how we would handle it the first time we discovered one of our youngsters masturbating (and they will). The conversation drifted into masturbation for children in general, and then we discussed our own childhoods and their differences. Finally, he said, "You know it really turns many men on to be able to watch a woman masturbate. I think it would turn me on and besides I'd learn so much." A startling idea—at least for me. But then Dick went on to explain why he thought so and it made sense. A man could learn very quickly the various ways to excite that particular woman if he watched what she did to excite herself. I liked the idea but it made me extremely uncomfortable. I had to tell him why.

As a child, I'd never masturbated. That's hard to believe but true. It was the dirtiest, nastiest, most wicked of all the no-nos, and it certainly wasn't Mary-like. Your hand fell off and your brain rotted. Of course, it all happened the first time you touched yourself. Your mother would know exactly what you had done as soon as she saw that your hand was missing. It was so bad that even thinking about it made you want to go wash out your mind with lye. So I didn't think and I didn't do it. But now my husband is suggesting not only that I masturbate but that I let him watch! There isn't a shelf made that's big enough to put all those hang-ups on at one time.

From his male frame of reference, it's not such a wayout thing. He'd just finished telling me that most boys masturbate as part of their growing-up, and that other boys know about it. The fact that other fellows are doing it makes the guilt easier to get over. Dick pointed out that you can see that their hand is still in its proper place at the end of their arms and that alleviates some of the fear. Men know that married men often masturbate if necessary—your wife is in the hospital for six weeks or she's cut you off because she has twenty-six headaches a month. You have a choice of masturbating, or wet dreams, or finding another woman. But women don't know this! While growing up, girls never talk about masturbating. They don't know if other girls are doing it or not, but they assume not. And they probably aren't doing it to the same extent as boys because the actual physical drive isn't there—we don't have to release excess sperm periodically.

After explaining to Dick why the idea wouldn't be

comfortable for me at the time, he could understand completely. "I'm so glad you told me," he said. "I wouldn't want you to do anything that was awkward for you just because you thought that's what I wanted." As long as we can communicate our feelings of why, then we can feel pretty safe in knowing that the No will be understood. It's a learning and a growing process on both sides. Since then I've thought a lot about my feelings on masturbation and about their origins. Hopefully, in time I'll be able to get rid of them completely.

We tend often to judge others by our own standards. We put them in our shoes, not vice versa. Wouldn't it be great if we could honestly look at our own reactions and say, "This is the way I feel, and I think I can see why," and then tell the other person that. A woman buys a slinky, see-through nightgown to surprise her husband, and instead of the delighted reaction she anticipated, she's turned off flat. "Take that thing off. It's disgusting, and it makes you look like a whore." Maybe his concept of married women honestly can't handle his wife acting anything other than Marylike or motherlike. Maybe his mother would never have worn anything suggestive in a million years, but if she did, he wouldn't have gotten to see it anyway, would he? There was another side to his mother (all our mothers) that he never got to see. Because of his upset image of the mother of his children now, he lashes out and makes her feel dirty. Wouldn't it be fantastic if he could tell her how he felt instead, and say, "Give me time to get used to a new image of you."

And then there's sperm! The whole idea of its wetness, its reality, its symbolization, along with other hang-ups, made oral sex a problem. Think about sperm for a minute. In the scientific explanation we received as children, sperm was the substance that united with the egg to create life. We all knew that when the man ejaculated the sperm was placed (never shot) in the woman's vagina and that was fine. But when you finish making love for the first time, things start happening that you never imagined. The sperm is not nicely in there uniting vaguely with an egg, or clinging to vaginal walls, or whatever it was supposed to do. It was running down your leg, getting on the sheets or your clothes; it had a slight odor; and there was even some on your hand. It was real and no one prepared you for that. It made you feel a little unclean and you wanted to wash it off. You couldn't say, "Yuk," so you said nothing. Then or now. Excess sperm is not a subject of polite conversation. Now five years later your husband suggests or indicates that he'd like to try oral sex. "In my mouth????? I haven't learned to handle it on the sheets." But you don't say that. You just shy away from trying oral sex by getting a headache and hope he'll forget the idea soon.

This is just as true for men as for women. Many men would like oral sex for themselves but are horrified at the idea of going down on a woman. Dick says it's for the same reason. They were as poorly prepared as we. The whole idea of "what's really down there" is mysterious. Whereas, women were fed the "gross" image, men were fed the "mystery" image. The nude pictures of women that boys sneaked a look at never unveiled what lay under that fuzzy mound of hair. Male genitals were out in the open; where were ours? Even if you managed to get a medical book out of the library and sat huddled with a bunch of boys over the color plate labeled *Female Genitalia,* it wouldn't prepare you to some day put your mouth there. Vaginal secretions? (Another great textbook term.) What if they gushed out all over you? What if they smelled bad or she had to go to the bathroom? (That's a big one for both men and women.) What if you got some in your mouth? What do you do when you get down there anyway? It's pretty obvious what to do for a man orally, but how do you know where to start on a woman. Listening to Dick, it's pretty easy to see how the cycle continued into our lives and into many others. Neither of us knew enough about ourselves or the opposite sex to be able to fill their needs, and we couldn't talk about it. Result: lots of unsatisfied people who still think if they enjoy sex too much it must be dirty. Lots of half-satisfied people, with vague yearnings toward something different or better, who can't break the ice and talk about it to the very person with whom they share their bodies.

For the two of us today there is a philosophy of sexual happiness with which we are comfortable. We still have many ingrained attitudes that we are trying to work out—there will always be some. But we recognize them and will continue to pick away the scabs they have left with each other's help. The most important part of this process and of our whole outlook is our ability to find comfort in what we have or what we can grow to—to feel safe enough to expose our hang-ups, yearnings, and desires to the other, knowing that we won't be scorned or ridiculed.

The other part of our philosophy is that sex between two people who love each other should be a joy, a form of Eros. For us, that means as it did to the ancient Greeks, that it should be life-giving. According to the legend, the world was barren and lifeless at one time. The god Eros breathed the spirit of life into the nostrils of clay forms of man and woman and that spirit of Eros is within us still as humans. It is forever reaching out with desire, with longing to breathe life into another. Life was made for joy, not for sorrow, and sex is a natural part of that life. Never again do the two of us want to feel guilty about enjoying what we can give to each other with our bodies.

One final thought. We've said a lot about the attitudes we've brought with us to our relationship. For many of you, maybe they rang a familiar bell. What about our children . . . your children? What will we do for them? Will we send them into marriage with our same hang-ups, our same ignorances? Do we want to see our own unhappiness or lack of satisfaction show up in their future marriages? We personally do not, and we're working hard with our children to see that it doesn't happen.

Despite the so-called sexual revolution, things haven't changed that much as far as formal sex education is concerned. Yes, the young people today do know more than we did, and perhaps they experiment more because they have the opportunity, but the things they are finding out from each other are often the wrong things. They know that they can use a shaken-up bottle of cola as a douche, and that a baggie with a rubber band will serve as a condom. They know that it's possible to fly to New York and back for an abortion in one day and be home in time for dinner. Their parents don't know that they've missed school. But the important things are still left unsaid by school sex courses or locker-room graduate school. What does it mean to be a man . . . a woman? What is a wife . . . a husband? What can you bring to that marital bed at twenty or twenty-one that will help both of you? What does it really mean to "make love?" What can it mean? What would I want to tell my son about me and about women, that would enable him to give his future wife the kind of happiness that Dick has given me? What would Dick want to tell our daughters to help them better understand a man's needs and his love? How much can we give them to bring a beautiful part of their lives out into the sunlight where it belongs, rather than spend another generation in the darkness under a rock? Who will tell them these things if not us? Who else cares or loves them enough? It's an awesome responsibility.

3.

Turning on Again

IF YOU SAT DOWN at the breakfast table every morning for ten years and found a bowl of corn flakes and a glass of milk in front of you, how would you feel about breakfast? Bored, right? If every third night for ten years you got into bed at eleven o'clock with the lights out, went through the same routine sex play, and made love in the same three positions, how would you feel about sex? Bored again. It would be hard to make today's teenagers believe that sex could ever become monotonous, but we, and perhaps many of you, can testify to that fact. In most cases it becomes stale because of the attitudes we brought unknowingly with us to marriage. It stays stale because of a lack of communication and because we don't know how to go about changing it.

We think there are four myths originated by Uncle Alphonse in the glacier age that prevail today. All four are designed to keep your bedroom boring.

Myth 1: "Once your sex life becomes stale, it has to stay that way." Oh, no! We turned ours around and we know of others who have. Scratch that one. It's just not true!

Myth 2: "We are the only couple who has this problem." Baloney! Since we became concerned enough to try and work on our sex life, we've talked to a great many people who are or were in the same boat. Masters and Johnson contend that fifty percent of the marriages in America are in some kind of sexual trouble, and that most could be helped. The boat isn't lonely. As a matter of fact, it's filled to overflowing.

Myth 3: "It's normal for sex to become routine after your early twenties, because people (especially women) don't have a high sex drive after that." Were we pleased when a doctor destroyed that one for us. Most men's sex drive peaks in their late teens and early twenties. They go into a slow, SLOW decline through their thirties and early forties, with a possible high spurt of activity in the early and mid-forties. From that point there is a gradually diminishing drive into old age. They can still be active and virile through their sixties, seventies, and eighties, witnessed by the fact that every once in a while you see a news story, "Man 88 Conceives Child."

The temporary decline seen for many males in their thirties is not due as much to waning sex drive as it is to economic and job pressures. This is the period in a man's career when he is most severely taxed physically and mentally. His responsibility to perform is at its highest level. He's reaching that crucial now-or-never stage in his work life and much of his energy is concentrated there. The drop in sexual activity is often no more than a combination of fatigue and worry. If both men and women were better acquainted with this fact, a lot of panic and insecurity could be avoided during those years.

Most females, contrary to everything I had ever heard, don't peak until their early to mid-thirties. This peak level remains constant throughout the forties except for a possible dip during menopause. Following that, they spurt back up again to the level of the male and gently decline with him through their senior years. They are most successful at receiving and giving sexual pleasure between the ages of thirty to forty-five. Some women enjoy sexual relations even more after menopause because the fear of pregnancy has been removed. There's no real reason for so many corpse-like female bodies lying in bed saying, "Hurry up and get it over with, Harry!"

Myth 4: "I am the only one dissatisfied with sex life in this marriage. My partner doesn't seem to care." Probably true. He doesn't *seem* to care. Maybe *she* feels you don't seem to care either. Why would it be easier for her to initiate a discussion about sex than for you? Dick pointed out that as we were going through our stale sex period, both of us were trying to think of how we could turn it around. The two of us were disssatisfied, but we never told each other. We just assumed thhat the other was happy or resigned to life as it was. We could have gone on that way forever.

In order to change anything about our lives, we have to face facts, face ourselves, and then find out where we are. Instead of walking around for years with vague rumblings of dissatisfaction, we have to ask ourselves a few honest questions first. What's our sex life really like? Is it dull, routine? Do I find it unsatisfying, unexciting? Do I really care if it is or not?

(That's an important question.) Would I want to change things if it could be done? Or am I satisfied to let things go along as they are? Dick and I, individually, had answered these questions mentally and decided that we did want to reach for more. We weren't satisfied with things as they were. We were willing to search for ways to change things. All we had to do was tell each other and then find the way.

We had answered the easy questions. Now came the hard ones. Whose fault is this? Is it mine? Is it his or hers? Or is it mutual? What am I willing to risk to change this situation? If I did work up enough courage to bring up the subject, what would I say? How would I start? How do I find out what to do? How did I get into this mess anyway? Those were the thoughts swirling through both our minds during that period, and for a while it seemed like it might be easier to just forget the whole thing and masturbate! But it really isn't because you have to remember that you love that guy or gal. At least we did, and knew that it was worth any price to have sex to be a vital and exciting part of our total love again.

So it meant then that we had to answer some more of those questions for ourselves before we could go on. What is our problem? For us it was birth control first, and then routine sex. We've already mentioned how we worked through the birth-control issue, but we were still left working out the hang-ups created by it, and the fact that our sex life was unexciting. Neither of us was being completely satisfied. Instinctively we both knew there could be something better.

When you've reached this point and isolated what you feel is the problem, you've got to answer those personal questions again. And now it really is tough to be honest. If you're a man and you've never thought or said, even jokingly, "My wife is frigid," or "My wife is turned off," you have to ask yourself if it could be your fault. Maybe you've never taken the time to discover and learn what she needs to satisfy her. Perhaps no one taught you that women need satisfaction as much as men if they are going to enjoy sex. Could it be your approach? Do you treat her as a person or as a thing in the total picture of your marriage? Do you take that time to think about her needs as a woman outside of the bedroom? If you merely use her and her body to satisfy your drives, she isn't likely to be terribly excited about making love to you. Is it possible that the old built-in attitudes of her childhood are what's holding her back? Or yours? That was part of the problem for me and for Dick, but you can't use that one as a universal dumping pit for all your troubles. "Well, she was brought up as a prude so what can you expect?" No fair throwing all your sexual troubles back on your mother-in-law's doorstep. But if her attitudes are the major problem, then it's your responsibility to find out what the hang-ups are and help her work through them.

Most of the attitudes that we mentioned in the last chapter, Dick and I have had to discuss. We had to begin talking somehow and admit there was a problem. And it was difficult initially to admit that we had any flaws, that we weren't the most broad-minded people who ever hopped into bed together. It took us years of gentleness and understanding to uncover and dig out all those ingrained ideas that were screwing us up. Now it's almost exciting when we discover a new one still buried down there.

If you happen to be an unsatisfied woman and you'd like a better sex life, Dick feels that you have to face a different set of questions and approach them with the same honesty. He believes that women withdraw more from a disappointing sex life than their husbands; they're more willing to let it be that way. As a result, honest facing of facts is important. First, do you believe that women have as much right to good sex as men? If you can't answer yes to that, then you'll probably feel guilty about taking any steps to improve things. Dick says it's more likely that you won't do anything because you're not going to stick your neck out for something that you don't believe in. However, if that's not a problem, then you're confronted with the same things that I had to face. Is this completely or partially my fault? Are my old hang-ups holding us back? Are his? For both of us this was the case. The only way we could solve our problems was through communications and honesty. We had to really look at ourselves and admit the hold those attitudes had on us. Once we could see the chinks in our armor, we had to hope for help, understanding, and patience from each other while we worked them out. Patience turned out to be one of the most important virtues, especially since attitudes don't disappear overnight.

More questions for women. Does he know that you're not satisfied? (This is where Dick sees many women withdrawing.) Is he a "slam-bam-thank-you-ma'm" lover who then rolls over and snores? Does he know how to turn you on? (Do you know how to turn him on?) Do you know how to turn yourself on so that you could tell him? Does he think women don't need to be turned on? Does he think about *you*? All solutions to these problems, except for the last, rest squarely on your shoulders. One more simple question—have you told him any of these things? If you haven't, you're withdrawing.

Perhaps your problems stem from the fact that you're a slow starter. It takes you a long time to climax (and there isn't anything wrong with that). But if your husband comes on fast, or isn't easily aroused again in a short time, you both need to learn some new techniques. First, you must communicate to him the fact that you warm slowly so that he understands the problem. Then both of you can learn how to handle it. The broadening of technique, we found, is easy.

One final question. Was your husband or wife turned on originally, but is no longer? If so, it is probably a problem of poor techniques. The potential was there, but one or both of you are failing to hit the right buttons to continue to turn the other on. Could they be turned on again? By you? The answer is probably a deafening "Yes."

Would you like to try an interesting experiment? Try to picture how your best friend, or someone else, would go about turning your mate back on. Visualize all the gals in your bridge club or that cute young secretary at the office, one by one, making love to your husband. Men, visualize all the guys in your poker club, or that good-looking young life-insurance salesman who dropped in last week, making love to your wife. Take time to think about it scene by scene. What would they do? How would they approach her? I'll bet some pretty good ideas will suddenly pop into your head as to how to do it yourself.

What Dick and I learned along the way is that neither of us came to this marriage perfect. Not everyone marries a Casanova, or a gal who knows exactly what to do for a man. I would guess that very few do. It's a joint learning process and many of us get bogged down, mainly because we're afraid to talk about how we feel. We were taught not to express our feelings, to hold them in. We either didn't want to hurt the other person or to show our own vulnerability and weakness. But then we recognized how foolish and destructive they were to ourselves. One major thing that we've discovered is that although it's hard to be honest, it isn't as hard as you thought it was going to be. And there isn't anybody else in the world, besides you two, who is interested enough in your sex life to do the hard parts for you.

Finding the courage to take the first step is very much like quitting smoking. Unless you want to do it badly enough, you know it's going to be a flop. One good way to build up your resolve so that you don't chicken out is to list your alternatives. If you have reached the conclusion that your sex life isn't all that you'd like it to be, and you're afraid to make a change, you have only four other choices:

1. Spend the rest of your life unsatisfied. (Neither of us wanted to do that.)
2. Take a lover. (This is risky business. And who's to guarantee that the milkman or that cute typ-

ist at the office is any better in bed than what we already have? Besides, part of the problem probably lies within us and we'd just be taking it with us.)

3. Get a divorce. (That's a pretty drastic step for most of us.)
4. Spend the rest of your life masturbating in the bathroom. (While that may solve the problem of satisfaction, it's also very lonely.)

So if you want to broach the subject of sex and you find yourself turning cowardly, run through your list of alternatives again and then act fast. For most of us, courage comes in spurts and fades quickly. Act while the spirit moves you.

We found two ways to break the ice. You can talk first and hope that something will start happening in bed, or you can act first, sexually, and hope that it will generate some talk. We tried both approaches simultaneously. All the following ideas we tried ourselves, and each was like a stepping-stone to the next. Each stepping-stone brought us a little closer to the top of that wall of silence we had built between us concerning sex.

The first thing that Dick did after thinking about our situation was to make the assumption that I wanted to change things, too. That was when he brought home the first marriage manual to see if he could arouse some interest. He didn't just toss it at me and say, "Here, read this. It'll do you some good." Any woman or man knows that's an automatic fight signal. I probably would have stomped away furious and never touched the thing. He just casually dropped it on the bed as he was unpacking from a trip. "I picked this up in the airport in Denver and it has some really interesting things in it." Now I had to read it just to find out what he thought was interesting. That left the way open for me to come back a week later and say, "What was it that you found interesting?" Or he could come back with, "Have you had a chance to browse through that book yet?" Hopefully you're off and running from there if you don't let the ball drop.

We found so many ways to use that book to stimulate conversation that it finally fell apart. But the mood always had to be right. Sometimes it meant waiting a few days to give the other person a chance to think or react; sometimes it meant waiting until neither of us was tired or irritable or depressed about something else. If we started off when the other person was in the wrong frame of mind, we found that we got nowhere fast. Most couples develop their own instinctive sense of timing, and sex fits the same way.

We ran that first book into the ground and then bought more as we found ourselves opening up. Dick would say, "Look at this position; it's something we've never tried. How do you think it would be for you?" This would either provoke one of two responses. I could tell him what I thought specifically about that position and the discussion could grow from there. Or I could say, "Ugh! I think that's disgusting!" Even a broadminded remark like that left an opening for him to ask why. That's how we initially began discussing the whole area of childhood attitudes, from which a deeper understanding of each other finally developed.

The most significant aspect was that we had a vehicle which enabled us to talk to each other about our lovemaking. Soon we started finding all kinds of vehicles to help it along. One was a story in our local paper about the controversy raging over sex education courses in the grade and high schools. This article gave us an opportunity to talk about our own education, and how we felt about it now. We tried to assess what the effects on us had been; where it had failed; how it had hurt us.

Another vehicle was dirty jokes, which prompted discussions about language and what words or ideas we consider vulgar. Dick would tell me a joke he'd heard at lunch and ask how I felt about it. He wanted to know what words offended me and why, what kind of concepts or what type of people did certain words or acts bring to mind. To a certain extent we continue to do this in other ways today. Just last week Dick brought home a pornographic tape and we listened to part of it. When he asked me how I felt about it, I had to admit that I was turned off. Not because of what they were doing, but because of the way they treated each other. The two people on the tape were using each other, and even though none of the acts were surprising or offensive to me, it was the crassness of exploitation that was offensive. It didn't fit in with my concept of love or Dick's either. And it was a good feeling to be able to talk about it and discover we had the same reactions.

Neither of us feels the least embarrassed that we've bought pornography and made use of it in many ways. Primarily, it helped lay out the entire range of sexual activities for us. It gave us a chance to find a place in that spectrum where the two of us could be comfortable. When we could see everything that was being done sexually we could decide where we fit in. How far could we go and still be comfortable with ourselves? By discussing it together, we realized that we didn't have to feel guilty about not doing everything that we'd heard or read about. I think lots of couples experience this reverse guilt. You hear about group sex or swapping, and vaguely wonder if there is something wrong with you because you could never do that. Dick and I found that we could honestly be very happy in our own bed, doing whatever we wanted to do. We didn't need other people in bed with us. We didn't need to whip or beat each other or urinate on each other, to get our kicks.

While we're talking about pornography, we must mention a fantastic idea for breaking the ice that was not ours originally. A good friend had been trying to initiate a conversation about sex with his wife, and nothing seemed to work. One day he walked into a porno store and bought everything in sight—books, magazines, tapes, even French ticklers. He took them home to his wife and said, "I really think we should sit down and look at all this stuff and talk about it. This is what our children are being exposed to in the mail, at school, and on the street. We had better prepare ourselves so that we'll be able to handle it when the subject comes up." Ingenious! What good mother could say no to that approach?

X-rated movies are another vehicle that can be handled in the same way that our friend used pornography. Go once "for the sake of the children!" You have to go together because who knows which parent will be confronted by their youngsters someday with questions. We used X-rated movies in a different way when we were becoming more open about our sex life. Dick suggested that we go one night and although I wasn't crazy about the idea we went. I was sure someone would recognize us and I needed his moral support to get me inside. I had visions of the lights flashing on at intermission, seeing my next-door neighbor sitting behind me, or bumping into our pastor on the street as we walked out. I solved the problem by wearing my coat over my head through the entire show. Do you have any idea how high the temperature is in such theaters?

Well, we didn't bump into anybody and now I don't think I'd care, anyway. We did talk about the movie all the way home and on into the night; it was one of the best vehicles we've ever found. Besides opening up conversation, you really can learn a lot from pornography and X-rated movies. Who can honestly say that he already knows everything? Not me! All that I learned was from *What Every Young Girl Should Know!*

Once we got over that initial hump, talking about our sex life became easier and easier. Dick made the discovery that women think about making love, have erotic impulses, or sexual fantasies during the day, just as men do. I had never told him that sometimes I think about screwing while I'm ironing, or attending a PTA meeting. (It's usually a lot more interesting than what's being said at the meeting!) He found out for the first time that housewives get just as horny as businessmen. When he was out of town and we were talking on the phone, I'd find myself saying, "I wish you'd come home soon. I really want you." He loved it. Why hadn't I ever expressed my desire for him before? For some reason, men find this much easier to do than women. I guess it's our training. Now when he comes home from work and kisses me, I can reach down, grab him, and say, "Let's duck the kids as soon as we get the chance and make love." While we are eating, he has a chance to dwell on the fact that I'm horny. It's amazing how ingenious he's become in finding totally absorbing projects for our children after dinner.

During this period of our openness, Dick began telling me things about his own drives and needs in a way that he hadn't before. He told me that he often thought about me at work and got an erection there during the day. He'd think about the last time we made love or what we would be doing the next time. On an out-of-town trip, he'd get terrifically horny and spend a lot of time thinking about all the different ways that he would like to make love when he got home. Now that we do talk about these things and tell each other how we feel, it's a wonder that there are still so many unsinged telephone lines left across the country.

If one of us was working up courage to try something different on the other that night, we'd try to put ourselves in a more sensuous frame of mind. Getting in the mood took various forms. Once after a bath, I sat for an hour watching myself in the mirror as I rubbed lotion all over my body. I kept thinking, "I feel so sexy that if I don't try oral sex with Dick tonight I never will." Sometimes just lying on the bed naked, Dick would try to imagine how he would feel making love to a new woman. How would she feel toward him? What would he do for her if he could start fresh sexually? Then he would do those things for me.

We found many ways to create greater sexual awareness and anticipation. For me, it was buying sexy lingerie, some see-through outfits, a body stocking, leopard bikini underwear, or going braless occasionally and letting Dick know when. Dick bought himself some mesh bikini shorts. They really looked great and made him feel like a different man. He described how, in these shorts, he felt as sexy as a woman might feel in a new black lingerie. Why not?

Every woman, should find her old love letters when she wants to feel desired. (Let's admit that we all have them, and that they're stashed behind last year's hats on the top shelf of the hall closet.) Read them. They make you feel great. Let your husband read them. It might please him to know that other men loved and desired you before he met you, but that he got you.

Let's suppose you are in a sensuous mood and you want to try making love some new ways tonight, but your partner doesn't know a thing about this desire. How do you start? We found some easy ways to get things moving, but first you have to know where you eventually want to end up that night. You have to educate yourself before you make a move. How was Dick going to arouse me as he'd never done before so that I'd want to come back for more? He read everything he could get his hands on and mapped out a strategy. He had to make sure he knew what he was doing so that once he got me interested I wasn't left hanging or hung-up.

The first night he used the vibrator is a good example. He had thought about it quite a bit during the day and decided that the best approach would be that of surprise. He'd wait until we were involved in lovemaking before bringing it out from under the pillow. Suddenly I heard a buzzing and was aware of the wildest sensation ever running across my breasts. I didn't have a chance to think about any negative reactions or hang-ups. I was already enjoying it. By the time he had covered my whole body with the vibrator, and I'd had some pretty thumping orgasms, the hangups were buried and forgotten forever. There was no doubt left in my mind that every bed should come equipped with its own vibrator.

The same kind of planning helped me experiment with Dick. Let's say that I had decided to use my breasts instead of my hands all over his back, stomach, and legs that night. How did I ease into something like that the first time? I offered to give him a back-rub. I was already in a nightgown that slipped off easily and the only way he would get a good rubdown was lying on the bed with me sitting straddled across his buttocks. Using lotion, which is sexy to begin with, I eventually suggested that he take off his shorts so that I could get lower down on his spine. From there nature just took its course. After a slow backrub, I leaned over and started brushing my breasts gently across his shoulders and back, then slid down to his buttocks and legs. It didn't take long before he turned over and I could continue on the front. Now what man can argue with that approach?

Backrubs are fantastic for starting all kinds of things. A man can use his penis as I did my breasts, or either partner can use his tongue. Even a plain backrub (and eventually front rub) with lotion can be fantastically exciting.

Climb into the shower with your wife some day, rub her back with soapy lather, and see what happens. Dick walked into the bathroom one night while I was reading in the tub and offered to scrub my back. A half hour later we were both dripping wet, making love on the shag carpeting of the bathroom floor.

Dick feels that if you're a woman and you want to make the first move, you must take time to prepare first. Learning what to do, and how to go about it so that you don't bungle the job the first time is just as important for women as it is for men. You might set the stage by flattering his ego that day. At night guide his hands to where you want them. Show him what you'd like done by doing it to him first, and then start him in that direction. If it's oral sex you'd like to try, push him gently down on you in the middle of love-making when he's already excited. Then be prepared to do the same for him. Your ego will survive if you have to take the first step. It really will.

If you're a guy making that first move, soften her up. Women seem to need tenderness so much. It's

44

not dishonest, and we're all sitting ducks for a little attention and romantic atmosphere. You might even start a week ahead, treating her as you did when you were courting her. Then pick a night when she is relaxed—not one when she's done eighteen loads of laundry, had the cub scout picnic, and painted the garage gravel grey—and have dinner alone, by candlelight. You might even get her a little looped with wine. She'll forgive you the next day. Then shower her with tenderness and more tenderness. At that point she wants to be loved not raped. So make love to her as you never have before.

In this chapter we've talked strictly about working through our own problems and creating our own ways of growing. Our problems happened to be fairly common ones, and our solutions may be of interest if you have had similar difficulties. However, there are far deeper sexual problems in some marriages that we aren't qualified to discuss. Psychological frigidity, premature ejaculation, and impotence are problems that cannot be cured by flippantly suggesting that you give your partner a backrub.

We're fortunate to have so many highly trained and understanding professionals who can help to resolve such problems. Neither Dick nor I would hesitate to ask for medical or psychological advice if we were faced with a situation that required it. Our marriage is too important to us to let pride or other people's opinions stand in our way. Whether it took the form of marriage counseling, clergy help, medical help, or a Masters and Johnson clinic, we would seek it out. When you see that Masters and Johnson have a 97.8 percent success factor in dealing with premature ejaculation, it would be hard to stay away, whatever the sacrifices.

It took patience to solve our problems. It took time to develop positive and freeing attitudes and to feel at home with our own bodies and with each other's. Since it had taken years for the hang-ups to grow, it took time to dissolve them, and I'm glad each of us understands that. Life in general is so much better for us now—just going to bed together is fun and exciting again. If we were to face the same situation again, we'd never wait so long to take that first step.

4.

Livening Up a Dull Sex Life

MAKING LOVE STANDING UP kills your arches! Unless, of course, the woman happens to be about four inches taller than the man. You may have more success than we've had. We happen to be a standard-size couple, male bigger than female, and whenever we try screwing upright I end up standing on my tiptoes for at least a half hour, and I am usually unable to walk for several days afterward because my feet just lock in that position. A stool isn't very much help; we've never found one the right height. Books piled up become a bit precarious. You have to clutch each other rather tightly to keep from toppling over backward, and you feel a little giddy in that position anyhow. Besides. Dick's cock keeps popping out at inappropriate moments which makes the whole thing totally unsatisfactory, despite what the marriage manuals say. However, I understand it's a marvelous exercise for those with flat feet.

So many things about lovemaking sound great on paper, but when you try them you really have to maintain a sense of humor. Recently, a best-selling how-to book proposed filling the bathtub with Jell-O and making love on top of it after it had hardened. Now this intrigued us, but being practical it immediately occurred to us that the family tub filled with Wild Cherry Jell-O might be a little tough to explain to our four very inquisitive children. You simply can't pull this off in the middle of the night and have all traces vanish with the dawn. How long does it take for 207 packages of Jell-O to harden? It may be fine for the dashing young bachelor with his own apartment who doesn't care if he can't bathe for several days, but it's not the kind of thing that goes unnoticed in a family of six. Of course, you could say you had volunteered to make the salad for the annual church supper, but then you'd have to throw in some cherries and mandarin oranges, scoop it into buckets, and carry it out of the house to somewhere. Our garbage men would lift one lid and never come back. On the other hand, you could say the supper had been canceled and try to flush it down the drain, and then spend a jolly hour in the basement watching your hot water heater go through its death throes. The whole idea still intrigues us; perhaps we can work out something. The next time we go away together, we can fill up the hotel bathtub and sacrifice showering for a few days to give it a chance to harden. After we've tried it, we simply ask the hotel to give us another room because ours has a bathtub full of Jell-O. We'll let you know how it comes out.

Livening up a routine or dull sex life doesn't start with bathtubs. It begins with the basics—attitudes, communications, deep love, and a comfortable and free feeling with your partner. We'll spend considerable time on communications later in the book, but freedom with each other is the mood we'd like to capture here.

Not many people know that they have a right to ask for what pleases them most in sex. It certainly took us long enough to learn this simple fact, and that must mean no one is a total lost cause. For example, we have a friend who has always hated having her ears touched. Her husband labored for years under the misconceived notion that one of the sexiest things he could do during love play was nibble on her ears. Unfortunately, this was making her loathe any foreplay and turning her off sex in general. Still, she couldn't bring herself to tell him; she had waited too long. To shatter his image of what was sexy after all those years would have been too harsh. Finally, she hit upon the direct substitute idea. The next time they made love she gently moved his head to the hollow of her neck and said, "Here is better." What a simple thing really! Instead of an outright confrontation that might have hurt him, an alternative that kept both of them happy.

If you're one of the majority of us who finds it difficult to say, "I don't like what you're doing," or "You're not satisfying me that way," there are many signals that you can use to accomplish the same purpose while leaving both egos intact. The *direct-*substitute approach that was just mentioned is one of them. Your hands are another. They are beautiful gifts not only for giving pleasure in sex but also for letting your partner know what you want. Use your hands to move your partner's head, mouth, or hands gently to where you receive the most pleasure, the maximum sensation. Let's say that your woman's hand is roaming slowly over your body. Put your hand over hers, guide it, and indicate by the pressure of your hand your most vulnerable spots. Lead her fingers to the underside of your penis, which is the most sensitive, and move them up and down in the stroking motions which are most pleasurable to you. Use pressure on her hand to indicate the amount of gentleness or roughness you desire in each of your hot spots. As you near climax, increase the momentum and force with which she strokes so that she can learn what you need from her.

Hands, and especially fingers, are marvelous tools for telegraphing messages in lovemaking. If you place yours over a man's fingers, you can guide him through the areas of the vagina and clitoris (which is so hard for men to find anyway) and show him exactly how much pressure to apply for the maximum sensation. If the most sensitive area of your breasts is the nipple button when it's moved in a circular pattern, guide his hand there with yours, put your index finger over his, and move it with the degree of pressure and speed that's best for you. He'll get the message pretty rapidly when he sees you going into orbit.

For those of us who find it difficult to talk directly about what we'd like, showing can provide another simple solution. Kiss his nipples the way you'd like yours kissed. Stroke the insides of his thighs exactly as you'd like yours done. Run one finger lightly over his entire body and then take his hand and start it moving down your body. Guaranteed pleasure for both parties.

We used a combination of both methods when we first experimenting with oral sex. The two of us had been thinking about oral sex for a long time but neither one had the nerve to be the first to blurt out, "Why don't you go down on me?" One night Dick gently began moving my head down when I was at his breast area. I knew what he wanted but I wasn't sure that this was my cup of tea, so there was a little stiff-necked resistance for awhile. As he described it later, it was like holding on to a kangaroo—down, up, down, up, boing, boing, boing—till I made up my mind that it wasn't going to kill me if I tried it. That first time didn't turn me on as much as it does now, but seeing the amount of excitement it generated in Dick was enough to make me want to continue. The same signaling process worked for me sometime later. Now oral sex is an exciting part of our normal sex life, but we'll go much more deeply into that subject in Chapter VI.

We talked somewhat in Chapter I about being solemn and somber in bed. In addition to sex being more fun when you're loose with each other, embarrassing little things often happen during lovemaking that require a sense of humor. Bodies stick together and make popping noises when they unstick. Noses get pinned shut while kissing so that you suddenly find yourself suffocating. Once while we were in the midst of some extraordinarily wild lovemaking, I gave Dick a charley horse by kneeling on his thigh accidentally. He went hopping around the room like a madman which could have been devastating if we hadn't both been laughing so hard. It changed the mood but not our closeness.

Just as signals and naturalness are important to a full sex life, so is lighting. The dark is a lovely place for lovemaking—sometimes. The light is even lovelier —sunlight, firelight, candlelight, or even neon, because you can see the other person's face and body and have the double joy of seeing the amount of pleasure you are giving as well as feeling. That seems almost too basic to mention except that we ran across evidence recently that proves there are many people who go through their entire married lives without seeing each other naked. They undress separately and only have intercourse in darkness. Others never undress at all, but make love in their nightclothes. How, I don't know, but I'm sure it isn't easy! Being the inquisitive type, it would seem to me that your curiosity would get the best of you after twenty years. What is that big long thing that keeps sticking me every night?

I love to watch Dick's body and face while we're making love; to see the muscles move and the skin stretched or slack over curves; to look at him smile at me. It excites me to watch him as he gets an erection. What a sense of excitement and anticipation to know it's hardening because of and for me. Dick wonders how any man could go through a lifetime and never have the pleasure of seeing his wife's breasts, the way her nipples become erect, to see her open and wet, waiting to receive him. If you've never opened your eyes and looked at your partner, or if you only make love with the lights off, you're missing a beautiful and highly stimulating part of sex. We feel that we're giving each other something unique and extraordinary when we make love. I'm giving Dick a gift, my body, which I'm proud to give, and the wholeness of myself. He is giving himself in the very same way to me. If this is a good and natural thing, and we believe it is, why give up seeing the reaction that it causes in each other's body and face?

Different lighting does marvelous things to enhance your own body and its reactions. Candlelight and firelight make your face look warm, glowing, and inviting; either light can cast a pattern of flickering shadows on naked skin that's most erotic. Any man would turn on after a few moments of watching the pattern of flames moving over his woman's nipples and breasts. And any woman would turn on being able to watch his hand follow that pattern across her naked body. Sunlight on your body is also fantastic, provided that you have a place that offers privacy. The warmth of the sun beating down on your back or stomach as you leisurely make love, combined with the feeling of being free, out in the open, is extremely sexy. However, the hitch in today's crowded world is finding a private place in the sun. Hotel balconies are great, we've discovered. Many are devised so that each is separated from the next by side walls ensuring total seclusion. Keep any pleasurable squealing at a low pitch or your neighbor above is apt to peer over the top of his terrace and see more than he bargained for.

We're fortunate to live near a beautiful forest, and in the summer we believe there's no lovelier spot to make love. Feeling that soft green moss on your bare skin, with the sun streaming through the trees and the birds singing, makes us feel that all's right with the world and certainly between us. We've driven for miles down bouncy dirt roads to find a deserted lake or stream, our own tiny Eden, and spent the afternoon making love under the trees at the shore. A swim nude in the sunlight afterward only heightens the feeling of lust and tenderness, and back to the woods we go to make love again.

Before our marriage, a helpful female relative once told my husband that it was always best to make love on a towel to avoid staining the sheets. The phrase used was, I believe, that you can make love like a gentleman or a frontiersman. For a while we dutifully followed her advice and had the cleanest sheets in town, unsoiled by lust, but our towels wore out very fast. Finally, we decided that making love on a towel has to be one of the most restrictive methods in existence. It hampers any spontaneity because you have to make sure you either stay on or end up on the towel. Moreover, the towel automatically restricts any rolling around or changing positions midstream. That's far too high a price to pay in this age of high-speed washers and dryers. We now have the cleanest towels in town and wear out our sheets in record time, but it's lots more fun. Seeing that small creamy stain in the morning always makes me think about the previous night, and I smile to myself, which is not a bad way to start the day.

Speaking of sheets, we have a black satin set that Dick bought me as a present. They feel fantastic. However, they have an unadvertised defect that I'll mention in a minute. The texture is what's exciting. I'm a bug on textures and find it very stimulating to make love on things that feel different—soft moss in the woods, a big piece of soft fake fur, cool leather in the summer, and long, soft grass. The new, long shag carpeting has a marvelous feel (almost furry), and the padding underneath makes it so soft you can almost bounce on the rug. We just recarpeted part of the house in shag and I'm sure the carpet dealer would have been highly shocked had he known it was being judged not only on color and softness when we picked it out, but how it would feel on my back too.

Back to the black satin sheets. One of the funniest things that's ever happened to us was on a night when Dick was creating atmosphere in our bedroom. We have a low table at the foot of the bed; he had lit several candles around the room and also placed a few on this table. Soft music was playing, the black sheets were on the bed, and the mood was ripe for love. Did I neglect to mention that satin is extremely slippery? Any slight movement and those sheets slither toward the floor in one direction or another. We were rolling, tossing, and screwing without regard for the sheets, and we didn't notice until the flames were a foot high that they had slipped toward the closest candle at the foot of the bed. There were a few wild moments while we managed to get the singed electric blanket and spread under control. Then the ridiculousness of the whole thing struck us. A moment before there had been a guy in my bed with a long, hard cock. Now there was a naked man with a limp one running around the room dumping the humidifier full of water onto the bed and me.

Candles and different lighting can be used to produce any mood you desire, but mental atmosphere can be created without any props. Dick can rub my knee slowly under the dinner table or look at me in that special way which lets me know I'm desired. Send that unmistakable message the next time you're out and he's guaranteed to pass up that last drink for the road if he knows what he's hurrying home for.

Probably the most extraordinary mood for lovemaking in our sixteen years together happened purely by accident—or maybe it didn't. Dick says no. Let's just say he took advantage of an unusual situation and put it to its best use. Early one evening I was talking on the phone to a mutual friend, a very handsome man, when Dick came into the bedroom and began taking off my clothes very slowly, grinning from ear to ear. He knew exactly what he was doing, who I was talking to, and the fact that it wasn't the kind of conversation I could end abruptly by saying, "I'll call you back tomorrow." He could also see the reaction he was getting. Fortunately, my end of the conversation required more listening than talking. By the time I was nude and he was kissing my breasts, I was reduced to a state of complete mental rubble. I couldn't have murmured a proper "um hum" at the right time if my life depended on it. Somehow that phone call eventually ended, but I don't remember how. Our friend never mentioned it again, but he probably thought, "That dizzy broad's having a seizure." And I still blush every time I see him. That's mental atmosphere for you! No props needed and it only cost a dime.

There are so many places to make love besides bed that you owe it to yourself to experiment a little. We can screw in exactly the same way, one night in bed and one night on a fur throw on the second story

53

porch and experience different sensations and moods. The feel of the night wind on your bare breasts or cock, the night noises, the openness of the sky above you, and even the look of your skin in the darkness contribute to exciting sexual responses. If you live surrounded closely by neighbors, it adds fun and intrigue to make love above them while they're having an unsuspecting drink in their backyard below.

A great deal has been written about making it in the bathtub—a good way to kill two birds with one stone. But unless you have an unusually long tub or a short husband it doesn't work too well unless the woman is on top. We really prefer the shower for two reasons. First, you can use more positions. (The one that seems to work out best for us is with Dick sitting leaning against a wall and me kneeling astride facing him.) Second, your privacy is insured, which is important when you have youngsters zooming around all day or teen-agers who never seem to go to bed at night. You can make as much noise as you want and no one can hear you. And the sensation of all that water streaming down on you is similar to that which you would feel if you were making love under a waterfall. But, gals, you'll have to make up your mind that you aren't going to worry about your hairdo! Part of the fun is playing Tahitian maiden in the stream, and who ever heard of a Tahitian maiden in a shower cap?

Many books have suggested getting laid in a lake or a swimming pool, but there's a distinct disadvantage for the woman. When a penis moves in and out of a vagina under water it takes some water in each time. Consequently, a good deal of the sensation is deadened for me. After a swim in the nude and all the fondling we desire in the shallow water of a lake, we head for the nearest raft, pier, or diving board to continue. Keep that raft in mind if you are at a small resort or cottage that's overflowing with people. No one will look for you there at midnight, and it's very sensuous to feel the raft rocking in the wake of the moon.

Before we leave the subject of lakes, a word should

be said in memory of one lake that will remain indelibly imprinted in our memories. Several years ago we were vacationing with two other couples at a small cabin in Oklahoma. Privacy definitely had become a problem. Finally, about eleven one night when we'd both become so horny that we couldn't stand it any longer, we decided to take a ride to be alone. The countryside was beautiful and isolated, and soon we found a narrow road that led to the end of a tiny, deserted peninsula. We parked the car and decided to go for a swim in the nude. We were so deeply involved in making love in the lake, that when we emerged some time later, we were surprised to find that our car was gone. After wandering around, one of us spotted a glimmer in the water on the other side of the trees. There was our convertible, submerged to the roof in this lovely, romantic lake, and there we were, dripping wet, five miles from the nearest cabin. Someone had released the brake and steered it downhill through a maze of trees that it was impossible for the car to navigate alone. When the tow truck retrieved it the next morning, we didn't find a nick on it. The enterprising person was also a good driver, but where he came from or went to, we don't know. I do know, however, that it was a very long walk back at three in the morning. It was even harder to offer a logical explanation to our friends as to how we could lose the car on such a small piece of land. I can still remember our flushed faces!

You really don't have to go to that extreme for a livelier sex life, any change in routine will help. A comfortable rocking chair in your living room can be a nice change from bed if you don't get too carried away—rocking. Those old-fashioned porch swings and gliders are also great. Hammocks are totally impossible unless one of you is capable of bending in the wrong direction. No, I retract that statement. I just thought of something we haven't tried. With the man in the hammock and the woman astride, it might work.

We use our bed for more than sleeping and making

love; it is one of the best places to talk. The atmosphere is intimate and conducive to relaxed conversation at any time, especially after lovemaking. Often when we've made love we'll talk afterward, get a snack and bring it back to eat in bed. That residue of affection remains; and we feel totally close and comfortable with each other.

Before closing this chapter, we'd like to mention the timing for making love. It's been the biggest continual problem in our sex life. We're still working on it after sixteen years of marriage. Dick is a night owl and can get by with five hours' sleep; I need seven or eight or I turn into a growling, howling witch the next day. Since we do have such good communication (the only time in our marriage that it's a drawback), we spend several hours after the children are tucked in, talking and sharing each other's day. By then it's about midnight or later, I'm getting sleepy, and Dick's just hitting his full stride. I can screw like an alley cat daytime or evenings, but after midnight I can be a very uninspiring partner or, more likely, a very crabby female the next morning.

We've found a few solutions, but are still searching for the perfect answer. One answer is more lovemaking during the day, but we have to devise ingenious ways to get four youngsters out of the house simultaneously. You can always hire a babysitter to take them on a long jaunt through the park for several hours under the pretext that you're going to take a nap or both of you feel the flu coming on. We've tried screwing in the morning before they awaken, but that has proved mediocre. Dick's such a heavy sleeper that it takes me forever to arouse him to the point that he knows what's happening and is eager to participate. It's usually more like he's having a nice dream. Moreover, I'm always conscious that the children could wake up at any minute. The other solution to our particular problem is talking for a while at night, making love, and then continuing our conversation until I'm half asleep. Of course, there are those wonderful times when Dick gets home late. I've been asleep for a few hours and slowly awaken to that hard cock entering me from the rear. Do I wake up fast!

Another brief thought on timing is the simple understanding that no two people always feel like making love at the same time. Everybody has particularly tiring days, or is worried, sick, or turned off occasionally. No one feels like making love all the time. In fairness to the other person, explain how you feel in advance before he suddenly appears with a hard-on, or she spends an hour soaking in bubble bath getting in the mood. You can simply say at dinner, "I've been awfully bitchy today. Maybe a good night's sleep will make me feel better." Direct and honest, and the other person can plan his evening accordingly. Be gentle in explaining and then attack as soon as you feel better. If it's your mate who's not in the mood, be patient and understanding. You'll be regarded not only by gratitude but also by better sex when it comes. But don't ever play games—that's not love.

5.

Beyond Intercourse

VISUALIZE TWO PEOPLE MAKING love! What image enters your mind? Don't you tend to picture a couple wound together in some form of actual intercourse and heading toward a climax? Probably we would envisage the same scene. A few nights ago when we conjured up a vision of ourselves in bed, we were kissing, stroking, and caressing each other; we hadn't joined in any position. In other words, we were (as the textbooks so coldly put it) indulging in foreplay. We were making love, we were not having intercourse, and there is a big difference. It was startling when we first thought about this, but soon it made sense within our concepts of love and sex.

What really is important to us when we make love? What is it that we hope to take from it? For us, it's several things. It's sharing our whole bodies in a most meaningful way; it's being able to touch, stroke, hold, and caress each other just because we feel love. Naturally, it's also a release of sexual tensions, which is an instinctive and exciting human function for both of us. At times sex is also simple and spontaneous fun. The important reasons for making love pointed back to foreplay first, and to the actual position in which we reached a climax second.

It was foreplay that created the mood of being loved and of wanting to show our love to each other. On various nights it created the mood of being needed, or cherished, or just wildly exotic. It never gave us the feeling of being used or accommodated, even on a night when one of us may have derived more pleasure from it than the other. There were two people together in that bed, each trying to give as much as he was capable of at that particular time. It suddenly occurred to us that the position we ended up in was of little consequence. As long as it was good for both of us, as long as we had comfortably found a way to show our feelings of love for each other, it didn't matter very much where or how the climax came. When we make love it's generally an hour-long affair with the penis actually in the vagina for only the last two to five minutes. The rest of that hour is for mood-setting, love-giving, and pleasure-fulfilling one another.

Did you know that most men come twenty seconds after entry into the vagina? One out of four can hold on for two minutes, but the majority ejaculate in a minute or less. That puts a different light on the term lovemaking, doesn't it? If Dick walked into the bedroom on Wednesday night with an erection and immediately leaped on top of me and inserted his penis, and it would be over in two minutes. That's copulation, not lovemaking! I'd feel used and Dick knows that. I doubt that I'd be very excited or eager to try it again on Thursday night. I couldn't possibly be aroused to a climax that fast, that way, no matter what position he used, and I think I speak for most women. As a matter of fact, given equal time, I'd probably do much better in the bathroom with the vibrator. We both understand that concentrating on the drive alone would never work for us. And that's why we feel so strongly that you have to love or care for someone that you're involved with sexually. All the positions in the world, masterfully executed, will never give the other person the feeling of being cherished and being wanted for himself instead of being merely a relief for someone else's glands. The only way that you can achieve this deep rapport is through foreplay, afterplay, and a willingness to give, not just receive. If you happen to find twenty-six positions along the way that really turn you on, that's frosting on the cake.

"Was it good? Did I enjoy it? Would I like to do it again? Did it make me feel as though I was loved?" Questions such as those should become the criteria by which we judge lovemaking. Not "How many ways can we put it in? How many orgasms do we each have logged up on the score sheet on the bedroom wall? How many minutes did it last?" Each of us is different and no two couples would answer those questions the same way. Nor would they want to.

The fact that Dick can last in one session for an hour or can hold back from climax for two to five minutes shouldn't matter to other couples. Five years ago he was lucky if he could last a minute because of the many pressures caused by the problems in our sex life. Now he feels that besides age, the real difference is being psychologically relaxed toward sex. He's not trying to match someone else's endurance record, or someone else's ability to come back two or ten times in one night. He knows that he has the ability to bring me to an orgasm whenever we both want, whether it's before or after he has climaxed. So he can enjoy making love without having to worry about me being left hanging. Dick knows that those damn locker-room standards have done much to hurt him and other men in the past. Whenever most men hear that some guy can keep it up for an hour, immediately they wonder what's wrong with them if they can't. No one assumes that maybe it happened only once in the man's life, or that it took him years to get to that point of so-called success, or that perhaps he also failed a few times along the way.

We went through a period when Dick was in his early thirties and he was working so hard, he could hardly get it up at all. We were making love about once in ten days and that was a big dip. We didn't worry too much because we recognized that it was probably the most logical thing in the world, considering the pressures under which he was working. We checked with our doctor and were told that nothing was medically wrong; nothing had changed between us, so we relaxed and waited. When the strain was removed we hoped the problem would disappear, and it did. It was a good thing I knew that a man's sex drives could be affected when his nervous system is under pressure. Otherwise I would have been worried. We learned to treat it as a temporary problem and worked around it in other ways. As long as he felt secure in his manhood, we knew that it was only a matter of patience and understanding on my part, and that meant a great deal to him.

Almost every man faces a similar situation during his life, often many times. It could be illness, business pressures, or almost any kind of tension. If the reaction is "Oh, my God, I'm becoming impotent," he's going to compound the problem through fear. That's when an understanding wife is needed, but first, as Dick says, he has to confide his fears to her. Then they can work it out together.

Sometimes when we make love for a prolonged period, Dick may lose his erection or have it soften. Usually I can bring it back. And if it doesn't come back that night, so what? He knows it will tomorrow and that's all that really matters. It's more important not to worry himself into impotency if it should

60

happen, or feel that he's failed me. He knows he can satisfy me in a number of ways and that's what counts.

At this point, we would like to talk about what makes us feel good and why. What are the ways and moods that we make love to other? What do we do to create those moods? What can Dick do to my body on various nights to make me feel like two or three separate women? What can I do to his body with mine to make him feel as though he's married to a geisha one night and good old me the next? Positions will be discussed but they are not the most significant aspect.

We've tried most of the combinations that are possible for two people who aren't double jointed. We bought a book some time ago that advertised 549 different positions, all sketched in living color. That was a waste of $6.95. They turned out to be subtle variations of the basic eight or ten, many of them requiring only a shift in leg placement. And anyone who's made love knows that you rarely get your legs in exactly the same place on subsequent occasions. There are only a handful of true basics—man on top, woman on top, facing front or back, side by side, or rear entry. It's what you do with each one that increases the number of modifications. You can keep the basic position, then stand up, kneel, sit up, sit in a chair, or both of you can stand on your heads. The possibilities are endless and anyone with a fair degree of imagination can figure out most of them without buying the book. Once some enterprising soul figured out that there are about 14,000 variations. The funny part is you've probably tried 12,000 and don't even know it.

Let's talk about erogenous zones; a better term for lay folks might be hot spots—you touch them, or someone else touches them, and they feel good. As a matter of fact, they feel great, they turn you on, they make you feel hot. We think of them as nipples, breasts, ear lobes, and the entire genital area for a woman and as the penis and scrotum (balls) for a man. Well, we made a marvelous discovery. Our whole bodies are one big hot spot depending on mood and how we are handled, caressed, kissed, or stroked. With a very small degree of difference, the areas are the same for both of us. Dick has nipples. Why shouldn't they feel as good when they're kissed as mine do?

Personal choice is something else, and you may decide mentally whether a part of your body can be stimulated or not. Your brain tells your body in advance what it will let you enjoy. "That's dirty. I shouldn't like it so I won't let myself." Some men honestly don't like their nipples kissed. But some won't *let* themselves enjoy it because they feel it's unmasculine (how sad!). I'm not crazy about having my buttocks stroked because it doesn't do much to me, but it doesn't turn me off. There have been nights when we have been making long, slow love, and I've been very aroused by Dick laying his body across my buttocks and gently brushing back and forth with it or with his cock. Everything depends on the mood and my frame of mind.

Under the right circumstances, any part of your body can be used to arouse your mate in a very pleasant way. I can run my index finger over Dick's body from his shoulder blades to the inside of his arm, and it will invariably turn him on. Why? Because he knows immediately that when I just use that finger, I'm thinking about sex. If he's sitting reading the paper and feels that one fingernail running across the back of his neck, he usually gets an erection, which is exactly the response I wanted.

Normally I'm extremely ticklish. If any part of my back is massaged, I become a giggling, squirming female in ten seconds. But, when we're making love, I can lie on my stomach and let Dick use his hands, his fingertips, his penis, or his whole body to run across the same area, and not feel ticklish. I just get hot.

We've found that any parts of our bodies can be used as arousal points, and any parts of our bodies can be used, if they protrude, to arouse each other. (Yes, even noses!) In the early days of our marriage we tended to think automatically of the same few hot spots, usually in the same sequence, whenever we made love. We began kissing, then stroking breasts, and finally fondling the penis, the scrotum, or the vagina. After that we either started over, used combinations of two, or moved quickly into intercourse. It was all over in about twenty minutes, and it was very pleasant. But after a few years of the same patterns, it was still pleasant, but dull. Like a plain bologna sandwich, it satisfies your hunger but there's not much pizzaz!

By discovering other erotic places on our bodies and other ways to stimulate them, we not only broke the boredom but also created a new mood each time we made love. One of our biggest discoveries was that both of us didn't have to be doing something at the same time. One night I could lie back and let Dick gently stroke my entire body with his hand, or with one finger, or maybe with his penis. As a result, I felt more like a woman, cared about and cherished. He was willing to do something for my body that demanded no reciprocation. He was making love to me not just having intercourse. And he got just as hot.

Another night I could do the same thing for him, using my breasts, my stomach, my hair, or even my toes. A toe moving over your body feels very much like a finger, but the mental image and the sensation it creates can be far more stimulating occasionally. Why? Simply because you know it's a toe. It's kinky. It makes you feel mildly wicked.

Every woman wants to feel cherished by her lover; a man is no different. He needs to be made love to in a soothing way to heal some of the bruises and scars that he picks up daily trying to provide for his family. Every so often he needs a geisha girl in bed instead of the efficient household manager who makes the washer repairman jump and who gets all the noses properly wiped. Men have marvelous fantasies about being made love to, and I'd rather fill those fantasies for Dick than have someone else do it. Many women fantasize, too. Some would like to strip just once, if they were sure they wouldn't be laughed at. Or they'd like to feel like someone's mistress, or maybe even a prostitute, instead of the nice girl who wipes the crumbs from the table and always get the grape-juice stains out of the shirts.

Not too long ago, we went to a local motel for a weekend to have some time to ourselves. Since the motel was across town and Dick was coming directly from work, we decided to meet there. As I checked in by myself, saying that my husband would be along shortly, I realized how fishy that must sound. I kept thinking about it as I followed the bellhop to the room, wondering what was going throug his mind. Probably some guy shacking up with his mistress for the weekend. I felt great when the room door was opened and I saw a red rose and a card propped up on the dresser. A few minutes later a rap on the door brought another bellhop with two drinks on a tray. Now, nobody does this for his wife! It's got to be some broad with her lover! Did I feel great!

I decided to act accordingly. Knowing that Dick had never been on time in his life, I took a long, soapy bubble bath and put on the shortest, sheerest, sexiest black thing that he'd ever given me. By the time I stretched out on the bed to wait and to contemplate the mental image of myself, I was really warm. I wasn't me—I was another woman entirely and I could hardly wait for him to walk through that door. As usual, he'd known exactly what he was doing. It was a fantastic weekend!

While we're on the subject of using different techniques to create various moods for lovemaking, we must mention the lotion massage. This was developed by Masters and Johnson as part of their treatment for premature ejaculation among other problems. It is a marvelous vehicle for breaking the ice and getting rid of some of those old hangups about touching each other. We think every newlywed couple should start off with this treatmentt as a means toward feeling free and relaxed with each other's bodies.

Both partners should be informed of the ground rules. First, only one person will be massaged at a time.

That person should feel relaxed and should have no guilt feelings because he or she is doing nothing to reciprocate. Don't think about it. Just lie back and enjoy what's happening. Second, there is a time limit of thirty minutes to each partner's turn. Third, there are certain positions to be maintained throughout.

Start with the man leaning back against the headboard of the bed in a sitting position with his legs flat and apart. The woman sits in the same position, between his legs, with her back against his chest, leaning against him. He begins massaging her body with lotion (Masters and Johnson suggest light lotion) starting with her face, cheekbones, eyelids, and working downward. He moves very slowly, knowing that he has a half hour to cover her whole body, ending with the entire genital area. He can reach every part of her body, even the underside of her legs and feet if she draws her knees up. At the end of the half hour, the couple switch positions. She sits against the back of the bed in his place, and he lies flat on the bed facing her, with his genital area and hips on her lap, and his legs straddling her on either side. She then uses the lotion to massage his entire body in the same way. I forgot the mention that this is done in the light—preferably candlelight.

The incredible thing about this simple technique is not that it's wildly erotic, but that we both felt a tremendous wave of contentment. Touch is a beautiful way of expressing warmth and tenderness for another person, aside from sex. It's the ability to feel a whole person, his eyelids and the skin over his rib cage, and to watch his eyes and the body react to the touching. The lotion gave the freedom to touch, to linger, to explore.

I guess that brings us back to the topic of position, doesn't it? We believe that every couple should have some degree of variation in the positions they use, if only to continue the mood they created during foreplay. If I'm playing my broad-on-the-loose role at the motel, then to maintain that mood I should be on top that night. In the woman astride position I can do more with my body, while Dick can lie back and enjoy it. If I'm tired or depressed, Dick sometimes makes love to me from the rear in the side-by-side position. Our bodies are very close with both his arms around me, and I feel that he is cuddling and taking care of me rather than just screwing me.

Any position should fill two requirements: It should be good for both of us and it should fit the mood. Some are better for one than for the other, and some are ridiculous (making love standing up). We should feel perfectly free to say, "That sounded good but it turned out to be an utter fiasco, so let's forget it in the future." It's not a reflection on our ability to perform; it simply was no good for us.

Often during intercourse we switch positions once or twice. Usually it's when we're both in the mood for fun and horsing around. One night after changing positions and merrily rolling around, we came too close to the edge of the bed without realizing it. With the next roll we fell right out of bed with a crash that I thought would bring down the house. Fortunately, neither of us were hurt. And after we stopped laughing we just kept going on the floor.

The other two things which determine the position we use are tightness of fit for Dick and some type of stimulation for me. The rear-entry position has the best fit for him but isn't good for me because his cock approaches from the back and doesn't hit my clitoris. If he uses his hand or a vibrator to stimulate me, everything is fine for both of us. But I had to tell him that rear entry wasn't too satisying on its own. Unless you speak up, your mate is not going to know what's good or bad for you.

Our favorite position has me on top, with both of us sitting up, facing each other. It produces the best stimulation for me, a tight fit for Dick, and the mutual freedom to see, touch, and kiss each other. We have found only one drawback—my feet go to sleep after a short time of kneeling back on them.

Let's talk about menstruation, specifically about whether or not to make love during menstruation. It should be your choice as a couple. More often it is the woman's choice alone. If she has a negative attitude toward sex, she says "no." But you should realize that the man's drive doesn't stop or slow down just because you happen to be menstruating. Nobody told his body, so it's producing sperm normally, and probably on the third day he's going to wake up with a hard-on. It's difficult for me to say, "Tough luck, you'll have to wait three more days." I love Dick and I want to do anything I can for him. It isn't really a matter of accommodation, it's a recognition of his needs. I'd *like* to satisfy those needs because I do love him. No one said I had to. Moreover, perhaps I miss sex during those five or six days.

We found several ways to continue making love during menstruation. During the first few days we do not have intercourse because my body doesn't feel up to snuff. But there isn't any reason why I can't help him climax orally, with my hand, or with the vibrator. We have heard about another method which we haven't tried yet. The man rubs his penis between the woman's breasts until he climaxes. When my flow becomes light, we sometimes make love in the tub or shower. Both of us feel totally comfortable with all these methods because of something that Dick once said to me. "This is your penis. Do whatever you want to with it, whenever you want." That statement made me think a great deal about our closeness and sharing our love. I do think of Dick's penis as ours, and I want to take care of it for us.

As long as we've mentioned vibrators, we would like to talk about them and some other devices that we use to liven up things once in awhile. We consider them toys because they signify fun and games for us.

For several years we had been using our flat, circular massage vibrator in sex. While it's the greatest thing in the world for back rubs, that large, round head poses something of a problem if you try to use it around a woman's vagina. It's similar to using a monkey wrench to take off a half-inch bolt. It just doesn't fit the job. And while the vibrator could be turned on edge, it was clumsy and sometimes uncomfortable when used for sexual stimulation. So we invested in the proper one for our purpose. Ours is long and narrow; the entire thing vibrates. It's specifically made for insertion in the vagina.

Everybody should have a vibrator. Not only can it be inserted in the vagina, but it also can be used to stimulate the clitoris, the nipples, or the area around the rectum. One of the hottest spots on Dick's body is the area between the rectum and the scrotum, and the vibrator is shaped perfectly to run up and down this region and drive him wild. It produces fantastic sensations when used to slowly stimulate the underside of his penis or its head, or when it is very gently pressed against or lightly rubbed over his balls. Another incredibly wild sensation is produced when we combine the vibrator with oral stimulation. If I suck the head of his penis while running the vibrator over the rest of it, he goes out of his mind. The possibilities are practically unlimited. If you have an extra $10.00 some day, I can't think of a better way to spend it.

There was a time when I felt a little squeamish about using any type of artificial device, but eventually I decided that it wasn't any different from putting on a black nightgown or using music or candlelight to stimulate Dick. The purpose was the same in either case, more excitement and more variety in our love life for both of us. Tongue in cheek, Dick came home with the specially shaped vibrator, but as soon as we discovered the pleasure derived from using it, our toy department expanded rapidly. Whenever we take trips, we bring along a little black bag which contains lotions and oils of different kinds, a few varieties of French ticklers, and a flexible rubber penis that serves a multitude of different uses. The latter can be inserted in the vagina when you are having oral sex or using the vibrator to stimulate other parts of the body. That's one black bag I hope the airlines never lose— for their sake, not ours.

Somehow, somewhere along the line, perhaps when Dick ordered the vibrator, we managed to get on the pornographic literature lists of several distributors in the country. At times the stuff pours into the house and some of it is really funny as long as you can keep it out of the children's hands. Did you know that you can buy French ticklers by the gross for $84.00? That is, if you happen to be in need of a gross of the "washable and re-usable" type.

There must be a hundred varieties of artificial penises. Some have bumps and feathers and ridges; others are plain pink or are artistically decorated with lifelike colored veins and arteries. How about the pneumatic penis that slips on over your own and can be pumped up with air? There's even a double-ended version for lesbians.

And if you're looking for a little gadget to slip on over your penis, there are stiffeners, extenders, and splints for sagging cocks. One version has its own set of balls attached. The manufacturers even thoughtfully include a tiny tape measure so that you can order the correct size.

Looking for a vibrator? Choose an old-fashioned penis shape; the bent penis shape; or a penis with a fringe on top. There's even a model on a long shaft with a tiny hand at the end that waves and another type which glows in the dark. Is your wife away on vacation with the children? How about the new vibrating artificial vagina which rhythmically expands and contracts while it vibrates? Whatever you might find interesting is available somewhere, and every month the manufacturers seem to come out with a "new and improved" version.

If you can't find any stores in your city that carry vibrators, pick up a couple of men's magazines. They will probably contain some mail-order advertising for these products.

Water beds might be considered another artificial aid to lovemaking. Some hotels now have them. The next time you travel ask for one when you make your reservation. They're truly comfortable to sleep on, and they're marvelous for screwing. Their flexibility allows you to try positions for intercourse that you couldn't use on a regular mattress. In addition, you just have to start the rhythm and the bed sustains it. It's difficult to describe the sensation because it's unique. But don't smoke in bed! Water beds have a nasty habit of gushing out hundreds of gallons of liquid if they come into contact with a hot ash.

We've already mentioned that Dick and I find the time after lovemaking most conducive to intimate conversation. If we've managed to create that feeling of love and being loved during intercourse, this is also the best time to hold onto and share it a little longer. I like to lie for a few minutes with Dick's arms around me. If he abruptly rolled over and went to sleep, I think I'd feel used, or if I did, he might feel that he had merely been accommodated.

There was a line in an old Paul Newman movie that summed up things well: "I may not be able to give you much in the way of material things, but I guarantee that every morning you'll wake up with a smile on your face." That's the way it should be.

6.

Oral Sex: Why Didn't Someone Tell Us Sooner?

THE VOLUNTEER COMMITTEE OF the Society for Conjugal Rhapsody Every Wednesday (SCREW) is having a luncheon at the Wally-Wally Club. The subject on their agenda for this month is "Oral Sex—Should We or Shouldn't We?" Mrs. Hardapple has been assigned the task of presenting information for the pro side of the argument, while Mrs. Drybottom has volunteered to speak for the negative side. The latter has fathered every social taboo over the past three centuries concerning oral sex: From nice people don't do that, to the Church's teaching that the only legitimate reason for sex was the procreation of children. Therefore, unless the sperm ended up in the vagina, you had committed a mortal sin. Mrs. Drybottom can spew out in machine order all the negatives. At the climax of her arguments she plans to devastate her opposition with one simple and profound statement: "Give me one good reason why we should try oral sex!" At this point she will triumphantly seat herself amid the finger sandwiches and the silence to smirk.

Mrs. Drybottom has never approached me with her question and, unfortunately, I wasn't invited to attend today's meeting. I would love to answer her "one good reason" with three simple words—BECAUSE IT'S FANTASTIC! If that isn't enough to recommend it to the ladies of SCREW, we can suggest other valid reasons to incorporate it into your lovemaking. Oral sex is probably the surest and fastest way for a woman to come to a climax. It produces my most intense orgasms. There are times when a woman may be left unsatisfied because her husband climaxed early and oral lovemaking can be a delightful way to resolve the situation.

It can be practiced by the woman as a consideration for her husband's needs when she is menstruating, or at any other time when it's not possible for her to have regular intercourse. How about those long weeks just before and after childbirth? Oral sex can help a man through these periods of abstinence. Not only is it the fastest way to bring a woman to a climax, it's also the fastest way to excite a man. If he's having trouble getting a good hard-on some night because he's tired or worried, oral will usually do the job quickly. And Dick says that it's also the most effective means to bring him back a second time. Women reap the benefits because men last longer on the second round.

It sounds as though we're selling something and we said we wouldn't do that. After you've seen a great movie or read a truly exciting book, don't you want to

71

tell other people about it so that they can enjoy it? We feel the same way about oral sex. It is a terrific part of our total lovemaking and we're enthusiastic about it.

Unfortunately, oral sex has been swept under the rug for so long that an air of perversion and dirtiness has surrounded it. "Nice people don't do that." Of course they do! And they have for centuries. In the past, they didn't tell Mrs. Drybottom about it because of the reaction it might provoke. We were genuinely surprised several months ago to find ourselves in a situation where people were actually willing to talk about it face to face. At a two-day seminar on marriage, the general subject of sex naturally arose and was thoroughly discussed. On the second day, however, the talk turned to oral sex. After some initial hedging, it was discussed openly and without embarrassment, and at least three-fourths of the couples admitted it was a regular and enjoyable part of their lovemaking. And those were people of all ages and from all walks of life. (Quick, Mrs. Hardapple, take those figures down!)

Probably the strangest phenomenon about oral lovemaking is that it's often a one-way street. Here is the one area in sex where the man is not the aggressor. After listening to several men's comments throughout the years, Dick has decided that most men love the idea of oral for themselves, but turn very squeamish when it comes to going down on a woman. Even in situations where the woman has been going down on the man for years, it's often difficult to get him to reciprocate.

Dick says it really isn't so hard to understand in light of the sex education he and most boys received. This is a case in which pure biology makes a difference. If a girl knew that oral sex meant kissing, sucking, and licking, once she got a look at a penis, it was pretty obvious what she should do with it. But what about the man? It's not so simple or obvious for him. Which thing do I kiss when I get down there? Where can I bite, where can I suck, without doing something wrong? I've never even seen what it looks like down there. He was strictly on his own. At that time, there weren't any manuals on oral sex. And who wants to look like a fool the first time he tries something?

Many men don't even want to try—not only because the techniques are cloudy, but also because they're afraid of what they might encounter when they get down there. The psychologist Eric Berne had a great phrase to describe the frustration many males feel. Men have "outdoor plumbing" but women have "indoor plumbing." Anything you don't understand is naturally going to make you hesitant, and female plumbing is a prime example. Is it going to be sloppy, wet, and gushy? If you've ever put a hand between a woman's legs when she's hot, you know that it's wet down there. Although most boys know that, they're not sure where the wetness comes from or why. What will it taste like? What's it going to smell like? Since there isn't any way to find out besides plunging right in, they'd just as soon pass.

Men aren't the only ones who hesitate about oral sex, however. Many women who are perfectly willing to go down on their men are not sure enough of themselves to have the situation reversed. They are reluctant because they don't know what it's going to taste or smell like. After all these years, I still can't relax and enjoy having Dick go down on me unless I've had a shower before we make love. And it was quite a while after I had been going down on Dick that it became a mutual treat. Most of the delay can be attributed to the reasons we've just mentioned.

A woman, however, may find herself frustrated by this one-way-street attitude. "I'm willing to do it for him; why isn't he willing to do it for me?" He may be a prisoner of all those mystery hang-ups and, understanding this, she may have to help him along initially. Perhaps she could find a way to let him see, touch, and explore her whole genital area before she asks him for oral sex. The Masters and Johnson lotion treatment might resolve the problem easily. This time, however, the woman could reverse the positions so that her genital area was in his lap and she was lying back facing him.

As far as cleanliness is concerned, it really is important for men and women. You should make certain that you are very clean before trying oral sex for the first time or it may be your last. Even the most devoted lover is going to be automatically turned off if he encounters offensive odors. We always take a shower, often together, immediately before any type of oral lovemaking. Washing well everywhere with lots of soapy lather, should take care of any odor. Don't forget the rectum. Even though you may not be planning to go near it, that area is at eye-to-eye level during oral sex.

Pleasant little extra touches are optional. They might make you feel more delectable and, of course, that will help you both to relax more. Women can perfume the insides of their thighs, men can use aftershave lotion. Don't, don't, *don't* use anything directly on your vagina or penis, no matter how sweet you'd like to smell! It stings like hell.

One of the companies that puts out vaginal sprays also makes a douche for women in raspberry, orange, and champagne flavors. Not fragrances—flavors! Look for it in the women's sanitary supplies section of your drugstore. Or if you have enough nerve, march up to the counter and ask the sixty-year-old lady with the glasses where to find it.

How about genital hair? It's probably cleaner than the hair on your head. After all, you probably shower more often than you wash your hair. But genital hair tends to get in the way and it sometimes gets in your mouth, so many people shave it off completely. We did this for a long time, and it raised a new and very funny problem for us. What would happen when Dick changed for a swim in the men's locker room? I kept teasing him about this until a few months ago when the tables were suddenly turned on me. I had made an appointment with my obstetrician. In two weeks there I would be, bald as a billiard ball, and I knew he'd ask me why. I couldn't say the razor slipped while I was shaving my legs. I stood in the shower every morning, yanking at the fuzz, saying, "Grow! Grow!" Thank God, by the time the appointment rolled around I had a half presentable crew-cut that didn't provoke any questions at all.

What about taste? That's a problem for men who want their wives to take the sperm in their mouths and swallow it; and for women who would like to have their husbands go down on them. We all wonder, "What's it like? How do I really taste?" There's an easy way to find out. Just taste yourself sometime. If you're a woman, check yourself with a finger the next time you're hot. If you're a man, find out after intercourse as you're cleaning up. Or if you want to find out what the other person tastes like, reverse the process. If you'd rather not have the other person know, it can be done easily and quietly, during or after lovemaking. And don't feel as though you're doing anything dishonest or sly. It's simply a matter of getting yourself used to something in slow stages before you try it full scale. It may make oral sex more enjoyable, and for that reason alone it's worth it.

Sperm does have a definite taste and smell, but in no way is it unpleasant. It's just that it doesn't taste like anything else. Dick says that vaginal secretions are no different; they have their own special taste and fragrance. However, he's found that there is one time during the month that the taste is stronger and is not as pleasant. For approximately two days while a woman ovulates, her body secretes an alkaline substance to aid the sperm along. It has a distinct taste and odor that's rather bitter and musky. If your husband is thinking about going down on you for the first time, it might be a good idea to have him wait until that short period is over.

If you're comfortable with the whole idea of oral sex, you will discover that there are more positions to get into and more things that you can combine with it than any other aspect of sex. Just as the clitoris is the most sensitive spot in regular intercourse, so is it in oral. Anything you've ever considered doing with your hands can be done with your mouth—and more. You can kiss, lick, or suck the clitoris gently or strongly, depending on your partner's preference. You can rub your beard or stubble lightly against it and produce a dramatic response. You can tickle the opening of the vagina, stroke, or suck with your tongue and you can use it to thrust in and out just as effectively as a penis to arouse a totally different feeling. If you hold the clitoris between your lips and then shake your head from side to side, it will cause wild sensations for your mate.

Dick seems to have such a good time popping, whistling, and shaking his head, that I wonder which of us is really getting more out of it. The possibilities, he finds, are endless as long as he remembers not to be too rough or to bite too hard.

Positions in which the woman is most open or accessible are, of course, best. If you can't reach it, you can't cause much sensation, obviously. For the same reason, having both partners on the bed, with the woman lying flat and the man trying to reach her from below doesn't work too well; the man is going to end up with a good kink in his neck. In this position, her hips should be resting on several pillows to make her more easily accessible. Or even better she should be lying on the edge of the bed with her legs hanging over the side, or on his shoulders. Then he can kneel on the floor comfortably and see and reach the entire area easily. Another plus for this position is that her whole body is stretched out before him. He can watch it move and see her face as he makes love to her.

In one of our favorite positions, Dick lies flat on the bed and I kneel above him, directly over his face. He has complete mobility and access. He can see all of me, reach up and touch me, and I can look down and watch him. Even though there isn't much I can do, we feel very close because we can look at one another.

When a woman is making love orally to a man the number of positions or techniques is almost infinite. Again, as with a woman, gentleness is the key. The whole penis or any part of it can be licked, kissed, blown on, sucked, or tickled with your tongue. It can be bitten or nipped if it's done lightly. The head or tip, and the rim surrounding it, plus the entire lower side of the shaft, are the most sensitive areas, so concentrate your efforts there. Running your tongue over his balls, or taking them gently into your mouth and sucking on them, will probably drive him right out of his head. Run your tongue in a straight line from the balls to the rectum, around it, and back again. This is an area on most men's bodies that really gets hot.

Combine any of the oral techniques of kissing, licking, or sucking with other techniques, and you have a whole new set of variables. Why not use your hands in combination with your mouth, or the vibrator? Suck the head of the penis while you stroke or squeeze the shaft. Hold that cock tightly in your mouth and suck it hard, while you run the vibrator over the lower half of it and then down onto his balls. Or lick and tickle the balls with your tongue, while you use the vibrator over the entire shaft and around the head and rim of the penis. The intensity of the sensations is so great that I don't think there's a man alive who'll ask you to stop. Sometimes a cigarette break for a few minutes at this point will enable him to cool down a little and give him a chance to last longer before coming.

Just as it's easier to see what can be done for a man, it's easier to do it. A woman is unrestricted in the positions for making love orally to a man, with one exception. With a hard erection, a man's penis sticks outward and upward from his body at an angle of about 45 degrees. Anything that forces that angle down is going to hurt. So as long as the head and underside are easily reached and you don't pull the cock down, any position is good. He can sit in a chair, lie on the bed, or stand up with you kneeling at his feet. Or you can lie flat on the bed with him kneeling above your face and straddling your shoulders. Probably the best position is lying flat on the bed, with the woman at right angles to the man's body. Both persons are comfortable and if she curves her hips toward him, he can stimulate her with his fingers while she is using her mouth.

A man has one great advantage over a woman in oral sex. She can suck him off in the car while they're stalled for an hour in a freeway backup, and no one will be the wiser. Except for the expression on his face, the motorist in the next car would probably think he was sitting alone, listening to the news.

We haven't mentioned sixty-nine yet—the subject of all those high-school locker room jokes. In case you weren't in the locker room at the time, we're referring to simultaneous oral sex. Both partners make love to each other at the same time, with one of them on top, or side by side, facing in opposite directions. The reason we saved it till last is because we don't use it very often. And not because it isn't good—it is! Part of the problem is that it's too good. When both of us are going at it full tilt, the sensations are so wild and so intense that it's hard to concentrate on what you're doing. It's also difficult not to get carried away and become too rough, particularly for me. When we make love orally I invariably have at least one orgasm, sometimes many. At the moment of climax a woman's body becomes taut and she loses track of what she is doing. If Dick's cock is in my mouth at that moment, I bite down hard without thinking. It's a natural reaction on my part but it really isn't much fun for Dick. So now when I feel an orgasm coming on, I am smart enough to push myself away from him and wait until it's over.

When you're in the mood for fun and games, nothing is better than oral sex. In fact, it becomes a game itself. Probably the most famous example, and I think it came from *Portnoy's Complaint*, was spearing a cupcake with a marshmallow center on the man's cock and then eating it off. I have heard a story about the man with a passion for oysters who stuffed his wife's vagina with them and then sucked them out one at a time. Seedless grapes sound somewhat more sanitary from a woman's point of view, if you're looking for an exotic way to have a midnight snack. Either example is pretty funny, if you happen to be in the mood. I remember reading somewhere about using whipped cream in an aerosol can to decorate a man's penis for dessert. Frankly that doesn't appeal to me nearly as much as cheese in an aerosol can. Before the psychiatrists bear down on me and have a good time with that one, let me just say that I don't have a sweet tooth. Besides, cheese is more masculine than whipped cream.

You might want to try the water technique. Fill your mouth with warm water and carefully slide in the man's penis. Swish the water carefully around like a mouthwash, and you'll drive him right out of his mind. It's very effective, but I have to offer a word of caution. Before you try it on your husband, practice slipping two of your fingers into your mouth when it's filled with water. It sounds simple, but it's not. The first time I tried the watch technique on Dick proved embarrassing. I went dashing off to the bathroom saying, "Close your eyes. I have a surprise for you." It really was a surprise because a minute later there was water all over him and the bed.

There really isn't much more to say about oral sex, except that we love it. (You've probably gathered that already.) For us it's exciting and a great way to broaden and diversify our love life. When you're that enthusiastic about something, it's hard not to encourage other people to at least consider it. How about a big billboard on the Los Angeles freeway?

TRY ORAL—YOU'LL LIKE IT!
(With a smiling face beneath.)

7.

Orgasms: Mine, Yours, and Nobody Else's

WHAT'S AN ORGASM ANYWAY? And what's all the fuss about lately? In the last year it seems that almost every magazine we've picked up has had an article on orgasms. There appears to be a battle raging but some of us didn't know there was a war. Clitoral orgasm vs. vaginal orgasm—which do you choose? Simultaneous orgasm vs. separate orgasm—which is more healthy for your psyche? Who can set a new world record for the most in the least amount of time? Will Marsha Mongoose make it tomorrow with fifty-one in eleven minutes? Who cares? Have you ever had the feeling that you'd just like to shake the world and say, "Hey, c'mon! Let's forget all this nonsense and talk about what's really important to me—*my* orgasm."

The great orgasm race, or who's running it, shouldn't concern us at all. But it does. Everywhere we turn there are new views and articles forcing us to make comparisons. If we could close our eyes for awhile and shut out the world, what would matter to us? Just our own private, personal orgasm, and the amount of contentment it beings us. Let's get some of the controversy out of the way so that we can get back to concentrating on our own and to enjoying it.

First, an orgasm is an intense, exciting, physical sensation for women and men. Next to pain, it's probably the most intense sensation that our bodies can experience. I could care less what's happening to my body medically or physiologically while I'm having one; the only thing I want to do is lie back and enjoy it while it lasts. Is an orgasm describable? Probably not. But when you've had one you know it.

Second, orgasms differ in intensity for each of us, and every orgasm is unique. Sometimes they can be so wild and violent that you feel you may blow apart. At other times they may be mild and gentle, leaving you with a feeling of mellowness and contentment instead of exhausted passion. If they are that different for one person, certainly they must vary even more between man and woman, between two women, or between two men. Male or female, the basic result is a feeling of tremendous satisfaction. The sensations of intense pleasure and satisfaction are very similar whether you have your orgasm during intercourse or through masturbation. (Score one for women's lib!) However, masturbation is lonely and intercourse is fun.

An orgasm is an orgasm. The stimulation that causes one is different for everyone. Stimulating the clitoris is unquestionably the fastest way to bring me on, but occasionally I can reach one simply by having the small of my back fondled. I know a woman who reaches them fastest having her breasts fondled, and another who can have an orgasm by kissing. It proves once again that each of us is an individual. We have to concentrate primarily on finding out what's best for us. As long as Dick knows what to do for me, and I for him, we're happy.

Does size and shape or thickness of your sex organs have any effect on your ability to perform or to be satisfied? No. A man has feeling in every inch of his penis and naturally the more pressure that's applied to it, the more sensations he'll receive. Even though a man does get greater pleasure and intensity of feeling from an orgasm in a tightly fitting vagina, he doesn't have to search for a new one every few years. No matter how loose or saggy a woman's vaginal muscles might become through childbirth, the fit can be tightened again by changing positions. The rear-entry position is much tighter than the standard missionary position, for example. If you are enterprising, there are vaginal exercises that can be done unobtrusively. They consist of tightening the vaginal muscles for a few seconds, then releasing them. A minor operation, not unlike pulling up the skin for a face lift, can also be performed.

The size of a man's penis, or how well hung he is, has very little to do with his ability to satisfy a woman. What he does with it and how, makes all the difference in the world. How hard or how deep he can bang away with it doesn't matter a great deal, because only 14 percent of women have any feeling within the vaginal entrance. For most women, it's totally dead. Isn't that surprising? So it's dead, and that makes the length of a penis relatively unimportant. The angle and the technique that a man uses, and the area that the penis rubs as it goes in and out causes the orgasms. The size of a woman's clitoris has no relationship to her ability to be satisfied. Dick and I had a hard time just finding the clitoris.

Many people seem to wonder how many orgasms they should have. Well, how many do you need? There are nights when I have one and I am the happiest person in the world. There are other nights when I can have three or more and be equally content. It depends on my body's ability to respond—where my saturation level is for that night. If I'm tired, it makes a difference. The mood makes a difference. How Dick stimulates me makes a difference. No two lovemaking sessions are really comparable, but one thing is the same. When I'm finished I know it, and I'm content. I don't care whether the woman in the next house or in the next motel room is having nine or ninety-nine that night. I'm happy and I'm not trying to compete with her.

Men have the same problem when it comes to multiple orgasms, but they handle it somewhat more realistically. Sure, they would like greater numbers because orgasms are as satisfying for them as they are for women. But while the desire or wish is there, physically it's not always possible for a man to come back a second or third time. When he fades he fades, and there's not much he can do about it for the moment. A breather and some time to rest may help, or he may need a woman's help to bring him back, but when he's finished for the night he knows it. He doesn't try to keep beating a dead horse, and maybe that's where we women have made a mistake in allowing the orgasm race to start for us. Our bodies probably are sending us the same message when we've reached our personal saturation point. Perhaps we're not listening.

The dangerous game of multiple sex orgasms could hurt our marriages. The new sexual freedom for women is great as long as it doesn't place an impossible burden on men to perform. "She's entitled to multiple orgasms. What's wrong with me if I can't give her six?" We might end up with a lot of worried and worn-out husbands, trying to prove a new form of masculinity, a new locker-room quota to get psychologically hung up on.

Every woman would like one or several orgasms every time. That's a natural desire, but we have to be realistic and recognize that it's not always going to happen. And if it doesn't, it may not be our husband's fault. It might be ours that night. Perhaps we're tired and can't get ourselves up for once. Why should that make us feel that we've failed, or that he's failed us? When we start saying to ourselves, "What's wrong with me if I don't have six?" we're in trouble.

Remember, sex is supposed to be fun, beautiful, and spontaneous, not a time trial with someone the winner and someone the loser. If you're happy with one, that's great. Forget the rest of the world. Let's quit trying to prove something in bed, and waving that bedsheet around as though it were some kind of banner for a new cause.

Another locker-room performance level that some "experts" feel we should meet is the simultaneous orgasm. If you'd really like to worry and take all the joy out of sex, try that one. It's almost impossible for two people to climax together by plan. Occasionally, it happens by accident and that's great, but when you have to work at it, it takes away the spontaneity and fun. I'd rather concentrate on my own, whenever it comes, and then on Dick's. The same is true for Dick.

It's a fantastic feeling to have a man explode inside you and be aware of it, or for a woman to surround a man's penis with her contractions. Whenever we do come together, we can't feel each other's and we miss it. Anyway, it's just one more contest, one more hang-up, and we're trying to get rid of some of ours, not add more.

8.

Funeral Rites for the Myths, Gaps, and "No-No's"

AS LITTLE CHILDREN WE'RE naturally curious about all aspects of life. We charge off merrily in pursuit of anything that looks interesting. Often children's normal wonderment and zest for exploration puts them on a collision course with the adult world's standards. Baby boys reach out for their penises with as much freedom as they do for their fingers and toes. Not until some grown-up points out that this is a terrible no-no, do they recognize the difference. How many of us were caught at one time happily playing doctor with the kids across the street and immediately made to feel ashamed or dirty? We were being normal children, full of curiosities about life, but especially about ourselves and our beautiful little bodies.

The "no THERE's" and the "no-no-dirty's" are quickly absorbed and learned by us as youngsters. We grow up to be model citizens who don't scratch their fannies on the bus no matter how much they itch, and we don't ask men where the sperm goes when they masturbate. Somewhere inside the big adult body that knows all the rules, the inquisitive little child still lurks, with his unanswered questions. But as we learn more and more rules, it gets increasingly difficult to ask those questions of anyone.

Nothing world-shaking is usually left unanswered after marriage, but there are several minor questions that nibble at your mind occasionally. One night several years ago when we were talking about venereal disease, Dick asked me a very funny question. He said, "I've never understood how women can sit down on a public toilet that thousands of strangers have used. Even if you're not worried about venereal disease, don't you want to know who used the seat before you?" I was so surprised that I just stared at him. "We never sit down. That's a basic lesson that mothers teach their young daughters." Now he was really confused. "If you don't sit down, then how do you go to the bathroom?" My first reaction was to blurt out, "We squat, stupid!" because it's so obvious if you're a woman and you've been doing it all your life. But then I realized that there wasn't any way he could possibly know that. Unless, as a child, he had asked that kind of question, it would never have arisen. And for years he had wondered what the chances were of a woman unsuspectingly picking up V.D. in a public restroom and bringing it home to her husband. With today's new knowledge we know that the chances are very slim whether we sit or squat.

There's another question that we don't like to ask about or admit to ourselves. What's the other person thinking about sexually? What goes through his mind when he's daydreaming about it? Does he think about other women? Would he like to make love to them? Does she think about other men? When we're making love, does she ever pretend that I'm someone else?

We all have sex fantasies at times, and women are no different from men. However, women tend to push them out of their minds because they think the fantasies are dirty or reflect disloyalty. Admit it, ladies! We've hidden our fantasies farther back on the closet shelf than the old love letters! They ought to be brought out, aired occasionally, and enjoyed. Men can regard their fantasies so much more naturally than we can, and as a result, they can enjoy them more.

Unfortunately, we always take the fun out of our fantasies by making ourselves feel guilty.

Take notice of how many men feel perfectly free to comment about another woman in mixed company. "Look at the build on that broad across the street!" You know he's not picturing her in the Miss Universe contest, he's probably visualizing her naked and climbing into bed with him. And there's nothing dirty or abnormal about that. It's a healthy, natural reaction to a good-looking woman. As Dick's often said, "When I get to the point where I don't appreciate a fabulous-looking girl, you had better worry. I'll either be dead, going gay, or malfunctioning badly."

If only we could open up those curiosity valves and ask our mates about their daydreams. Think how much we'd learn about them, and how we could use those dreams to aid our sex lives. If only we could feel safe enough with each other to admit our own mental wanderings without guilt. When Dick and I began to talk about fantasies, it proved to be a freeing experience for both of us. For the first time we felt that we could be totally open, and that the other person would understand. With the realization that fantasies were a natural thing for both of us, we could feel secure in the knowledge that they weren't a sign of dissatisfaction or disloyalty, and they weren't going to be held against us or thrown up as a subject of ridicule in some future quarrel.

And we have learned considerably more about what makes each of us tick sexually. At the same time, we've had a lot of fun sharing these fantasies. We found, for example, that nether of us has ever had any thoughts about engaging in homosexual activity. We've both wondered what it really would be like, but who doesn't wonder? Dick had been exposed to it as a boy, and we know several homosexuals today; but individually we discarded it as not for us. We've talked and thought about affairs with other men or women since we've been married. And we've discussed how each of us would feel about extramarital relations. Don't we all speculate at some time about whether we've been the only one in our mate's life for the past ten years or more? Wouldn't we really like to ask? Often we're afraid to hear the response. "What would I do if he said that there had been others?"

Of course, the most fun is finding out about the other person's earthly fantasies. "If you could pick anybody in the whole world, with the exception of me, who would you sleep with?" For years I've happily idled away a few minutes here and a few minutes there, conjuring up different men who turn me on. My very first true love, for whom I still hold warm, happy feelings. Neil Diamond—he writes such fantastic music and sings it with so much soul that he must be great in the flesh. Rod McKuen—does every woman curl up with his love poems and think he wrote them for her alone, or is it just me? Rod is usually the star at the theater inside my head.

Occasionally a character in a play or movie will turn me on. Not necessarily the actor who's playing the part, but the character himself. Dr. Zhivago is a perfect example. I absolutely fell in love with him and not Omar Sharif who played the role. King Arthur in *Camelot* had the same effect on me. Not Richard Harris, but Arthur.

Every so often the fantasies are more real and closer to home. If I pass an extraordinarily handsome man on the street, or meet one at a party, I might spend a few minutes thinking about what he might be like in bed. Doctors and clergymen as a group tend to turn on many women. Perhaps it is because women go to them with their problems, and usually find a sympathetic and understanding ear. I think emotional involvement is more necessary for women's fantasies than for men's, since we tend to romanticize and visualize being in love more frequently than we fantasize being in bed.

Sometimes the daydreams are purely sexual. If so, the characters are generally nameless and faceless. What would it be like to have two men make love to me at the same time, or go to an orgy, or strip in front of a strange man? These fantasies arouse my curiosity more than my sexual longing. I wonder what it would be like, yet I have no one in mind particularly.

Dick's fantasies are far more interesting than mine. He says that because I'm used to my own, and it's always more fun hearing about someone else's. He's right, of course, because ours are basically the same. Maria Schell has a special place in his fantasies, because she's so earthy looking, and also because she plays such honest, human parts. That appeals to Dick's instinct for reality and openness. Similarly, that reflects back on our marriage since neither of us could survive long in a plastic relationship. Brigitte Bardot turns him on, and long ago, Marilyn Monroe did. Those are two of his strictly physical fantasies.

Very seldom do Dick's fantasies involve people we know, and if that is the case, they are very much like mine. A cute new secretary at the office, or a new woman that we meet might encourage some occasional thoughts. A new face or personality is always intriguing. Usually he tells me, and it doesn't provoke any jealousy or resentment. I quietly make sure we never see that person again! No, seriously, there really is no problem now that we both realize that fantasies are a natural occurrence.

Dick's sexual daydreams are like those of many other men: Visualizing two women making love to him simultaneously; orgies occasionally, and wondering about what they'd be like; screwing, being made love to orally, by whoever might be in his mind at that moment; watching a woman masturbate; and occasionally going to bed with a woman who has really huge breasts.

Although both our fantasies included an orgy or three people, neither Dick nor I was included as one of the partners present. If he daydreamed about two women making love to him simultaneously, I wasn't one of them. If I pictured myself at an orgy, Dick wasn't there. And neither of us ever thought seriously about wife-swapping. When we talked about the subject, we found out that we didn't want to share each

other with someone else. Dick can completely understand that I might think tender thoughts about an old
love, but that doesn't mean he'd enjoy the idea of
actually helping this man make love to me. Neither
would I. Maybe that's the nice thing about fantasies,
and perhaps that's what makes them so healthy. You
know that they're fantasies. You can take them down
from that shelf whenever you want and enjoy them for
what they are. But then you put them back where
they belong and get on with the real business of life
—loving that flesh and blood person that you chose.

9.

Masturbation—Sh-h-h,
Have You Seen Our Mothers?

WHO MASTURBATES? WELL, BESIDES the two of us,
I'm not really sure. Masturbation isn't a subject that is
frequently discussed on the golf course or at a tea.
Why is it that we can masturbate with no hang-ups,
but talking about it is so sticky? I feel as though I'm
about to skate out onto a very thinly iced pond, knowing that ice may crack around me and, knowing too,
that the kindly old lady on the shore in tennis shoes
isn't likely to throw me a life jacket if I start to sink.

We know that we do it, and we have a few friends
who are brave enough to admit that they do. Statistics
show that most people masturbate: two-thirds to three
quarters of all women do as well as the majority of
men. Dick claims there isn't a man living who could
say that he'd never masturbated once in his life. So,
maybe everyone can join us out on the ice now. Even
you, little old lady in tennis shoes. Remember that
first summer at camp when you were so homesick?

If so many of us do, then why is it so terribly hard
to admit? For us, the answer rests once again in our

childhood upbringing. The fears, the dirtiness, the sin concept were drummed into us quite effectively. And no one, until recently, has pointed out any legitimate reasons for masturbation. Until Masters and Johnson and a few others stated that it could be a valuable tool to aid sexually unresponsive wives, nothing good had been said on the subject. Since then, many people, including me, tried to see masturbation in a new light, and soon more and more valid reasons were uncovered.

As I said before, this was a very difficult hang-up for me to overcome, and I am not completely liberated yet. Although I agreed with everyone I was reading. I still felt as though someone were watching from afar with horror. Dick has never had any problem with masturbation, and we were trying to figure out why. He believes that most men can be more comfortable with it simply because they have been doing it longer and more frequently. They come to regard it far more naturally. Years ago he came to terms with himself on the dirtiness and sin aspects and was honestly stunned (and a little sad for me) when I told him that I'd never masturbated. Because it was such a natural and prevalent act in his eyes, he assumed that I had tried it, too. Hadn't everyone? Until two years ago, I was one of the 25 percent in that survey who hadn't masturbated, so I had a lot of catching up to do.

After reading and hearing about some of the recent viewpoints on masturbation, we felt that they were sensible. They were less oriented to the sin concept and more oriented to the understanding of human needs. We had gone through years of trial and error trying to find out how best to stimulate one another. I probably could have learned a great deal by myself in a few short hours of masturbation, he couldn't tell me that. If we had both been open originally, and if I had been more receptive, we could have saved a lot of time wasted on the hit-or-miss method. That realization was the first truly valid reason to rethink some of those hang-ups and early teachings.

Another intriguing reason was the statistics that

we ran across. Ninety-five percent of the women who masturbate have orgasms, and it's possible to train your body to become more responsive. In other words, if you had never had an orgasm through normal intercourse with your husband, masturbation could aid in teaching you how to spark your own body and learn its many trigger points. Then once you had orgasms and knew how you got them, you could help your husband understand your body better and hopefully bring you to orgasms during lovemaking. Now who could argue with that approach? It really made sense to me, and if we could find a way to make love better, then I wanted to start giving it some serious thought.

The whole approach is just as valid for men as for women. Dick feels that even though most men are comfortable with the idea of masturbating, they haven't applied the knowledge gained from it to make their sex lives better. And they could. There are many ways that men masturbate: the quick jack-off that is primarily done for relief. There's also the long, more relaxed, pleasure-oriented situation that allows men not only to enjoy the feeling but also to learn about their bodies and their responses. During these experimental sessions, many men have discovered that they can stop just before reaching orgasm. They let the stimulation die down for a few minutes and start to bring it up again. It is possible for them to continue like this for an hour until they are ready to end it with an orgasm. They do have the control when they want to. Why shouldn't they apply those techniques which they've taught themselves to lovemaking? Dick believes that men can teach their wives how to help prolong intercourse, and therefore make it more enjoyable for both of them. I have nothing against making love for an hour, do you? If that's not a valid reason for looking at masturbation in a healthier light I don't know what is.

Men can teach women where the hot spots are on their own bodies. Most men have no trouble reaching an orgasm, but there are still good, better, and best ways to do it. Most men know what they are; they have been experimenting for years. Why not tell us so that we can do the best job possible when we make love to you. I would not have known that the rim and head of the penis are more sensitive than the shaft if Dick had not told me. "Here, not there, is better. This way, not that way." I might still be yanking on his penis as if I were milking a cow; I might never have touched his nipples or his balls if he hadn't started me in that direction.

There are many positive, healthy reasons for practicing masturbation. One is to relieve the sexual tensions that build up when there is no other outlet. Since we've already admitted that women also get horny, it's equally valid for them. However, society tends to be more understanding about men doing it since their bodies keep chugging away, manufacturing sperm, whether there's a legitimate way to discharge it or not. Males have three alternatives: They can have intercourse, they can have wet dreams, or they can masturbate. If intercourse is ruled out for a prolonged period because of illness, pregnancy, childbirth, or traveling, there are only two options open. Wet dreams, or nocturnal emissions, occur automatically when the sperm builds to a point of overflowing while the male is either half or fully asleep. For some men this happens once a week or once in ten days; for others the frequency may be different. Dick says many adolescent boys begin masturbation after their first wet dream; they find that it was a pleasant experience and thus tend to help it along in the future. Perhaps wet dreams could be regarded as the body's way of masturbating subconsciously. In the past we've tended to treat them with almost the same amount of disdain as masturbation. We (especially mothers) would rather pretend they didn't happen even though they are the only legitimate release we've allowed for teen-age boys.

Let's discuss a theoretical case: You're a woman for whom intercourse has been ruled out for a period of time. (Perhaps you're about to have a baby or your husband is on a business trip for two weeks.) What would you like your husband to do with that excess sperm and the drive to release it? If Dick were stuck in Tokyo for two weeks, I'd rather have him get some relief by masturbating than have him deposit that sperm in some geisha girl who happens to be available. Whether it's in downtown Hackensack or downtown Hong Kong, girls are available. Be realistic and ask yourself what was his alternative.

Maybe he was lonely and bored in Hackensack, or maybe he was tense and insecure at the office and needed to relieve some of those tensions. Or perhaps he got an erection thinking about you. You can't hop in the car, run downtown and screw him at lunchtime, can you? And he can't just lie down on his wall-to-wall carpeting and have a wet dream. Maybe he walks into the men's room and masturbates to help him get through the afternoon. Either way, is it wrong?

On the other hand, if Dick did get sent abroad on business and I couldn't go along I would probably be somewhat jealous. He's having fun and I'm stuck at home with three children who have dirty socks and one with bubonic plague. I'm lonely and I'm probably horny after a week. Loneliness, plus horniness, plus dirty socks equals bitchiness for me. Maybe a car will run over me tomorrow, I'll die, and then he'll really feel bad when he gets home for having such a good time. Poor Dick is going to walk through the front door to find the surliest man-eating monster waiting for him and never know why. Before those natural small jealousies combine with other tensions to create the monster, why not keep the tensions at a minimum. During his absence, Dick would much rather have me masturbate to get rid of the horniness than meet the fire-breathing dragon on his return. I can't say I disagree. It does make me feel better and when I do, the dirty socks don't seem so overwhelming.

Two years ago, after thinking through all the valid reasons for trying masturbation, I decided that there were certain times when it would be healthier for me to masturbate than not. But I had to make my squeamish hang-ups believe that. It seemed best to try it a few times and see how I felt. I knew that if my hand fell off or I went blind, then my hang-ups had been right all along, and I could always revert to my old way of thinking. Fortunately, as the benefits of learning more about my body became apparent to both of us and we could see positive results in our sex life, many of my old attitudes melted away. It had been one of the most difficult sexual subjects for me to talk about, the toughest hang-up to face. Once it was in the open, our marriage reached a deeper level of communication.

One night when we'd been talking and asking each other questions, I said, in half jest, that I'd love to watch a man masturbate just to see how he did it. Dick quietly said, "Would you like to watch me?" After thinking about it for a minute, I said, "Yes, I really would." "Would you be comfortable watching me?" "Yes." And so that night I watched and learned more about my husband than I had in years.

Surprisingly, there was no feeling of embarrassment before or after for either of us. I experienced tremendous curiosity and excitement because I was able to uncover another facet of the man I love, to see a new side of his masculinity. And I also felt a great surge of thankfulness that he was free enough to want to share this with me. For Dick, it was secure and comforting to be free and totally devoid of hang-ups with someone he loved; to be able to completely open up to me. Moreover, he was happy that I could accept his maleness with no revulsion or disgust.

I learned so much that night. Watching an erection occur, it seemed as though a blind prehistoric creature were rising from the depths, swaying back and forth looking for a source of life and nourishment. The total thrusting forward of Dick's body just before climax seemed to symbolize a reaching toward someone or something. Because we're so involved during intercourse, these were things about Dick that I had missed through the years. This seeking and thrusting of his body made such an impression on me that night that I've been conscious of it since then in a new way whenever we make love.

Another thing that surprised me was the roughness with which he could handle himself. Thinking of my own sensitive areas, I had a tendency to treat his penis with gentleness in the past. There was no way other than showing me, that he could convey what a tough organ that cock is. Since that night I've been able to handle it much as he did, without the fear that I was going to snap it off. As he said, "It's not so fragile." It was interesting, too, to watch the extreme gentleness with which he handled his testicles.

That night was a learning and a sharing experience together; it's helped us be more open, and more understanding. If I can ever rid myself of my remaining hang-ups on masturbation, I'd like to share the knowledge of my body with him in the same way.

We talked a great deal since that night about masturbation for men and women. We wanted to learn more about the ways and thoughts that accompany it; they vary depending on the existing mood and the need. A man can begin masturbating while he is half asleep, as the result of a dream or fantasy, and then continue when he is fully awake and aroused. He can have a pleasant thought about a woman who just walked by, or remember the last time that he and his wife made love, and suddenly find himself with an erection. He can consciously evoke or create a prolonged fantasy—a ten-minute movie that plays on the inside of his eyelids, with himself and the woman of his choice as the stars, prompted by no sexual thoughts.

The degree of satisfaction or relief from masturbation seems to be the same for men and women. A climax is a climax whether you are having intercourse or masturbating, but the degree of sexiness is completely different. My hand stroking Dick's penis is sexier than his hand. His body next to mine is 1,000 times more exciting than any fantasy. Even though both masturbation and lovemaking leave you satisfied there's no comparison in the atmosphere that the two acts create.

I was fascinated to learn about the different methods a young boy might employ to relieve himself. According to Dick, just as boys differ, their methods differ, from the common to the bizarre. Many boys keep a "jag rag" hidden away in the back of the closet. Some masturbate into the sink, into the toilet, or most often in bed at night. The lights are out, the blankets are on, and chances of discovery are slim. And if a boy has been given a poor image of his own manhood regarding wet dreams or sperm, it's easier not to face himself in the dark. At the other extreme is Portnoy who glories in reassurances of his manhood. "How high will it go? Can I hit the bathroom light?" It's really so natural for a boy to wonder just how much power he contains and what he can do with it. Dick says that many boys put their thumbs over the head at the last minute to get more power. Some masturbate in the shower using soap (doesn't beat up the penis so much), and there is little chance of detection. Some put a pillow between their legs and rub against its softness or against the sheets.

Masturbation wasn't talked about very much when we were youngsters, but I do remember hearing about a rather intriguing gambling game called Circle Jack. On rainy, boring afternoons, boys sat around in a circle on a floor throwing dollars into a pot in the middle. Then they started masturbating simultaneously and whoever came first won the pot. It's an unusual way to supplement your allowance, and I hope those boys don't have problems with premature ejaculation today. Dick has never heard of it, but I know I couldn't have made it up.

Girls have and use an equally wide variety of ways to masturbate. Many are dangerous or stupid, but during adolescence there is no one to tell you because it isn't talked about by adults. The most common and safest way is hand stimulation (before it falls off). Supplementing the hand are all the things that can be inserted into a vagina. Everyone had heard about carrots, bananas, and cucumbers, but how about hot dogs and candles? You know how soft a hot dog is and how easily they break. Think how embarrassing it would be to have your mother drag you off to the doctor to have half a hot dog removed. You couldn't exactly claim that it had dropped out of your bun at lunch by accident!

Since this is all hearsay on my part, I can only hope that youngsters are getting smarter, but I doubt it. Their sources of information about masturbation are no more open than they were in our day. Most of their knowledge is acquired in the locker room and at the slumber party. While carrots with ridges might feel great, it would be a smashing idea to wash off the pesticides first, and, of course, that advice sounds like something only a mother would say. See the problem? Mothers tell you not to masturbate, but they don't tell you how to protect your body if you're going to do it anyway. What mother is going to buy her daughter a vibrator so that she won't have to use a banana?

There are other perfectly harmless ways to masturbate that probably will always be popular. Using soap in the tub (but not the deodorant soap) or soapy lather in the shower have been popular since tubs and showers came on the scene. Even though you're not supposed to touch yourself THERE, you have to wash, don't you? That's when a girl is tempted to wash just a little longer or harder to see what it feels like. Unless you have a tub and shower combination, masturbating by letting the stream of water from the shower hit your clitoris is a little tricky. In a stall shower it's impossible, and under the best of circumstances in the tub, it's like instant drowning. Besides, if you can get the shower stream focused on your vaginal area, the rest of your body freezes.

If you're an adult woman and can approach the idea of masturbation as beneficial at times, you aren't likely to fool around with cucumbers or sausages. You're going to get a vibrator; it can't give you DDT poisoning or fall apart inside you. Moreover, it was made specifically for that purpose. There isn't a faster or better way to be stimulated manually, and if you're trying to find your hot spots and build up your stimulation rate, that's the only sensible way to do it. At the same time, it can be incorporated beautifully into your total sex life for more fun and excitement.

As for us, where do we go from here now that many of the hang-ups are gone? On to more and better understanding of our bodies and each other, I hope. Whatever we can learn about ourselves and then bring to our bed or to our total marriage has to have merit, If masturbation can help us do that, then it too has merits. Over the past few years it has made us much more open with one another. What part it will play in the future we don't know, but we aren't closing any doors.

10.

Affairs—Or, Why Are You Trying to Scare Me?

WE'D LIKE TO ACQUAINT you with a friend of ours, whom we'll call Fred. He lives with his wife and children in a lovely suburban ranch house, with a well-kept yard, and a swing set in the backyard. Fred's a good guy and everyone likes him. He's active in the community, donates money to his church, and takes the children to Sunday school and cub scout picnics. On weekends Nancy and Fred entertain friends, play cards, and generally exude marital happiness. They're active people whom you'd probably like if you met. Most of Fred's acquaintances think he is a good husband and a good father—the type that's the bedrock of any community.

There is another side to Fred which his friends and home never see. Fred likes to play around on the road, and he plays hard. His line of work demands that he travel extensively, and the plane door barely closes behind him before he puts a make on some girl.

By the time he's reached his destination, he may have himself a date for that evening with someone he's met on the plane or with one of the stewardesses. If that fails, he can always fall back on one of the many women he knows in any town that he's previously visited. And Fred also has an unending list of available prostitutes or their cover businesses. At a sales meeting Fred knows exactly where to get the three girls who will serve drinks in the nude at his cocktail party. The theme is hospitality and "Help yourself to whatever takes your fancy—drinks, hors d'oeuvres, girls." Because he has a liberal expense account, the cocktail party is usually held in a suite, with bedrooms available for immediate use.

Since Fred likes his prospective customers to be happy, he always has a few special women in the different cities, who liven up parties with their unique talents. He knows one who has developed phenomenal muscles in the lips of her vagina. When Fred's friends fold a five-dollar bill like a tent and set it on the surface of a narrow coffee table, she entertains them by picking it up with the opening of her vagina. It's such an astounding feat that the game can last for an hour. Obviously the girl keeps the money and makes a good deal more that night as the men present test out those superbly trained muscles on the real thing.

When Fred returns home from a trip, he utters the normal complaints about what a rough week it's been, and about the hard pace and competitiveness involved in selling. He's exhausted, particularly because the fun and games were added to the rigors of the regular working day. Nancy complains mildly about his having to travel so much, but understands that it's important if they're to get ahead. They both settle back into the routine of suburban life and they will probably live happily ever after. Unless Nancy catches on to Fred!

Why are we telling you about Fred if he's so un-usual? Because he's not! I admit that Fred is more colorful than most traveling husbands—he does have a flair for playing in high style—but he's not unusual.

Most men who have traveled in business have known, met, or at least heard of the Freds. More common are the subdued Freds, who play quietly and often whenever the opportunity presents itself.

It sounds as though we're trying to scare the daylights out of you women and you're right. We are! And you men, too. Not all the women who seem to be available on the road are prostitutes; many are married themselves. Wouldn't Fred be surprised to find that Nancy plays occasionally while he's gone?

We don't live among a particularly loose or perverted segment of society. We live in a normal American suburb and have normal friends, and yet a large number of people we know have something going on the side. It may be a full-fledged affair between two of them in the same town who never travel, or it may be a husband who looks for a little action on a trip. But extramarital affairs are happening everywhere, and their growing number signifies that something is wrong. A man doesn't pick up a broad in an out-of-town bar just because she's available. There has to be a reason. A housewife doesn't decide that she'll find a way to meet her dentist secretly because she's having a boring afternoon. With the risks involved for both, there has to be an important reason why.

In my travels before marriage, I became convinced that at least half the married men on the road played around. After talking to Dick and to many of our friends, I'm sure that the percentage is even higher. Not only is it completely above board and out in the open among businessmen, there is a code of ethics operating among those who cheat on their mates. "You don't take back to the hometown anything that you've seen or heard on the road." As a result, there are many Nancys who appear to be happy suburban housewives and who probably have no knowledge of what's going on until their husbands slip once. Then the whole marriage becomes a disaster area, because they were unprepared to face reality.

Since most wives have no way of knowing what's available, or the pressures that may be put on their men to play the game, they have no way of fighting it. If a woman thinks about the prospect at all, it's usually dismissed with a "not my husband" attitude. She can't envision the situations that may confront her man when he's away, or she doesn't perceive the things that occur between the two of them which may be driving him to seek those situations. I'd much rather know and consider what may lie ahead for Dick when he leaves town for a week. At least I can send him out of the house having done the best job I can with our relationship. He can leave knowing that his wife is happy and satisfied, and that she can probably make it through the week no matter how many handsome, horny doctors she has to see. Long ago, we decided that there was a best way for us to survive hazards of the road. When Dick leaves town, we're both drained and wearing a glow. It seems to help.

Visualize Sarah who has been married for ten years, and now takes both her marriage and her husband Sam for granted. Her man is meek and mild, and he doesn't even travel. She can relax about infidelity until death do us part. Every morning at 8:30 she waves goodby with the dishrag in her hand as she wipes crumbs from the counter. She hasn't had time to put on makeup because she likes to sleep that extra fifteen minutes. There may or may not be rollers in her hair. Who's going to see her anyway? The pink bathrobe with the slightly frayed lace that she wears every morning is perfect for cleaning up the kitchen because she can throw it in the washer if it gets dirty. Sarah has money for clothes to wear when they go out. She likes to save her pretty hostess gown for Christmas Eve and for special occasions. Sarah certainly wouldn't want to look like a slob when there were people in the house.

This is the last vision of Sarah that Sam takes with him to work each morning. Twenty minutes later he is walking into a large office building on Main Street. With him on the steps, in the elevator, and in the office are attractive women—young secretaries, typists, file clerks. They're bright and cheerful to look at;

they're wide awake because they've been up since 6:30 A.M. getting ready to go to the office. These girls chatter about work, what happened last night, what they did that was interesting, where they went, what book they read. They never talk about babies' formulas, or diapers, or washing machines. They'd much rather skip breakfast if it meant they didn't have time to put on their makeup, because it's important to them. And Sam is important to them; he's not a dull insurance adjuster with nothing much to say. When Sam is excited about getting a large fire claim settled, they're excited. "Go, Sam. Good job, Sam!" They're involved in his work eight hours a day.

Sarah at home in the pink bathrobe, doesn't stand a chance. And the saddest thing is that Sarah doesn't know it and she has never thought about the comparison. "I love Sam. He loves me. What is there to worry about?" So the logical thing to ask Sam when she hears the back door open after work is, "Will you take out the garbage?"

Sarah decided long ago that settling fire claims is dull work. So that night after dinner they discuss Sammy, Jr.'s appointment with the orthodontist, and what Gertie, a neighbor across the street, had to say about that snippy young fourth-grade teacher. By eight o'clock they are watching TV and during the late news, Sarah excuses herself to head for bed. She's had a rough day with the children and knows that if she gets to sleep before the news is over, Sam won't wake her up. Besides, they made love three nights ago so Sam should be content for the time being. The next morning Sam leaves for Main Street at 8:30, and Sarah, relaxing in her pink bathrobe, has another cup of coffee and reads the women's section of the newspaper. "It's a good life. So what is there to worry about. Sam doesn't even travel."

As Dick puts it so beautifully, "Oh, Sarah baby, are you in trouble! The hourglass is running out! When Sam starts collecting nineteen-year-old blond typists who feed his ego, you'll never understand why. You'll weep and call mother. You'll moan, 'I gave him a good life. The food was always cooked on time and the house was clean. What did he see in that little tramp?' " It would be better to ask yourself what that little tramp saw in Sam that you missed, Sarah. And ask yourself *now,* before you find yourself fat, forty-five, and putting up the storm windows alone. Or maybe Sam is smart, and only needs to have his ego fed occasionally. Maybe you'll never know at all, Sarah. And maybe like some women, you'd rather not know. Let Sam play on the side as long as he is discreet, and our friends don't find out. And as long as he doesn't bother you about sex any more. Many women consider this a fair exchange and can live with it as long as it doesn't interfere with the security of their home life. Perhaps your pride can make that kind of a trade-off, Sarah. But what if it can't? What if you really care about Sam? When do you stop being smug and start to worry?

I worry, and if I do, Sarah should, too. I started worrying before marriage whenever married men asked me for a date. I kept wondering what was wrong with their marriages. The worry didn't stop when Dick began telling me what he had seen on trips or what he had been exposed to. I worried more when he told me how often clients ask him to find a girl for them or expect him to join in the fun. It's hard to believe, isn't it, that your husband might be asked to procure for someone else on the road or in his own town? But it happens.

Traveling with Dick on business trips when other wives are not taken along is an eye opener. I am always amazed that the code of ethics of not taking stories back home includes me. If Fred decides to bring his girl friend from home instead of his wife, he assumes (rightly) that I'm not going to go back and tell Nancy. So there we are traveling to the meeting with Fred and Suzie, instead of Fred and Nancy. Are Dick and I going to go home and possibly break up Fred's marriage by talking about it? No! And we worry—about ourselves and what's happening to marriage, and how long we can all stand up under the onslaught.

Dick is just as startled when I tell him about two women friends who seem to be happily married, but each has been having an affair for years. Why? It seems to be easier for us to understand why the Sams start to look elsewhere than it is for us to comprehend why the Sarahs do, but the statistics show that almost half the Sarahs are also having extramarital affairs. Are they sexually unsatisfied by their husbands, or mentally bored? Are they married to men who have taken them for granted, and therefore need someone to put the romance and ego-feed back in their lives? Do they live with busy executives who work night and day in a world that excludes them? Is it loneliness, or boredom, or sex, or love that forces them to look elsewhere? We have a friend who began an affair because she said that once before she died she wanted to be treated like a real woman, and not another asset. Her husband is a highly successful businessman who thinks in terms of acquisitions. They loved each other when they first married, but eventually he treated her merely as a good social acquisition in his busy world. He gave her everything except love and understanding, so she found it elsewhere.

I worry about marriages, mine and others, when I talk to a good friend who is an ex-stewardess. If her experiences aren't enough to curl Sarah's hair, not much else will. Every possible sad story of misunderstanding wives is thrown at stewardesses by men they meet flying. How these women have the courage to get married after what they've seen is surprising. Perhaps they absorb all the stories and decide with their eyes wide open that those things won't be replayed in their own marriages. Maybe their experiences help them never to become smug. My friend tells me that when she flew, the national divorce rate was 1 out of 5, but the divorce rate for stewardesses was 1 out of 29—the lowest of any female occupation. She can only conclude that after what stews have been exposed to, they approach their marriages differently and more realistically. They know too much to take marriage for granted. As she says, "In training school, when they go to the extent of teaching you all the different ways you can tell if a man is married, they're telling you very plainly about the state of marriages today. After having dozens of very married men ask me out, I have a pretty good idea of what they're not getting from their wives. I'd have to be crazy to send my husband out on a trip after a fight or with a hard-on."

We really like this woman. She's aware, concerned, and pragmatic. She loves and trusts her husband, but she also thinks of him as a human being. Assessing the situation, she's realistic enough to know that if she allows too many areas of discontent to develop in their marriage, there are plenty of available women willing to fill in those gaps—for a night or a lifetime. She's not afraid of marriage; she's only afraid of smugness.

It may be our own smugness that causes surprise when we hear about a good friend who is having an extramarital affair or is getting divorced. Or it may be that marriage is tougher today, and as a consequence, affairs are more common. Dick and I feel that part of the problem is that we come to marriage so badly prepared. There are not many twenty-year-olds who realize the amount of giving and understanding necessary to make marriage work for a lifetime. Few of us have the ability to communicate our needs to our partner, so we cop out by throwing up our hands in woe saying, "She or he doesn't understand me." Today tensions are greater for the working husband, for wives, and for family life than they were in our parents' generation. Unfortunately, we haven't been better prepared to cope with them.

Let's take our heads out of the sand and admit that it's difficult to maintain an exciting, loving relationship between two people for forty years. On that premise, do we then quit before we start, or do we try to face the situation honestly and work at it realistically. Are extramarital relationships more common today, or does it just seem that way?

Tensions are certainly higher now than ever before,

and mobility offers an escape that wasn't present fifty years ago. Your grandfather probably felt like whacking grandma at least once in his lifetime, or walking out and laying someone else because she didn't understand him. But the opportunities weren't readily available then. But today if Fred has an argument with Nancy over the spending of their savings, and he leaves town angry, he shouldn't have too much difficulty finding a sympathetic ear elsewhere. If Nancy is left at home upset for a week, she probably has a second car and can visit places and with people that grandma had no access to.

The majority of people live in large communities today. Grandma was hampered because she didn't have a car, but even more because her friends and neighbors knew what she did with her time. Now a drive across town can often be as safe as driving to a new town. Nobody knows you and the chances of successfully pulling off a secret liaison are much better. There weren't any motels in grandma's day. Where could she go besides the haystack? It was not only risky, but it also must have been damned uncomfortable.

Loneliness plays an important role in affairs for both men and women today. What's life really like for the salesman who's constantly on the road? What's it like for his wife? For him, it may consist of dinner alone in a restaurant with a paperback novel for company and then TV in the hotel room three or fours nights a week. A conversation in a bar with anyone is a welcome break. He's lonesome and he misses his wife and children. It's harder for married men and women to travel alone because they've become used to sharing. Dick finds that meals are especially lonely times. At home he's with the people who love him most, even though the children may spill milk in his lap and chatter incessantly.

An affair can start very innocently. The man who loves his wife is just as susceptible as the man who doesn't care. Picture the man who's been covering his territory for three days, but today was particularly bad.

The big sale that he was expecting fell through, or the buyer from his biggest manufacturing client chewed him out because the last order was fouled up by the shipping department. He's very depressed, there's no one to talk to, and he can't face that paperback yet. He stops off at a bar before going back to the hotel simply because the atmosphere is a little more congenial. It's not crowded and there's a woman sitting alone at the bar. After a drink or two, conversation develops. "You're new here. What are you doing in town?" She may not be a hooker, she may be a woman who's lonely, too. But right then, she's someone to talk to, and suddenly he doesn't want to go back to the hotel. He has a sympathetic ear and no thoughts of infidelity. He has found a temporary balm for his loneliness and insecurity.

Over a few drinks he might tell her about his day. She'll probably listen and sympathize. "Isn't it a shame that sales managers have so little regard for their men today? It was certainly unfair to blame the shipping department's errors on you." It really doesn't matter much what she says, if the words are soothing. He asks her to have dinner and after more drinks and soothing of his jangled nerves, he finds himself in bed with a compassionate stranger. He's overcome with guilt. "I didn't mean to do this. What would Nancy think?" But he could never go home and explain to her the innocent sequence of events that led him to that bed. How could she, at home with the children, understand his loneliness and weakness? So he lives with his guilt. Somewhere in the back of his mind is tucked away the knowledge, that if he's ever lonely and down in Biloxi, there's a sympathetic ear waiting.

Knowing that Dick has to travel at times and that not every day is going to be a good day, we try to minimize our loneliness by calling. When he's away, we usually talk every night, sometimes for an hour or more. The cost is staggering, but it's the only way we've found to alleviate that loneliness. I want him to be able to tell me about all the things that went wrong so that I can soothe him, not a strange woman in a bar.

It's a warm feeling, no matter how far away he is, to know that night he's going to share my problems, and my day. And if everything has gone wrong it's good to hear him say, "Don't worry about it. We'll take care of it when I get home on Friday." The money that we spend is unimportant compared to the warmth and closeness that comes from those calls. We can always find other ways to cut back on our expenses to pay for them. I'd rather have a happy marriage than a new coat next month, wouldn't you? It will keep me warmer in the long run.

Another major factor that seems to cause affairs is the lack of understanding of the opposite sex. Men and women are different and have different needs. It's important to understand how we can unknowingly drive our partner to look for someone else. For women who have a deep need to feel loved and cherished (and that means shown), life can become unbearable if they are consistently taken for granted, no matter how many material possessions their husbands may provide. Dick and I have a friend whose husband thinks of her as a highly efficient partner in life. Efficient hostess, efficient household manager, efficient wife and mother. He loves her but he never tells her. When her unmet needs finally became unbearable, she started looking elsewhere, and since then she's had a series of affairs. "Someone, anyone, tell me that I'm a woman and that you love me for that." If she ever finds that person, I don't think that she would look back over her shoulder as she walked away from her marriage.

The same lack of understanding applies to many wives. It's almost impossible for us women to relate to the frustrations and tensions of our husband's lives, unless (and this is a big unless) men are willing to share them with us, and we are willing to pry their feelings out of them. Men have an aversion to admitting they are frightened, or insecure, or lonely, but they are, just as often as women are. Women learn to express their emotions more easily during childhood, and they're allowed the luxury of crying. It takes an extraordinary woman to allow her man to feel safe enough with her to cry or to pour out his fears. Perhaps that's why the most common excuse that men use when looking for consolation outside their marriages is, "My wife doesn't understand me."

There is a particular period in a man's life when he needs more understanding and love than he has ever received. It is the time of the male equivalent of menopause. And it is only in recent years that more women have become aware of it.

Many men feel they have reached a plateau—around age forty. Careerwise, a man knows whether or not he's going to make it. The dreams and aspirations that he once had are now fading and he must adjust to and live with his realities. Although most men have to put their dreams to bed, that doesn't make it any easier. The years of climbing, scratching, and competing have taken their toll. Younger and brighter men are coming up to his level and then passing him by. He's weary of the battle. His ego is wounded and it needs to be cared for and licked back to health by someone. Who will do it if not his wife? It's a difficult period for men, just as female menopause is for us. We fully expect an abundance of love and understanding at that time in our lives, and we should be aware and willing to help our men through theirs, too.

At the same time, even though it's not true, he believes he may be over the hill sexually. He's through procreating and his children are almost grown. He may now think that they only need him to finance their educations. His insecurity makes him wonder if anyone needs him much anymore—his wife, his children, his employer. To whom is he important and vital? That word vital is the key. Men have a much greater fear of impotence than women do, and the thought of losing that vitality or potency is terrifying to many men. And yet it isn't something they can talk readily about to anyone, even to the most understanding wife.

For many men, thoughts of proving themselves

one more time or of being important to someone one more time start forming. And this one more time (whether it be one or many) causes many to fall out of the marriage bed. These males experience a longing to be virile again before old age creeps in and a great need for reassurance as a person. Frequently they sport new hair styles and flashier clothes in an attempt to project a new youthful image. The symptoms may be present whether the man has secret affairs or not. Many women cuttingly refer to their husband's dashing appearance with sarcasm. "Bob's going through his second childhood." He's not. He's fulfilling a desperate need within himself, and a wise woman could help him fill it with more ego stroking, more attention, more love, and more sex. Especially more sex. Although many women are appalled by the sudden increases in their husbands' desires, they can do more to satisfy that need in the conjugal bed than anywhere else. They could be more inventive and give more than they ever have before. After all, the need is greater than ever before. And perhaps, if women could try to be more understanding and more receptive we could prevent a few heartaches in the future. We all need someone who thinks we're worthwhile. In addition, we women might receive a little more love, patience, and understanding from our mates when we find ourselves going through menopause.

Men have a completely different sexual makeup from women. We kiddingly or grudgingly admit to this difference when we comment about Sam needing some again soon, but we don't really try to understand it. Dick swears that men have an innate drive for variety and excitement in their sex lives, and that this is why many men who love their wives also look for one-night stands. It adds the flavor and newness that's missing in the matrimonial bed without disrupting the marriage. If sex is dull or boring, or just an accommodation for the wife, it becomes easier to understand why her husband looks for new stimulation with other women. He may be entirely satisfied with every other aspect of his married life, but one of his vital needs is unfulfilled. He probably doesn't want the long-range involvement of an affair, and his wife satisfies his ego needs and give him love. She still hasn't learned about stimulating sex, but that can easily be filled by any good whore on the road.

We women don't seem to know or understand the importance of varied sex for a man. If we did, we could put many prostitutes out of business. We still have the love aspect going for us and they don't; the two together are an unbeatable combination. One of Dick's favorite quips is, "A man doesn't really want to go across the street for hamburgers when he can have steak at home." Sex with love is better than sex alone.

Teasing, freshness, newness are important. But even more so, Dick believes, is the freedom and willingness with which we give our bodies. We can understand why women ration sex if it's never been good for them. If it's always been "slam-bam-thank-you-ma'am" for Sarah, then even Dick can understand why she goes to bed early to avoid Sam. I'd rather see Sarah and Sam have a little fun, but I can sympathize with her. But neither Dick nor I can understand the women who use sex as a barter. "I'll let you make love to me if you give me this or do that." Let him! He could rape her if he wanted, but most men are too civilized to do that. Dick hears from half the men he knows that bartering is an established way of life in their marriages. It usually isn't tolerated for long. If a man's going to pay for it, he may as well go elsewhere and get his money's worth. Basically, bartering is the same as prostitution. Although a woman might scream and rant if she discovered that her husband had hired a whore, she is using her body in the same way, if she barters.

Since we have mentioned prostitutes, let's discuss and talk about them. Why do men go to them? What do they do that we won't do? And most important, what have they learned about men that might be valuable to us in our marriages? School is in session for girls only.

Most women have a morbid fascination about prostitution; we've wondered what prostitutes do, how they get their contacts, and what they charge. That's why books such as the *Happy Hooker* and *Redpants* are successes. It won't be the little old men sneaking up to the drugstore counter to buy them. It'll be us.

My esteem for the age-old profession of prostitution has soared in the last ten years, and that's because I am better informed. I used to think that whores were wicked women who lurked in back alleys and dark stairways snaring unsuspecting men. There are still many lurkers, but some of the women are charming and delightful people whose professional ethics are very high. You might have one as an acquaintance without knowing it. I did.

Several years ago at a business meeting, the wives were aked to help with some of the paper work and the preparations. For a week I worked with a lovely, pleasant, intelligent girl, and we became very friendly. I knew she wasn't one of the wives, but assumed that she was either a local Kelly girl, or one of the full-time staff for the group. One night after talking about what a great worker she was, I asked Dick if he knew anything about Claudine. "She's a high-quality prostitute who flew in for the meeting and had some free time during the days, so she decided to help out. She really likes the men in this group. They give her a lot of business, and that's her way of saying that she's grateful." How do I reconcile her with my image of the sleazy lady in the back alleys waiting to entrap my husband?

The first few minutes the next morning were a little awkward for me, but we soon started working. I was amazed by Claudine's openness. Once she realized that I knew what her profession was, and that it didn't send me screaming from the room, she was able to talk to me about it in a very practical manner. It was a job that she enjoyed immensely and it was also very lucrative. She was carefully building up her investment program with sound stocks for the future. "After all," she said, "I won't be good at this forever."

Besides Claudine and another girl whom I met under similar circumstances, my education has been broadened mostly by Dick. On his way home from one business trip, he had a fascinating three-hour plane conversation with the girl sitting beside him. She was flying into our hometown for a convention. It was not long after they started talking that she made her "invitation." Dick declined explaining that this was his hometown they were flying into. Soon they began discussing her profession. She was an attractive divorcée in her late twenties with three children. Receiving no alimony or child support, she drifted into high-level prostitution as the best means to support her family and still have the daytime free to spend with her children. She was investing most of her profits in the stock market and in real estate with the family's future security in mind. She simply said, "I make $30,000 a year and I only have a few good years left. I have to plan for our future."

Dick was stunned by her income and asked her what the various rates were. She said that depended on the size of the city in which you operated. For a woman in her prime, in the right territory, a quick, straight lay taking only a few minutes usually ran about twenty-five dollars. Of course, better hotel lobbies and bars are more lucrative than back-street dives, but you have to have the dress and the poise to fit them. A suck-off with a lay, which still didn't take much time, costs about fifty dollars, and the all-night rates (or several hours) are between $100 and $300, depending on the girl. These charges could be doubled for large conventions and for cities like Las Vegas. Word-of-mouth advertising saves high-class prostitutes a lot of time, and most good pros develop a regular clientele over the years.

Dick was most interested in finding out what she felt were the main reasons that married customers come to her regularly. Why did men look for a whore, and what did they seek from one? Many men came because they were lonely, insecure, frustrated, and tense. In addition to relieving some of these feelings through sex, often she was asked to listen. A prostitute is safe in a man's eyes, he can tell her anything without shocking her or being subjected to ridicule.

Sexually, the same degree of freedom applies to a man. There are many things he can ask a prostitute to do that he could never ask his wife to do. He can safely act out his fantasies, no matter what they are, knowing that she won't be shocked or laugh at him. He can ask her to masturbate and let him watch, or he can ask her to let him masturbate. Many men want to be kissed and tongued all over their bodies; it makes them feel as though someone really cares enough to service him.

Sometimes males want to be childlike again and have someone soothe and mother them. Dick's seatmate said that there was a place called Mother's Whorehouse in her hometown, which employed some women in their sixties to serve this need exclusively. Men go there strictly to be pampered. Mother will cook dinner for you, bring you breakfast in bed, talk to you, rub your back, and listen to your troubles. You can get laid if you want, but that's not the main drawing card. More importantly, you can be a little boy again with a cuddly mother if there is hurt somewhere in your heart or mind.

Another important question that Dick asked concerned V.D. Weren't prostitutes afraid of contracting it? She said they were deathly afraid of V.D. because it put them out of commission for at least a month. High-class prostitutes have a good way of checking first to make sure that they are as safe as possible. They ask a man to undress and lie on the bed while they wash him. He thinks it's a nice gesture and it's also exciting and stimulating. Most girls have either a basin of warm, soapy water in the room or a sink, so that the washing is done quickly and easily. In reality, she's checking him for V.D. very carefully.

Needless to say, that flight home was probably one of the more educational and enlightening trips Dick's taken—and the most enjoyable. Both of us benefited from her openness.

As the plane landed, she offered to be available whenever Dick had business again in her city. He declined, but she said that she understood. Her parting shot was priceless. "You know," she said, "I really like you. You're a nice guy and I can see that you're happily married. But you still should come see me. I could teach you many things that you could pass on to your wife. It would be good for your marriage, and I wouldn't charge you!" Now who's more broadminded? She or I?

If airline stewardesses know a lot about the state of our marriages today, imagine how much more prostitutes must know. We could learn to avoid some pitfalls, if only we could listen to them with an open mind. Which brings us back to our marriage today, and how the two of us view affairs. Maybe we should define our terms before going any further. Both affairs and one-night stands are extramarital activities. In our minds an affair is an ongoing relationship that entails more than sex. It may go on for weeks, months, or years, and it fills a major gap in the life of the straying partner that isn't being filled at home. An affair includes sex, of course, but more often, the major reason for straying is some lack of understanding at home. This is very different in our eyes from a one-night stand which is normally sex oriented. A man has a driving, but temporary need, usually sexual, and he picks up some girl and gets himself laid. She takes care of the need for the moment, he has made no commitment, and he will probably never see her again.

Ten years ago those marriage vows to be faithful to one another until death were absolutely rigid for Dick and me. There was no flexibility, there was no consideration or comparative understanding of human weakness, and there was no forgiveness. I was probably more rigid than Dick about infidelity. After witnessing the effect an affair had on some close friends, it was difficult for me to be objective. I remember uttering some strong statements. "If I ever found out that you'd been playing around, I'd leave you in a minute. You'd come home and find us gone." That kind of statement doesn't leave much room on either side for any human understanding. We were newly married, and it was hard for us to accept any reason why a man or woman would be unfaithful.

Our attitude has softened considerably in ten years. It's become more flexible, and I hope more realistic, because of what we've seen, what we've heard, and what we've lived through ourselves. Because marriage is not the rosy dream that we visualized at twenty, and because we found that it was a day-in and day-out job making it work, we can better understand our own weaknesses. If Dick found out tomorrow that I'd been having an affair with a friend, I think he'd first ask himself why and then ask me. What would happen afterward would depend on the why, and how we could cope with it. If I found that he'd been playing on the road I think (I hope) that I'd ask myself first, "What is it he needs from me that I haven't been giving him?"

We think we know how we would react. But neither of us knows for certain. Both of us sense that we'd be more able to take a one-night stand in stride than a full-blown affair. The purely sexual escape could be understood for a number of reasons: One's guard is down because of loneliness, frustration, liquor, and suddenly the situation is a fact. But an affair would signify deep trouble in our marriage and would be much harder to cope with. Not only would it mean that a major need was not being fulfilled, but also that it had gotten to the point where we couldn't contain it any more. Even more tragic for us would be the realization that neither of us had been able to communicate it to the other. In addition, there would be a third person deeply involved, and we don't know how we could cope with that situation. We can only hope that we could meet the problem as *our* problem, and that we might be able to salvage our marriage. Many people have done it, but they've had to push their pride out of the way to succeed.

Dick and I know that we're still growing together.

We've openly and honestly talked about the past with each other and found there was nothing that couldn't be said and understood. Where our life will take us in the future, we have no way of knowing. We realize we're very human and very weak. I hope if we find ourselves confronted by an affair, we can swallow our pride and not drive each other further away. And I hope that we can ask why first and try to remember one of our old family jokes. "Whenever you point your finger at the other guy, three fingers point back at you."

11.

Postscripts and Tidbits
on Sex Appeal

"HELLO. THIS IS YOUR Jewish mother speaking. Remember when you were six, I told you there was no excuse for holey underwear? So how come you had frayed edges on your panties when you were trying on dresses the other day? And you, Sam, sit down. I almost fainted from the garlic on your breath this morning when you came over for coffee. Did you sleep in the same bed with my daughter that way last night, or did she give you pizza for breakfast? Here, I brought some Sen-Sen. Don't thank me! Keep the package. You need it! And that stomach! Sarah, your father at his age is in better shape than this lump of a husband. A little handball wouldn't kill you, Sam. I arranged for you to play with Papa on Thursday afternoon instead of lunch. No, don't thank me! I did it for your own good!"

Wouldn't it be great if we all had a Jewish mother to whip us back into line from time to time? We all have an image of ourselves, but sometimes life gets busy and we let the image slip for awhile. If we get really lazy we let it slip forever. Occasionally we need someone to blast into our lives and say, "You look like a slob!"

How about that mental image? How do you picture yourself? The outdoor, all-American type? The chic, tailored woman? The innocent baby doll? Whatever your type, you probably dress accordingly. Did you ever stop to think that that man you share room and board with may have an entirely different image of you? Ask him how he visualizes you when he's daydreaming at the office? What if he sees you as the mod, today woman, and you see yourself as the clinging vine type? If you keep wearing frilly blouses and white lace stockings, you're going to frustrate the poor man to death. We mentally typecast ourselves, but we seldom check with our men to see if the role fits.

For example, hair has caused women image problems for centuries. Females love to change hairstyles. Invariably, the change throws their husbands for a loop. "Hey, who's the blonde broad in my kitchen? And where's the little brunette tomboy I left at breakfast?" It takes them time to adjust because they've never been able to change images that fast; sometimes it makes them a little nervous. For years I wore my hair shaggy and windblown, which fits my life-style. Dick loved it because his image of me has always been that of the outdoor girl, running through the woods barefoot, hair blowing in the breeze. One day I became so bored with that hairstyle and image, that when Dick came home that night he found a sophisticated young woman making dinner, hair lightened three shades and swept up in a sleek chignon. I thought that he'd be delighted at the change, but he was shocked. What had happened to good, old, tousled me that he could hug without messing up? For hours he was afraid to get too close for fear that something would wrinkle or crinkle, or that my hair would unwind itself. I sat on his lap and the hairpins stuck in his cheek. It took me a half hour that night to plaster and pin all my hair into place so that I could sleep rigid on my back like a petrified mummy. The next morning after working the kink out of my neck, I decided I really wasn't so bored with the old me, after all, and Dick breathed a monumental sigh of relief. Periodically the bug bites again, but it never seems to last more than a day or two.

Sometimes we have a mental image of our mate, with which he or she couldn't feel comfortable. If we insist on this look, friction generally arises. For years a good friend of ours has been slowly easing his wife into a new image. He likes to think of her as a swinger, and he would love to have her dress the part. Way-out, mod clothes and lots of eye makeup. I think he pictures her in the Virginia Slims ads, striding along saying, "You've come a long way, baby," over her shoulder. She's very conservative and would feel much more comfortable in a matched sweater and skirt. Both are good natured about the situation, and they can tease each other without malice. She cheerfully allows herself to be dragged in and out of boutiques, but she puts her foot firmly down when he suggests something that she honestly can't wear. He, in turn, keeps quiet when she appears for the company party in a tweed tailored suit instead of flashy pants. For them, the difference in images is a small and sometimes amusing part of their life, which doesn't create a problem. They've both taken the time to understand why the other sees himself in that image, and why it's difficult to change. For some couples, however, the problem of clashing images is major.

Several weeks ago, we were at a gathering where a free-for-all between a young husband and his wife took place. Both had had a little too much to drink when he made some casual but sarcastic remark within her earshot about her dressing like Mother Hubbard. Evidently it was a subject that had been heatedly discussed before and which immediately provoked a reaction from his wife. The barbs flew back and forth for a few minutes until she finally burst out, "Well, if you're so hot to dress me up like a whore, why don't you get yourself one and leave me alone!" She

119

stormed out of the room. He moaned, "How can you reason with anybody that closed-minded?" Then he rushed out after her.

The rest of us felt rather uncomfortable after they had gone, and Dick and I continued to think about it on the drive home. They had blown a seemingly small problem out to such large proportions by their lack of understanding of one another, that it must affect other areas of their lives. Dick said, "Can't you see them every time they get dressed to go out? She picks out something she knows is going to rankle, and she is uptight before getting dressed. He walks into the room and says, 'Not that grey granny again,' and their evening is off to a flying start before they leave the house. Why don't they sit down and rationally tell each other how they really feel about her clothes and why? Perhaps then, they could find a compromise." Dick's solution sounds easy, but it isn't always. Again, as in sex, somebody has to be the first one to initiate that conversation in a calm tone. Both parties have to be willing to really listen to what the other is saying despite their hang-ups. The problem in that marriage seems to be a lot deeper than the clothes issue.

Frequently, the situation is reversed, with the man being the conservative one. His wife tires of her housewife image and buys herself what she thinks is a sensational outfit. She feels great until he walks into the house and makes some cutting crack such as, "Who do you think you are, the babysitter?" He hurts her pride, and the conversation goes nowhere but downhill. Maybe he feels threatened by a sudden youthful image of his wife, but there must be a better way to handle the situation.

Luckily, we've never been troubled with the image problem as it relates to clothes. In the early years of our marriage, we often shopped together. We both love shopping, and we learned a lot about how each of us sees the other and ourselves. If I got excited over a lace-fronted dress shirt for Dick, he'd tell me that it wasn't him. He'd feel uncomfortable wearing it. If he pulled a low-cut, slinky dress off the rack and

120

asked how I liked it, I could tell him that although it was stunning, it wasn't for me. Lacking the necessary equipment to fill out a dress slit to the waist, I just couldn't wear one. After I'd tried one on for him he completely understood and forgot about that style for me in the future. Gradually, we began to know what each of us liked and what we liked and what we like on each other. Now when I buy clothes for Dick, I have a good idea what he'd pick for himself. If he brings home a dress for me as a surprise, I know it will be something I'll also like. Nothing seems to deflate a man's ego faster than to learn that his wife has returned a present, whether it is a nightgown or a pantsuit, that he bought her.

Occasionally we get our images crossed, but we try to be good sports about it. Dick's hair provides a good example. For the past year I've been advocating a more youthful, less conservative style. He has let his hair and sideburns grow longer and fuller as have most men, but he still combs it the same way. I keep teasing him about how great he looks when he comes out of the shower, or when he has been working outside and his hair has fallen across his forehead. I think it looks sharp; he thinks it looks messy. Finally, after chasing me around the house to get his comb back before work, he sat me down for a heart-to-heart talk. "I'm not a mad artist or a philosopher or a university professor, I'm a businessman, and I have clients to face every day. I'd make them and myself nervous if I walked in looking like Chico Marx, or Flopsy, Mopsy, and Flora. Besides, the hair itches when it's down to my nose. But above all, it's not me. I like it this way, and it's comfortable for me." I got the message and I learned to leave well enough alone.

Women's clothes can be a painful subject in a lot of homes and in men's conversations around the lunch or poker table. Whether females like to admit it or not, we let ourselves be herded along with the rest of the sheep into wearing the new fashions, regardless of what they might be. And after marriage many of us dress for other women instead of men. Why do we get so smug when we're trying to keep one?

The midi is a perfect example. Admittedly, it was the ugliest thing foisted upon the fashion world in my lifetime, and yet many women finally succumbed because it was high style. For once, men were very vocal about a women's style change, and I doubt that there were many of us who didn't know exactly how they felt about the midi. The point is that we let ourselves be swept along, and men no longer doubted that we dress for other women or ourselves, and not for them. Dick says a lot of men just filed that away mentally for future reference.

Our sex appeal is often diminished by a lack of cleanliness. Men are sometimes more guilty of this than women. "I've been working in the yard, but we're staying home tonight so I'll shower in the morning." That attitude is not only inconsiderate, but also dangerous. Nothing kills off a sensuous image faster than bad breath, smelly armpits, or smelly genitals, especially in bed. We do know a few men—the "take-me-as-I-am" types—who want their sex natural. Unless they have wives with acute sinus problems, they aren't engaging in much foreplay or oral sex or getting much in return. Not many women will put up with the naturalists' approach to sex for long.

It's not always men who have rarified odors, however. Women can be as inconsiderate without knowing it. About five years ago, a funny thing happened that temporarily threw me for a loop. I brush my teeth frequently. And unconsciously, I had changed one of my eating habits. When the problem arose I never connected the two. Fortunately, Dick's not subtle or shy. One night as we were kissing he said, "Don't be upset, but I have to tell you something. Every night around dinner time you have this awful smell around your head when I get close to you. It seems to go away later, but it's pretty bad."

Needless to say, it made me very nervous, and I immediately made a dentist's appointment. I was certain that I had a rotten tooth hidden away somewhere.

No luck, not even a cavity. Next I trotted off to the Eye, Ear, Nose and Throat man, but he could find nothing wrong, either. Happily, he was a patient, kindly old man and he took pity on me. "Are you sure it's not your breath? Let me smell it." Well, it was in the morning and my breath was fine. He asked me to tell him about my eating habits. "The past several months I've been skipping lunch, so I usually have a snack late in the afternoon while I am preparing dinner. I nibble on some pepperoni sticks and a few crackers with Roquefort cheese to tide me over until dinner." Roquefort cheese! No wonder Dick thought I was rotting away when he walked in! The answer was so simple and so funny, but the consequences would have been very different if he'd never said anything.

My love for garlic and pungent foods hasn't decreased, nor had Dick's increased. I have learned to keep a bottle of mouthwash in the kitchen and pocket-size sprays planted in my purse and stashed all over the house.

We can't afford to take our sensual images for granted. The area that we're most apt to let slide is our weight. And men and women are equally guilty. A little flab, a little roll, a little dimply rump are signs that get easier to overlook through the years because they appear gradually and individually. By the time we notice, we are a clothes size bigger, and we have to exert a monumental effort to get our bodies back in shape. It might be simpler to give up and buy the next size or have your tailor let all your suits out, but it's not very sexy. —

We've been told that swingers and wife swappers tend to stay in better shape than we straight folk. It makes sense because they use their bodies to a definite advantage and come to regard them as their most valuable and precious tool. On the other hand, we are inclined to forget that our bodies are the most valuable piece of equipment we bring to our sex lives. It's easy to get out of shape if you lack the incentive or you are lazy. No one likes to diet or start the morning with sit-ups.

What we have to do is re-create the sexual images of ourselves so that it is easier to swallow that yogurt or get through the day on grapefruit. Dick and I like spaghetti and cream puffs as much as the next person, but a few mental images make it less difficult for us to reach for the celery sticks.

This method may not work for you, but it's done wonders for my morale and willpower these last ten years. Whenever I see the inevitable roll developing, I play a very serious mental game. First, mental visions. Does Merle Oberon at sixty look better than I do at thirty? Or I envision Dick's mother. She has a fantastic figure for a woman in her sixties and has worked hard to maintain it. Will I look as good when I'm her age? If I can't scare myself with that comparison, I go to the bedroom and stare at myself in the full-length mirror—stripped, with every light on and the lampshades off. The flab! The thigh bulge! The pot! Quick, to the store for carrot sticks and cottage cheese! I wish I could put a photo of that pose on the refrigerator door without scandalizing all the youngsters in the neighborhood who constantly raid our refrigerator.

Another great lift for diet lags is to set up a mental affair. This works equally well for men and women, but one part of you has to be very persuasive and the other part has to be very gullible. After you've taken that hard, honest look at yourself, decide how you feel about your body. You used to think it was sexy, you were proud of it, and it made you feel desirable. How much has it changed? If an attractive man or woman saw you naked, would you be ashamed of that body today? That's incentive number one to go back on the diet.

Number two takes a little more imagination and gullibility. With the picture of myself firmly in mind, I play out a little fantasy. I've just learned that my old college flame is coming to town in a month. He wants to see me, and from the tone of his voice I can visualize both of us being swept up in forgotten passions. But I can't let him see me in this shape. He'd throw up. So I plunge into a mad month (it's important to set a deadline) of jogging in place, toe touching, and quietly eating double helpings of string beans for dinner. I polish my toenails, put cream on my hands, and fly through my housework wearing Dick's weighted belt as the deadline draws nearer and nearer. And, of course, I never say a word about it. It's my secret. By the time the month is up, I'm usually back in great shape. Dick reaps all the benefits from my nonexistent affair, and I splurge on a new bikini. It's a lot of fun and takes much of the pain out of calorie counting. The trick is to really make yourself believe the fantasy for the time, or you'll grab the first available piece of cheesecake.

This game could work for men if they could stop being so analytical and be more romantically inclined. Imagine Raquel Welch waltzing into your life instead. Wouldn't that tear you off to the nearest gym or handball court to work out? Actually, this type of mental game is similar to the way that many men feel as they go through the start of middle age. During that time, it's more an unconscious desire to renew virility and to maintain sex appeal. Males may buy the flashy clothes while I'm getting rid of my dishpan hands for my imaginary lover, but basically it's the same principle at work. They may not be sure of what lies ahead for them sexually, but they're going to be ready.

A parting shot to anyone who diets. Diet and suffer in silence. First, it's much better for your image to have the other person think that you maintain that fantastic shape with no effort. Dick's never been particularly turned on by watching me do push-ups before breakfast, but I have heard him brag to friends that my size hasn't changed since he met me. Secondly, everyone hates perpetual dieters; they are excruciating bores. They never seem to lose much weight, but they talk constantly about how hard it is to do. Men seem to be able to handle the stoic, silent grind of getting in shape better than women. But in either case, whiners aren't sexy to listen to or live with.

Once I have my body back in shape I feel more desirable. And Dick's going to be the recipient of those feelings. Every so often, no matter how good our shape, we have to make a conscious effort to rekindle body awareness. Married couples are inclined to take their partner's body for granted after a time. But a strange body will generate excitement instantly. If that were Raquel climbing out of the tub instead of me, it's doubtful that Dick would stroll in to pick up a Kleenex and stroll out again without looking twice.

Men and women have to work to put back some of the mystery which surrounds their bodies; this is especially difficult for women. Dick believes that we women have confided too many of our beauty secrets to our husbands. In so doing, we've sadly killed off part of our sexual image at the same time. They know we wear girdles, pad our bras, wear wigs and false eyelashes, and color our hair. There are few sights less sexy than watching a woman struggle into a girdle, no matter how dazzling the end result. They know that sweet smell in the air isn't really us, but the perfume Aunt Minnie sent for Christmas.

You can't live behind closed doors in a marriage, but you can help prevent that image from cracking too badly along the way. When you walk into a party dressed to kill, the other men may compliment you, but your husband probably won't because he had to watch you struggle for twenty minutes with the false eyelashes. And he's the one you really want to impress. You can't avoid getting dressed together, but you can do some other things to rekindle that body awareness and appreciation. This is the time to wear that black, almost see-through nightie. It lends an erotic aura to an ordinary Tuesday night. Dick's mesh briefs have the same effect on me. I can almost see through them but not quite. Go bra-less when your husband comes home from work and watch the reaction as he puts his arms around you to say hello. He'll be much more aware of those breasts under your blouse at dinner than he would be if you strolled by naked that night on your way into the shower. Dick turned the tables on me one night after a series of bra-less occasions. Driving to a party he informed me that he wasn't wearing any shorts under his slacks. Of course nothing showed, but I was fascinated watching him every time he moved to see if it would. It isn't hard to think of ways to rekindle that awareness once you make yourself conscious of your own body again. And it goes a long way toward keeping the variety and excitement in sex that most men would like.

For the sake of that body and its image, leave some things to the imagination. Maintain a little dignity and privacy in your lives together. We've had a ritual for years that we both honor. Every once in awhile I go off to the bedroom alone for a few hours. It's often a night when Dick has some paper work to do and won't miss me anyway. I'll do my nails, my toenails, take a bubble bath, cream my skin. There's no reason why he has to watch me hacking away at my cuticle, or shaving my legs, or grinding away the last of the summer's calluses with a pumice stone. When I'm finished I usually feel pleased with myself, relaxed, and desirable. And who benefits most from that feeling? The paper work can always wait another hour.

The worst insult you can bestow upon your image is to allow your mystery to die forever on the toilet seat. Never, never, never go to the "john" while he's shaving in the morning! Even if you have to waddle through frying the bacon with crossed legs. Nobody has that strong a stomach at 7 A.M. or that much love.

Your hair is part of your image, but sometimes it has a direct effect on your sex life. Many men like the untouchable look on their wives when they are out on the town. But they're not quite as happy with that image when it applies to the bedroom. When women become untouchable in bed because they have been to the hairdresser that day, men get a little ornery. "It has to last for the party on Sunday. This is only Friday, so don't muss me up." Who are you trying to look good for and please? Is it the other people at that party or the man with whom you live? Dick and a lot of men are also turned off by the hair-spray syndrome. He hates putting his face against my hair when it feels like a Brillo pad. And it drives him wild when I walk into the bathroom while he's shaving and fill the room with hair spray.

All women like to look their best. We're vain and that has its good points. But you can't roll around in bed having a glorious time and expect your hair to stay upswept, teased, or curled. And you can't make love in the shower, the tub, the lake, or on your back if you're worried about your hairdo. You have to make a choice or find some new options.

You can learn to do your hair yourself and enjoy life more. You can buy a wig for those mornings or evenings after, or you can make love in the woman-astride position after a visit to the hairdresser. Who knows —some night you may be having such a good time that you will fall over on your teased head and won't even mind. Ideally, the best solution would be to wear a hairstyle that wouldn't be affected by your sex life. Maybe that's why the shag haircut became so popular, and why long, straight hair has been in style for so many years.

Our images are far more important to our sex appeal than we like to admit. Too often we don't give enough thought to them after marriage. Witness the many bad jokes about flannel nightgowns, curlers, cold cream, beer bellies, and pear-shaped executive fannies. Usually there's a kernel of truth in all those jokes that we'd rather not face.

Marriage by its very intimacy tends to make us take each other for granted, but we have to try to fight it with our eyes wide open. Let's use our fantasies in a constructive way to do so. Would you let Paul Newman see you getting ready for bed in a flannel nightgown, a head full of rollers, and the white mask of death over your face? Of course not. Would you men dine with Raquel Welch, attired in your Saturday yard clothes, which smell like the locker room at the local YMCA? That's also unthinkable. But who is really more important in your life? Raquel or the woman you've snuggled up against for years? Paul Newman or that man who's *really* lying there waiting for you in bed? Over the course of a lifetime, in which of those two minds is your image more important? Sweet dreams, Raquel! Good night, Paul!

Growth Through Communication

12.

Living in Openness

ON A SUNNY GLORIOUS day in June, a young bride and groom, both radiant, meet at the altar to join in marriage. Their lives seem to stretch out before them like a shimmering road, straight and smooth. They foresee no insurmountable problems, only a future filled with happiness, love, and sharing. They are probably the only two people in the church that morning who share that unrealistic vision of their future. The rest of us, whether we have been married a week, a year, or a lifetime, know from our experiences that marriage is far from that first rosy dream. It takes effort, sometimes agonizing effort, to mesh two lives together. It takes infinite understanding and the ability to communicate with each other to make that road smooth, and it takes these same qualities to pass through the roadblocks that appear unexpectedly in every lifetime.

Those of us sitting in the pews who have the ability to communicate within our marriages never underestimate its importance for a minute. Those who don't have communication know by the toll that it has taken in their own lives, that its absence can stifle a relationship. They also know that marriage does not necessarily mean the end of loneliness. For two people who cannot talk, deeply and openly, it is the start of a new loneliness, which is even more piercing.

It will not take the newlyweds long to discover that a few realities were missing from their dream. Within the next few days they'll begin establishing patterns of communication that will determine much of their future happiness. And, most likely, they won't realize they are doing it. During the first morning of their honeymoon, she might comb her hair in the bathroom. A few minutes later he goes into the bathroom to brush his teeth and finds hair all over the sink. It always repulsed him when he found his sister's hair in the sink, and it repulses him now, first thing in the morning. Will he walk back into the bedroom and tell her that? No, of course not. They've only been married a day, and he loves her. He decides to bring it up at some future time.

Later, she goes into the bathroom to check her makeup and notices that he forgot to put the top back on the toothpaste. Blobs of paste are stuck all over the sink. It bothered her when her roommates did this, and it bothers her now. But she quietly cleans up thinking that she'll mention it sometime. But not now, not today. And maybe they'll be two of the fortunate few who will say to each other calmly and soon, "Something you do bothers me. This is what it is and this is why. Can we talk about it?"

It's simpler for many couples to sweep the hair aside or wipe up the toothpaste indefinitely, than to talk openly about something unpleasant. At least it's easier until the honeymoon glow wears off, and the thought of facing that hair first thing every morning becomes one more grating, irritating part of daily life. Eventually, when enough of these complaints build up they will be voiced, but not as a genuine reaction to hairy sinks. More often, it is two years later in the midst of a fight over something else, that the dam breaks and the flood pours out. "You leave the tooth-

132

paste smeared all over the sink for me to clean up every day. Your pants are always thrown over a chair and they get wrinkled, so I have to pick them up and iron them again. And why can't you put your socks in the laundry bag instead of leaving them on the floor? Maybe your mother waited on you, but I don't have time to do everything in this house and still be your valet. You just take me for granted and treat me like a servant!"

She's not communicating a list of legitimate gripes or differences, she's declaring all-out war. The man's response is as predictable as it is familiar. "Taking care of this house is your job. I have a living to earn, which never seems to be very important to you until you're spending the money. The way you go through it, you'd think I owned Fort Knox. And I never see you worrying about taking care of my things. You leave the car looking like a pigsty, full of dirty tissues and old paper bags for me to clean out. You lend my tools to your brother and to all the neighbors; nothing is here when I want it. And when I do get them back, they're rusty. Talk about being treated like a servant! You expect me to go out and kill myself earning a living, so you can sit around the house all day drinking coffee with the girls. If you'd spend less time talking on the phone, you wouldn't have any trouble keeping the house cleaned." Both of them have opened up enough areas to fight about for hours, but they still aren't communicating. Now they're just trying to score equal hurts.

When we got married, Dick and I found that we brought with us deeply ingrained attitudes, habit patterns, and lifestyles. And these can cause tremendous problems in a relationship. With good communication there are very few problems that can't be handled; without it, most are compounded.

How important is communication in a marriage? To us it is vital. It is as important as love and more important than sex. Without it, I doubt that we would have been able to work out our sex problems. We came to marriage with love, but that love might have dwindled or diminished if we had not been able to feed it through the years with new insights and a deep understanding of one another.

We've grown and we've changed in twelve years. Obstacles have arisen that we could never have foreseen standing at the altar. We couldn't have kept our love as strong as it is without constantly working and striving to know each other better. We have communicated our fears, longings, disappointments, and dreams to each other. And the struggle isn't over for us. We'll continue to grow, to change, and to face new obstacles in the future. We recognize now that communicating is a lifelong job. I can't start taking Dick for granted tomorrow because I know everything about him today. He can't box me into a mold and say, "After twelve years, I understand her." Both of us are going to change over the next thirty years. We will be constantly exposed to new things that will realign our thoughts and feelings.

My family's way of communicating differs considerably from Dick's, and so we came to marriage with dissimilar expectations of family communications. During my childhood, family discussions centered on daily occurrences, school work, world news, the neighborhood. But we never talked about how we felt. I can't remember saying, "I'm lonely," or "I'm scared." I never told my parents when I had my heart broken in high school; I told my best friend and I cried on her shoulder. My sisters and brothers never confided their secret dreams or longings to each other, although all of us were friendly.

My mother and dad didn't express their inner thoughts or feelings in front of us. Perhaps my dad said to my mother, "I'm worried about my job. There are new, younger men coming in, and I'd afraid I'll be passed by." But if he did, we never heard him. My father is proud, but not vocal, and I adopted many of his attitudes. "It's my problem and I'll work it out myself." Because he didn't share his problems with us, we didn't share our problems with others. One of my mother's favorite sayings is, "You don't hang your dirty wash on the line for others to see," and we never did. I don't think my family is unusual.

Dick's family is completely opposite. They talk constantly about everything, and they share most of their thoughts and feelings. If a crisis arises, the whole family participates in finding the solution. There is no subject the children can't discuss with their parents. They are close and trust each other, and that's why they are so unusual. Not only is the atmosphere at their home warm, but people also care more about what others think and feel than what they are doing.

Dick's dad is the kind of man who wears his heart on his sleeve, and you always know exactly how he feels. If he is up, he is way up, if he is down, he is way down. But in either case, the whole world knows how he feels, especially his own family. From him, Dick inherited a very precious gift—the ability to cry, the ability to show his emotions without fear or shame. And Dick's mother has the ability to listen with great empathy and compassion, which she has passed on to him.

Becoming a member of Dick's family was a cultural shock of earthquake proportions. I liked what I saw but their frank concern for everyone and for everything almost drove me crazy at times. It didn't seem possible that a group of people could spend so much time just talking. Everybody genuinely wanted to know everything about each other, and it seemed impossible to keep up with their present situations. Each day brought new problems for some member of the family, and these were treated as family problems. Pat's difficulties with a boyfriend and Dick's worry over whether to change jobs were matters of vital concern to the entire clan.

Being a very private person, I wasn't sure that I wanted them to know what happened in my life each day. Nor was I certain that I needed their help. I had always accomplished things alone and I was accustomed to relying on myself. It wasn't that difficult to share my thoughts and feelings with Dick, but with his whole family? For months I thought they were all very nosy about each other and about us. It took me time to recognize that there is a big difference between meddling, or curiosity, and caring. They cared about each other and about me, and once I accepted that, I felt good. When other people care about you, you're never lonely. And I found that they respected my privacy. No one tried to force me to open up if I wasn't ready.

Sharing feelings with anyone besides Dick was hard at first. It was easier for me to let the world know when I was up, and why, than when I was down. I always believed that if I expressed my disappointments or worries, I would be accused of complaining and whining. I was very reluctant to voice any negative feelings. Eventually, I realized that I wasn't being honest with the people who loved me. If I told them I was depressed, it gave them a better idea of how to handle themselves in the situation.

Did you ever go flying into someone's life like a ray of sunshine and have that person bite off your head for no apparent reason? Actually, you didn't do anything wrong, but suddenly somebody's angry with you, and you have no idea why. Frequently, children are the innocent victims of such anger. We yell at them for some petty thing that might not have bothered us if we weren't concerned and upset about something else. When I used to find myself blowing up at Dick or the children because I was already in a rotten mood, I recognized how unfair it really is to keep all your negative feelings to yourself. Now, whenever we can, we both try to forewarn the children and each other of the storm clouds. As the youngsters burst through the door after school, a warning comes from the kitchen. "I'm in a terrible mood. It has nothing to do with you, but if you're smart, you'll tiptoe until further notice."

Just as I had some difficulty in adjusting to Dick's unusual family, he had some problems relating to my more typical one. And my parents had a difficult time relating to him. He made my mother nervous for years; whenever she told him about some trivial incident, he'd ask her how she felt about it, and she didn't know how to answer that. "I know what happened, but tell me how you feel about it. No, how you really feel." I think she spent the first few years of our marriage just backing up, trying to figure out what he was after.

My dad's first meeting with Dick was also bewildering. Since Dick and I lived away from my hometown when we decided to get married, Dick hadn't met either of my parents. Although they knew about him, we didn't feel it would be fair to telephone them and announce that the date was set. Dick thought that it would be a good idea if he not only got to know them, but also to have a talk with my father privately about us. He flew into town and took Daddy to lunch. He spent three hours telling him exactly how he felt about me, how he saw himself, and how he envisioned our future. I think he stunned my father with his honesty.

On the other hand, I had a grandmother who played an important part in my growing years. She had always operated completely on the feeling level and was one of the warmest people I've ever known. She understood Dick the first minute she laid eyes on him and adored him. He'd say, "What do you think, Gramma?" and she'd say, "Come and have some strudel, and I'll tell you." They would disappear for the rest of the day. The two of them have been bosom buddies since, simply because neither one of them learned how to play games.

Although we came to marriage with different feelings and attitudes toward openness, that was no area for compromise. I think it's reasonable to say that anyone who has lived in an atmosphere of open communications has no desire to settle for less. Dick would have had to regress to operate on my level or my family's level of surface talking. Seeing his openness made it easier for me to be that way. I grew to his level slowly during the first years of our marriage. The more I saw openness working in our life together, the more convinced I was that it was the only way to live.

I discovered that I wasn't losing anything by sharing my private thoughts with someone else. Slowly I learned to feel safe expressing them, knowing that he cared enough to really listen and hear what I was saying. And the sharing helped him to understand me better.

We've both grown in openness, which doesn't mean that we don't have disagreements, or that neither of us ever does anything that upsets the other, or that things don't build up inside. It does mean that the boiler doesn't explode as it did in the imaginary fight at the beginning of the chapter. When we reach that point, one of us can say, "Forget the toothpaste and the socks. What are you really trying to say to me? Do you think I've been taking you for granted lately? Let's talk about that then?" And we can talk about it, without bringing up everything from the dent in the car two years ago to our mothers-in-law.

When two people live together, complaints, honest ones, are natural. So are disagreements. Our two lives can't always run smoothly. Since both of us are busy people, every so often we lose sight of the fact that the other may be getting bogged down. This is a time when complaints are appropriate. They serve as signals that something's wrong, and we need to slow down to find out where. If you hold in the feeling that you're being slighted or taken for granted, you will get angrier and more frustrated. Eventually you will explode.

We've never had one of those knock-down-drag-'em-out fights, but we know that we never want to. We've watched friends, families, and couples tear each other apart that way, and we've seen how hard it is for them to forgive each other after the hurt has been done. It is possible to have a disagreement without having a fight, but only if there is communication on both sides. It means honestly saying what you feel and honestly trying to *listen* (to hear and to understand) to what the other person is expressing. To some people the idea of disagreeing without fighting may seem impossible, but it's not. It is a matter of stating a difference between two people and leaving out all the unnecessary hurtful remarks.

Without communication, marriage and life together is harder, and understanding is almost impossible. The love that you once had for someone can be destroyed through sheer frustration. There is no area of our married life that isn't affected by communication: our bed, our job, our children, our social life, our leisure time, our relationship with relatives and friends. All could become potential areas of discontent and friction when there isn't good communication between us.

Throughout our married life, the two most frequent complaints we have heard other couples express are: "He never talks to me," and "She doesn't understand me." Openness seems to be lacking in many of our friends' marriages. They appear to be more comfortable communicating on a surface level about children, job activities, washing machines, and "Where shall we go for our summer vacation?" I, and millions of others, grew up happily despite the lack of openness. But there is a better way, and why settle for less if it's possible to have more?

Now if we look at our parents' generation, the chinks in the picture of surface living start to widen into gaping cracks. After the busy, daily hubbub of raising a family is over and the children have left home, what happens to these people? What do they share together? What happens to the woman in menopause, whose children are married or at school, who is trying to wrestle through her problems?

What happens to the man facing retirement with nothing to occupy his time and with no one to understand his loneliness? That future would frighten us. Today, our lives are filled with activities that might compensate for any lack of deep openness with each other. But what about tomorrow? Communication doesn't suddenly blossom between two people at age fifty or sixty-five. By that time, a couple is probably locked into a pattern of mutual silence. The sad question then arises, "Isn't there or wasn't there something more to life than this?" Dick and I believe that we have only one lifetime to live together, and we want to live it to the fullest. We want to live our marriage with gusto; we do not want to look back in our old age with regrets, thinking, "It's over and I feel I missed something."

Is it possible at any time in a marriage to begin communicating if you haven't done so before? Can you start fresh? Again, as with sex, the answer is: "What is it worth to you, and what price are you willing to pay?" But how do you know whether or not you're communicating with each other? What criteria do you use?

We know there are no common standards, but you can easily find out how deep the communication level is in your own marriage. Ask yourself how many things you *can't* talk about together. How many taboo subjects are there? What topics immediately provoke an argument or cannot be comfortably discussed by one or both of you? Can you talk together about the following things:

What's really bothering me—Can it be discussed in a reasonable (but totally honest) way without fighting? Can I make the other person understand my viewpoint, or how I feel without having him get angry? Without getting angry myself? Without both of us retaliating with an equal number of gripes?

Sexual longings, desire, and needs—Can we express to each other what we need or would like to make our sex life better? Can we talk about all aspects of *our* sex life without getting uptight?

Disappointments and failures—Can I honestly tell my partner how I feel about myself when I've failed? Or how I feel when someone or something that I depended on disappoints me? Or when I disappoint myself because of weakness or pride?

Needs—Can I express my needs? Can I tell my husband that I need to be shown more often that he loves and cherishes me? Can he hear and understand what I'm saying? Or will he tell me to get a good night's sleep and I'll feel better tomorrow? Can I tell my wife that I need more patience and love from

140

her now because I'm scared of growing old, useless, and impotent? Or afraid of losing my job? Will I be laughed at?

Changing viewpoints—Are we so locked in our images of each other that a change in one partner's thinking patterns or lifestyles brings out fear and uncertainty in the other? The man one day realizes that the length of a teen-ager's hair does not determine his worth. But his wife wails, "What will the neighbors think when they see Jimmy looking like a hippie?" Can we recognize, understand, and accept growth and change in our partners?

Masks and images—Can we admit to each other (to ourselves) that we do wear masks and adopt certain "proper" images in our lives to cover or to hide our true feelings, or to make ourselves more acceptable to others? Can we admit to each other than we wear masks in business, in our social life, and even in our homes? Can we take them off in front of each other?

Insecurities and fears—Can we talk to each other and say, "I'm afraid. I'm afraid my friends won't like me. I'm afraid of not succeeding in my work. I'm afraid of growing old and not being needed. I feel threatened by the younger generation, and by my own children because I don't understand them. The changes are coming too fast for me." Can we share these deep, gut-level fears?

Loneliness—Can we admit to ourselves that we feel utterly alone, unloved, and uncared for at times, and that it's a devastating feeling? Can we express that feeling to those we love? When the world we care about seems to be drifting away from us, and we're frightened, can we reach out for help?

Honest gripes—Whether it's a legitimate or an imaginary point, can we say to each other, "I still love you, but I don't like you when you belch after dinner; it embarrasses me." Can our gripes be heard and understood without causing a donnybrook? "Oh, boy! Wait until you hear the ones I've been saving up." Can we talk together about those aspects of each of us which are irritating?

There are hundreds of questions similar to these that you might use to test how open and honest the communications are in your marriage. It astounds me how few of those questions I could have answered with my own family growing up or with my own family today. Between Dick and myself, there are none that can't be or haven't been talked about and answered.

One of the biggest barriers to deep communication seems to be the multitude of masks that we're taught to wear by society. Unfortunately, it's hard to drop them when we are alone. We formed an image of ourselves and of one another long ago; it's more comfortable to keep it than to change ourselves or our mates.

Consider the young housewife of ten years ago vs. the same housewife today. When I was young, my concept of marriage included being a good wife, mother, and homemaker. The image had a fixed set of rules and standards. I would take care of my husband, raise healthy children who ate all their vegetables, keep a tidy house, and bake cakes. Everyone would cluster around the oven as the cakes came out saying, "Ahhhhh, Good Mommy!" After a few years of marriage, as my interests broadened and grew, my cake visions were the first to change. There were other things I enjoyed doing more than spending the entire morning whipping up a homemade cake. I found that I could take a fascinating course in anthropology at the local university and still make a cake, but now I used a prepared mix. Everybody continued to say, "Ahhhhh, Good Mommy!" Then I discovered that I could sneak in a frozen cake once in a while with the same result.

I decided after several years of on-the-job experience that washing out babies' diapers and cleaning the oven weren't fun at all. There were literally thousands of things that I'd prefer to do. The same could be said of washing the fingermarks from the walls, of cleaning out closets, of sewing ripped pockets. I discovered that I really didn't like housework. It was unstimulating, repetitive, and time consuming. But to say that aloud and have my image crack was another thing! I'm supposed to thrive on this work because my mother and grandmother did. How do I tell Dick that the girll he married is a dyed-in-the-wool phony? She hates keeping his house clean.

Had I never told him, we'd probably both be miserable today. Every pair of dirty socks that flew into the laundry basket might have built a new level of frustration. But I did tell him one day, and I was honestly surprised at his reaction. Instead of calling his lawyer, he said, "I'd hate it too, if I were you." That was surprise number one. Number two was that he had vast areas in his life that he hated as much. He hated doing some of the mindless detail work at the office, when he wanted to work on more stimulating things. He hated putting on storm windows and doing the yard work when he could have been at a football game. More importantly, there were outside activities that he found exciting, and there were things that he wanted to get involved in which didn't include me and us. He, too, hesitated mentioning them because he felt that his place was at home with the family every night.

Hallelujah! His image was as badly cracked as mine! We both knew it, and everything was still all right. So we decided to help each other, and the hell with what the rest of the world thought. If my grandmother felt it was terrible that I used cake mixes or frozen cakes, Dick would stand behind me and swear he liked them better. If his dad frowned because Dick hired a teen-ager to put up the storm windows while he watched the ball game, his dad would have to try and understand us and not his image of what we should be. If the neighbors raised their eyebrows when the grass was cut every two weeks instead of every week, it was just too bad. As long as we understood each other, that was all that really mattered.

We also decided that as soon as we had more money, we'd use it to free ourselves from some of the sheer drudgery that both of us detested. We had set aside money to buy a new car next year, but it would be more fun to use it now. We could take courses, buy books, or hire babysitters at night, so that we could get involved in outside interests—either together or individually. We could easily resign ourselves to driving the old car another year, if it meant that I could paint while someone else cleaned the oven, or that Dick could take up a new hobby in his spare time while a carpenter put up the shelves in the basement. It's amazing how much easier life becomes when you jointly decide not to let anyone lock you into a lifetime mold again.

Another major barrier to communication is listening. It is very difficult to learn to really listen to what another person is saying and then to put yourself in his shoes. I know, because I've been trying to develop the ability for years without achieving total success. Dick came to marriage a better listener than I, and I've spent all these years trying to catch up.

Very few people listen well, although they think they do. We tend to hear selectively. We only pick up and respond to those parts of a conversation that we want to hear, either positive or negative. For example, Dick may say, "I'm not criticizing you, but what is happening to the mates for my socks?" I immediately become defensive, because I think he's attacking my ability to handle the laundry competently. I didn't listen to the part about not criticizing me. He was merely asking what was happening to the odd socks. Were they always one load behind, and would they catch up someday? Had they worn out? Should he get some new ones? My inability to really hear all of what he said, caused my defensive reaction.

The majority of us tend to think our own thoughts while listening to others. We're marking time until they take the next breath or finish, so that we can give our viewpoint. While we're reacting to and mentally mounting our own arguments against the first point that they have made, we miss points two, three, and four. And perhaps these could have made a real difference in what the person meant, and thus our reaction to it. When listening to people who talk or think slowly, I mentally finish the thought or sentence for them, and then draw my own conclusions. I sometimes don't even hear how they actually finish it themselves. We've all seen this happen at parties when a good discussion begins. You can almost see people edging forward on their chairs, ready to make the next point as soon as the speaker draws a breath. Nobody's really listening to anyone else. These debates degenerate quickly into free-for-alls, with everyone talking at once and no one listening. That's fine at a party, but not in a marriage.

Fortunately, Dick is not troubled by this flaw of mine. He has the ability to sit patiently and let the speaker finish without interrupting. He tries to hear not only what the person is saying, but also what he might not be saying before answering or commenting. Coming home from a party occasionally, Dick would gently point out how many times I had interrupted or jumped the point on someone. "Who me? Did I do that?" I found myself becoming more conscious of how often I did take away the conversation from someone else. It's a hard habit to break but it can be done. It takes awareness and an occasional reminder.

Both the selective listener and the jumper-in can benefit in marriage from a listening device that is employed by a friend who is a psychologist. To help a couple keep conversation on an even keel and to make sure that each person hears everything that the other is saying, he asks that the speaker not be interrupted. Then the listener is asked to restate the speaker's main point. "If I heard you correctly, you said that you needed more privacy and that I should leave you alone more." "No, you didn't hear me correctly. What I said was, 'With all that I have to do, it's hard to find time for privacy and my own interests. I'm asking you to help think of ways that might give me more time. It had nothing to do with you.'" We so often misinterpret or misunderstand what is being said, that this little gimmick is a good tool to remember when conversation starts to get heated.

Dick and I frequently have to stop each other and go back over the same point several times before we make ourselves clear. "I don't think you're hearing me," sometimes sounds like a broken record in our home, but it does work. If you force the other person to wait until they understand what you're trying to say, it will prevent hurt feelings.

We all have hot buttons that keep us from listening and communicating. A hot button can be any subject or person that causes an immediate negative response whenever it's mentioned. The mother-in-law often causes a hot-button response with many wives. The husband says, "Is your mother coming over again this Sunday?" She angrily snaps back, "What's the matter with my mother coming over? You've never liked my mother. Why don't you admit it and stop making cracks about her?"

Perhaps he was only asking so that he would know how to plan his Sunday afternoon. Maybe he made the statement without innuendos. But for some reason, she heard it as, "Is your mother coming AGAIN?" Possibly, they had a fight about her mother's influence or frequency of visits in the past, and she's nursing a hot button that he's not even aware of. For some reason, every time he mentions her mother they have a fight, and he can't figure out why.

In the past, we had a couple of hot buttons similar to that one, and it took some hard work to get rid of them. One centered around politics and an image of mine that had changed over the years. When we were first married, we shared the same basic political philosophy. Dick was better informed, but I felt that I had valid opinions, too. As some of mine began to change, a problem arose in our discussions. Whenever I expressed any political views, I'd find myself getting an in-depth lecture from Dick. At least that was the way I felt, and I don't like being lectured to. I'd find myself clamming up and waiting for the lecture to run its course. I had stopped listening.

For about a year, if Dick said anything that even vaguely involved politics, I'd grit my teeth and withdraw. Finally, one night I told him how I felt. He had no idea he'd been lecturing or that I now detested the word, politics. Because I hadn't communicated my feelings, he thought I was still listening with rapt attention. We both felt badly. After we hashed out the problem, it disappeared overnight. Now it has become a joke in our discussions. "I don't care to have my mind confused with the facts on this issue. I'm very happy operating intuitively."

With many people the hot-button subject never becomes a joke. We often see wives or husbands withdraw when their spouse begins to expound on a certain topic. Both of us can recognize the signs because we've seen them in ourselves. That long-suffering mask of blankness comes over their faces, and they retreat to their private world until the ordeal is over. The audible sigh is usually the sign of a hot button to which you're resigned. "Here we go again with the 'Kids Are No Damn Good Today' lecture." Wouldn't it be better to openly deal with the problem than to continue to fight or to retreat for a lifetime? You might stun the other person with a statement such as, "Do you know that you drive me crazy when you do that?" But wouldn't you rather know? Most of the time we can't bring ourselves to tell the other person about the irritants or hot buttons. We're afraid of the reaction it may provoke, or we're afraid of hurting him.

Second-guessing is another obstacle to communications. When we second-guess people we judge in advance how they will respond or feel. If we think something will hurt their feelings or make them angry, we keep it to ourselves. In our marriage we've found that we were often totally wrong in our second-guessing. I thought Dick would be angry or hurt when I told him about his political lectures. He wasn't, but he felt badly for both of us that I had let it go on for so long without saying anything. We judge for other people—friends, associates, our families, children, and spouses—in all areas of our lives. Because we feel that we know them so well, we're sure we know how they would react. Based upon that assumption, we decide what we'll tell and how honest we'll be. We're often wrong.

For years, Dick assumed correctly that I didn't care for business entertaining. Most wives don't, but it's a necessary evil. What Dick assumed, incorrectly, was that I wasn't willing to entertain clients. The audible sigh that he heard after he said that we were entertaining the Gumps again this Saturday was a natural reaction on my part. Last time, while Dick and Mr. Gump spent a jolly evening getting some business done, Mrs. Gump bored me to tears for three and one-half hours with every gory detail of her last four major operations.

When Dick mentioned another dose of the Gump maladies in my life, I moaned "Arghhhhh!" But that didn't mean that I wouldn't go. Or that I'd be rude and tell Mrs. Gump that I'd heard about a marvelous new operation for the removal of faulty vocal cords. I understood that Mr. Gump was important to Dick, and I wanted to help, but I had to let off a little steam, too. He interpreted my "Arghhhhh!" in a much more negative way than I meant it, and for a time, he took Mr. Gump to dinner alone. This didn't work out nearly so well because poor Mrs. Gump was left unhappy at home alone. She had lost the best audience she'd had in years—me!

When Dick and I finally discussed the situation, he understood what I was actually saying. And he realized he had second-guessed me in interpreting the "Arghhhhh!" as an, "Oh no! Not me!" I'm sure that there will always be Gumps in our lives, but we can handle them better now that we both understand the other's viewpoint. And we've found a few ways to make these business evenings more palatable. We arrange a rather fast dinner, and then we take the Gumps to a play on a weeknight. Dick can accomplish his business during the dinner hour, Mrs. Gump gets to go out, but she has to keep quiet during the play, and our good-byes are said early because tomorrow is a workday. The pain and discomfort is minimal on our side, and the Gumps are still happy.

Often when we second-guess people, it's because we love them. We don't tell them anything which we think will hurt them, or which we don't think they are capable of handling. For instance, a man may find his sex life totally unsatisfying or unexciting with his wife. If he prejudges that she is perfectly happy with the situation as it is, he's closing the door to communication and solution. Or he may feel that if he tells her (in kinder words) that she's a lousy lover, he'll destroy her and their marriage. He's made a judgment for his wife without consulting her. As a result, he may be resigning both of them to a long, unsatisfactory sex life.

Assumptions always indicate a breakdown of communications, whether they prove right or wrong. What we may think is our intuitive understanding of a situation, is often not only wrong but also can be dangerous. If Dick comes home for dinner, silent and withdrawn, and spends the evening that way, obviously, I'm going to sense that there's something wrong. If I ask him and he says, "Nothing," that only makes things worse. That word is the world's greatest turn-off. It makes me assume that whatever the problem is, it has something to do with me, but he won't tell me what. If the silence continues for several days, I'll find myself thinking about very little else and begin to assume all sorts of things. "What could I have said or done to upset him so much that he shuts me out?" Many women eventually will come to the conclusion that there's another woman and that their husbands don't love them anymore. Silly as that assumption sounds, it's a logical one for a woman. Then suspicion, distrust, and anger enter the picture, and in a few days the whole atmosphere in your home has changed.

The reality of the situation is probably very different from the assumption. Dick might be faced with a major problem at work, and he might be struggling through the possible solutions and their implications. When he said, "Nothing is wrong," he made an assumption for me. He assumed that it would be kinder not to burden me with his problems, or that I wouldn't be interested. He saw no reason why both of us should worry for three days. It would be better to tell me about the problem after it was solved. It never occurred to him that I would rather know exactly what was wrong, than spend days imagining my own reasons for this silent, changed man in my life. He had no idea that in trying to spare me, he was actually being cruel.

"Nothing is wrong" is a phrase that should be stricken from every married couples' vocabulary. We try to ban it from ours but still have occasional lapses, because it is an easy cop-out. If you have a headache, say you have a headache. If the boss chewed you out and you're depressed, say so. If the children are going through an impossible new stage, frazzling every nerve ending in your body, tell him. Give the other person the comfort of knowing it isn't his fault. And if it is, tell him why, instead of making him try to guess for a week. By that time, he'll have built up enough ammunition of his own to blast you out of the house. And you'll deserve whatever you get for playing games.

If your behavior has changed and there really is nothing wrong, your mate deserves more than a one-word explanation. Every so often, either Dick or I will be in a quiet mood for a few days. There is no cause, no gripe, no reason; it's just the way we feel. If we honestly tell each other that, there's no problem. "I just feel like being quiet. I'd like to go off by myself tonight, and read or daydream for awhile. I'm not upset. It has nothing to do with you. I'm just in a funny mood." That lets your mate off the hook, and he can play poker with the boys that night or watch a good show on TV. But he doesn't have to feel guilty or sit around and worry.

There are times when everyone craves privacy, especially because of the busy pace of our lives today. We should be entitled to time alone without guilt. Forcing two people to share every thought, every activity, every free moment together for forty years is unnatural. Forcing togetherness is letting yourself be frozen into another image of what married life should be like. Someone else made up that image and has been peddling it for years. It's not realistic to assume there won't be any individuality between two people, and Dick and I don't have to live that way. But we do have to communicate to each other how we both feel about the need for privacy. Through that communication, hopefully, we can agree on a lifestyle that's comfortable for both of us.

As we mentioned earlier, there is a high price to pay for total communication in a relationship. But we feel it's worth the cost because the rewards are so great. The price is paid in time—in countless hours spent with the TV off, learning about each other. The price is paid in the dismantling of our masks and games, of our fronts and armor. But most of all, the price is paid in vulnerability.

All of us are afraid to open ourselves completely to another because we fear rejection or ridicule. If I open myself entirely to you, and if you turn away from me, I have nothing left. It's a terrifying thought. As a consequence, we protect ourselves with masks and games so that no one can get inside the real person. Starting in childhood, we learn that it's safer to wear the proper mask, and so we continue to build our defense into an impregnable fortress around ourselves.

But what about marriage? If I say that I love someone enough to spend my life with that person, what am I really sharing besides room and board, if I don't share myself? How can I care for someone and fill his needs, if I don't really know him? How can I say that I love someone if I'm not willing to let him know me? If I'm unwilling to share my innermost thoughts and needs with this person, aren't I actually saying that I don't trust him? In sex, am I really unwilling to respond to this man because he's a stranger to me? I know his body and I know his habits, but I don't know him.

Who will be the first to open and take that risk of rejection? Somehow, we have to begin to trust. If we open ourselves a little, we invite our loved one to open a little. If we find that we survived, that no spear

151

was thrown, and no laughter echoed throughout the room, we can open up a little more without fear. It's a gradual process to reach total openness. We have to slowly peel from each other the layers and layers of defenses that have accumulated. But the rewards are so worthwhile: the freedom to move, to breathe, to be yourself again, and still to have someone love you. It's like running through the .woods naked, unencumbered, and free.

Freedom is the reward for two people who can be completely open. It's the freedom for Dick to cry on my shoulder when he needs to cry, yet be a man. It's the freedom for me to tell him the worst things I see in myself and know that he won't abandon me or destroy me with criticism. It's knowing that no demands will ever be made on our privacy, that there will be no prying or forcing of disclosures that aren't ready to be revealed. It's knowing that the other person is waiting with love, not just curiosity, to help us resolve our problems and heartaches. It's knowing that the truth can always be told, and that no matter how painful it is, someone is trying to understand and accept it. It's knowing that loneliness will never be a part of our lives again. There is someone who really cares how we feel.

It's the freedom to be free, to be part of someone else and still to be ourselves, to be totally secure, knowing that we are anchored in trust. It's never being taken for granted again. It's never again feeling that one role in life is superior to or more important than another. It's a partnership with two people deeply committed to each other, trying to do their jobs to the best of their ability, and knowing that each is appreciated fully by the other.

It's never fearing that we will be misunderstood. Given enough time, we can help each other really hear what we are saying. The faults and habits of two people trying to live as a unit need grate no longer; they can be accepted as human characteristics of two imperfect people. Arguments and fights can disappear;

they can become disagreements between two individuals, each having a valid viewpoint.

It's freedom from the heavy burden of role-playing; it's standing up for what we believe is right, knowing that there is always someone supporting us. And knowing too, that no matter how tough the going gets, we won't be abandoned. It's that strength which enables us to drop our masks with parents, friends, associates, churches, schools, and society and which allows us to say, "No that's not what we want. That's not what we believe in. That's wrong for us."

Most important, it's the confidence, the peace of knowing that we never stand alone when confronted with any problem. It's recognizing that the world can't touch us, can't hurt us, can't pull us down, as long as we have each other. And that no single force except death, is greater than our strength combined. That's freedom!

13.

Identity Crisis in Marriage . . .
Who Am I? Who Are You?
Where Did Gramma Go?

LIFE FOR US AS a young family today is drastically different from our concepts of what it would be like. Reconciling our traditional views of the roles we would play in marriage with the realities of our living patterns today has been very difficult for us and for many of our friends. Our concepts of a mother's role, a father's role, a husband and wife team, and general family living were based on the ways that we saw our parents and grandparents live their lives. We began marriage with a fixed image of the roles that each of us would play and soon discovered that they didn't fit at all. The ground shook beneath us as we tried to find our places.

"Who am I?" and "Who are you?" became searching questions for us as we tried to determine what our roles were in our life together. And "Where did Gramma go?" symbolized a new lifestyle that we were not well prepared to meet.

As Dick and I were growing up, both of us were surrounded by family living. Relatives were always visiting. Great aunts came to play cards, uncles pitched in to paint the garage, or offered to take the young boys to ball games. Holidays or birthdays brought the entire clan together, with the women helping in a steaming kitchen and the men talking in the living room. Cousins were underfoot everywhere, sometimes dozens of them, and a family get-together was a frequent and joyous romp for the children. We knew all our cousins and saw them often. Winters brought talk and family gossip around the kitchen table and roasted chestnuts for the youngsters. Summers brought picnics and vacations with other families in the clan.

And there was always Gramma. Grammas were accessible. They lived around the corner or down the street or across town. Their kitchens smelled of coffee-cake baking, and they let you eat a piece before dinner. Grammas wanted you to stay overnight. At their homes, you could look forward to two solid days of uninterrupted attention. You walked to the delicatessen to buy crusty rye bread with Grandpa, stopped to visit Great Gramma and eat sugar cubes (she never thought they made your teeth fall out), and came home to listen to Gramma's stories of the olden days. It was one big, warm, fuzzy world, and children and grownups knew where they fit into it.

Today our daily family life bears no resemblance to that close, accessible family. Our youngsters are secure with the concepts of family life that they have formed. It's Dick and I, caught between two separate cultures, who were, and still are at times, confused as to our roles. And we seem to share this confusion with many of our friends.

Our family unit has never been as small as it is today. We live in Dick's hometown, yet we don't have one relative living in our city. Even Gramma and Grampa have retired and moved away. The cousins, aunts, and uncles are scattered across the country, separated by hundreds, sometimes thousands of miles. Our children may see a set of cousins once every four or five years. And if they see either of their two sets of grandparents more than once a year, they're lucky.

The mere isolation of ourselves as a family has brought changes to our roles that neither of us could have visualized as we were growing up. I don't remember having anyone other than a relative as a baby-sitter when I was a child. On the other hand, our children have never known anyone but the hired baby-sitter—the teen-ager who stays for the evening, or the woman who lives in while we are on a trip. We know, too, that this is a common lifestyle among most of our friends because of the frantic swapping of sitters' names. The hired baby-sitter poses a problem for us, not for our children. Because of our backgrounds, neither Dick nor I feel it is healthy to leave the children with new baby-sitters often. We don't have the same confidence that we would if Gramma were in charge. And yet, we realize that every so often it's good for us to get away alone; there are also times when it's helpful, even necessary, for me to travel with Dick on a business trip. As a result, we feel torn, and I particularly worry about how much freedom I have to come and to go. Where does my responsibility rest—with Dick who may need to get away and would like his wife with him or at home with the children? Which role do I play? From the children's point of view, there is no problem. For them it's the most natural thing in the world to have baby-sitters; they've grown up with them just as we grew up with Gramma. In fact, our daughters can't wait until they're old enough to sit for other people and earn money.

Another difficulty which has affected our lives is the domestication of the male. When I get sick, who has to pitch in and help? Dick, of course, because Gramma no longer lives around the corner. If I'm decked with pneumonia for a week, he has to cook, run the house, and keep our world spinning until I can take over again, or he has to find someone competent who can. And all these responsibilities are in addition to his work. He can't take off for a week because I'm in the hospital having a baby, or serve as a volunteer on a three-day Girl Scout camp-out with our daughters. There is no Gramma or Aunt Marian to step in and help.

Even if Gramma did live in town, there is no guarantee that she would be able or willing to step in. Gramma's image has changed. She's just as likely, today, to be selling real estate or working as the Welcome Wagon lady as she is to be baking coffeecakes. Many friends have told us that when they had their first child, Gramma let it be known that she was not stepping into the built-in-baby-sitter role. She had her own life to lead, and it was easier to send a check once in a while to help out than to get tied down.

Now that the scattered family is so prevalent, many young fathers step automatically into a domestic role that their fathers would not have considered. However, it does tend to confuse their image. If asked what a father did in our childhood, we might have answered, "He works, comes home, reads the paper, and talks." Today, our children might answer the question differently. "He works, comes home, and if Mom's sick, he cooks dinner and does the laundry." Or, "He works and helps out at home, because Mom works, too."

The change in lifestyle from our parents' generation to our own is not the only factor which confuses Dick's role in the home. His occupation, plus the fact that our children cannot watch him work, further confuses his masculine or provider image. Dick's job entails mental rather than physical labor, and is in an intangible field—communications. He neither makes something nor sells something. There is nothing that you can hold in your hand and say to a child, "This is what Daddy does." Even if our youngsters visit his office, they see only men writing and talking. It's difficult for a small child to relate this to "work" as he knows it, or as we knew it in the past.

We've heard the same dilemma voiced among our friends. "How do you explain to your children what you do, and that it has value?" Lawyers, stockbrokers, insurance salesmen, government workers, researchers, social workers have the same problem of explaining an intangible concept of work to their children. There is no physical labor, there is no product involved, and sons cannot imitate their fathers in the traditional sense.

In our school district it's amazing how few children in the early grades know what their fathers do. When asked about Daddy during "'Show and Tell," the replies are often funny but sad. "Daddy doodles on paper all day." Or "Daddy talks on the phone." In the child's mind, this is very much like play, not work. "Why is Daddy so tired when he comes home? Why does he have headaches, and why does Mommy tell us that Daddy's had a hard day?" What could be hard about talking on the phone and doodling on paper?

A blacksmith's son watched his father toil. When the child grew up, maybe, he could be as strong as his father. Perhaps, he could use that heavy hammer. That was a masculine image—clear and simple. What masculine image do our children have to imitate today if Daddy is not a pro football player? Our Daddy doesn't even know where the hammer is kept; it's Mommy's hammer for fixing small things around the house, or it's the carpenter's hammer for fixing the big things for which Daddy neither has the time nor talent. Who does our son emulate today, and from whom does he derive his masculine image?

How do our children develop a sense of the value of money? A farmer's boy doesn't waste food. He has seen the endless hours and labor involved in growing it. But our food comes in cellophane packages, pre-wrapped at the local supermarket. Money to pay for it comes easily from writing on a small piece of paper called a check. And Daddy earns money by going on trips, flying on airplanes, and staying in exciting cities in fancy hotels. This is the ultimate in adventure for our children—to go on a trip and stay in a hotel. Lucky Daddy not only gets to travel all the time, but he gets paid for it.

The conflict of images between father and child is startling. Daddy may be beating his brains out instead of his muscles, but the children cannot connect this mental activity with real work. And despite our nagging that "money doesn't grow on trees," youngsters can't easily put a proper value on it. It seems to come with such ease.

There are several other ways in which our lifestyle differs from that of our parents and grandparents. Some of these will directly affect how our children see themselves in later life. The most significant change in lifestyle of which we are aware is the absent male. I don't remember my father or grandfather going on an overnight business trip while I was growing up, nor does Dick. It seems that they were home almost every evening. Dick, however, travels a moderate amount. In addition, there are evenings when he has to work late in town, and there are nights when he's involved in civic or community activities—there are fund drives, school board meetings, dinners with clients, and hobbies. In general, the father's presence in the home is a fraction of what it was for us in childhood. And as his presence diminished, his areas of influence also diminish. Phantom Fatherhood has become the new lifestyle for us, and for many of our friends.

Not only does this change Dick's role in our home drastically, but mine increases proportionately as his diminishes. Since he may not be there when a problem arises, I find myself disciplining the children in situations that he would have traditionally handled. Who teaches them how to fight the neighborhood bully if Daddy's not around? Mom. Who teaches them ethics and acceptable modes of behavior? Mom. In the past, those traits were learned from what a child saw in both parents. Today, if he sees one parent infrequently, what he picks up as a future lifestyle is going to be heavily out of balance. Since Phantom Fatherhood is a situation that many of us cannot avoid, drastic measures have to be taken to get things back in balance in our homes—unless we are willing to accept a Mom-oriented society. Dick and I are not comfortable with that concept. We feel it's healthy for our children to grow up absorbing a meaningful male and female viewpoint.

As Dick's role in our family was becoming blurred and confused, I found that the traditional concept of my role was uncomfortably obsolete, too. Not only was I assuming responsibilities which he had been forced to drop for lack of time, but also my time was fragmented over many areas. There were choices, pressures, and responsibilities in my daily life that my grandmother never dreamed of, and neither had I. I might be asked to run a major charity drive in the community that took months to plan and to execute; drive a carload of youngsters to a swamp to study ecology as part of a school program; or make two hundred telephone calls for the local voter registration drive. This was in addition to Gramma's normal day of cooking, cleaning, and running the house.

And it was added to the responsibilities that I'd inherited as a result of Dick's absences. While I had twice the time-saving devices and appliances that Gramma had, it seemed that I had half the time.

I think it was about five years ago that we stopped cold and put our lives and our roles into perspective. We had been talking to Dick's mother about the family and different projects and activities, while she shook her head in bewilderment. "I don't know how you two, or any young people today, can do everything that you do. It's wonderful, but it makes me dizzy to watch you." I was about to laugh and answer, "It's easy, we take tranquilizers!" when I stopped cold in horror. It was true, we did take tranquilizers occasionally, and it wasn't funny at all. I'd see Dick grab one as he flew in from a business trip, dropped his suitcases, and immediately turned around to head for the school play that night. As I swept the last of the cub scouts out

159

the door, I would reach for a pill before finishing my telephone calls for the university fund-raising project. The baby was crying, the Muscular Dystrophy envelope was still sitting on my desk waiting for me to collect on our block, and I hadn't started dinner yet. Tranquilizers had become a crutch at times to help us balance all those balls in the air at once, and suddenly it no longer seemed funny. Tension was a way of life for us.

"Who am I really?" is a question that we each asked ourselves that night. "Who are we, where are we going, and what do we want out of life for ourselves and for our children?" We realized that both of us had been shooting off like Roman candles in all directions. We had assumed that we could be all things to all people—good fathers and good mothers, and still be good for each other. It was a haphazard course with confusion of responsibility and, at times, of roles. The tranquilizers took care of the rough spots temporarily, but what about the future? Wouldn't we be better able to help ourselves and each other, if we knew where we were heading and if we could get a clearer picture of what our real roles were?

It was incredible what a vast and important part of living we had failed to communicate to each other. There were so many questions that we'd never thought about discussing, but these affected our daily living patterns. When one of us was crabby, we chalked it off to crabbiness, instead of recognizing that we were both involved in too many activities to function without friction. Resentment had built up in some areas because we had never asked each other the questions, "What do you expect from me? What do you need from me?" In retrospect, we could see that much of the tension in our day resulted from ignoring one basic problem. We had neither clear-cut patterns for our lives, nor clear-cut roles to work from comfortably. It was time to start.

First, we had to realistically look at our situation. Because of his job, Dick was one of today's Phantom Fathers. There was nothing that we could do about that. He had to earn a living. In the area of outside community involvement there was more leeway, and we had to decide just how much responsibility I could assume before friction started. How much outside activity did Dick need to fulfill himself as a person, and when did it begin to corrode family life? Since his job required that he travel, we had to decide how we could keep his influence and position as head of the house, strong and understandable for the children.

We realized that we needed to know how much the other was capable of, and what we could depend on each other for. Could I handle the money in the family? No, but I might be able to take the responsibility for most household maintenance and the yard. If it got to be too much, I'd yell for help. We defined our roles more clearly as we saw them, and we made sure that both of us saw them in the same way. We tried to plan given areas of obligation for each of us, knowing that these might change as our circumstances changed. The work load at the office might be heavier three years from now and demand more of Dick's time and, therefore, increase my responsibility at home. At that point, we'd reassess any new situation and try to shift some of the responsibilities to cover the changes.

We attempted to understand and communicate our common goals as a family. What were we reaching for ultimately? Was it financial security? A better lifestyle? Fulfillment as individuals? We had to decide what was most important to us as a couple, and then try to determine whether we could pay its price. What were our goals and needs as individuals? Once we had communicated these to each other, we could attempt to fit them into our family goals. We could determine how much flexibility each of us had, and how much time and money to pursue personal interests.

Most important, we were aware that we had to understand far better what each of our jobs involved to avoid any possible future resentment or friction. We had to know and appreciate the pulls, pressures, frustrations, and rewards present in each other's day.

We recognized that our lives had to be more of a

team operation in this hectic, changing world, and that we had to constantly communicate weak spots and mounting tensions. Otherwise, the team work would fall apart and we would probably be back on tranquilizers!

As significant as that realization was for us, equally important was the awareness that we needed to do more to help our children understand us. We needed more time filling in the gaps and supporting each other. It was necessary for me to interpret for them what their father did, what his day involved, and what his life away from them was like so that they could more fully understand him. They had no way of knowing why he came in utterly beat on certain nights, or why there were times when he didn't come home. "Daddy's working hard" wasn't a sufficient explanation. Why was Daddy working hard? For us or because he likes to? What were the family goals that Daddy was working toward—that we were working toward together? Explaining that to them was a job we had skipped before, and it had to be done.

If Dick, by necessity, had to be absent much of the time, how could he remain a strong force in the children's lives? By devoting more time solely to them when he was home—quality time, not just TV time together. By talking to them occasionally from the office, to let them know that he was thinking of them, or that he did remember that today was report-card day. He spent more time talking, exchanging ideas, discussing problems with them than ever before. As a result, he became a more active force in their lives. He became as open with them as he is with me. Their time together became infinitely more valuable from the viewpoint of understanding than the trip to the zoo that he might have missed.

Since the children could see what I was doing a good part of the day, Dick assumed the responsibility of helping them interpret what a mother's life meant. He explained that many of my telephone calls were made in an effort to raise money for a hospital, or for crippled children, and this activity was important to all of us. He spent and still spends a great deal of time talking to the children individually about what a woman is to a man: What I am to him, and how we help each other in life; how and why he needs me in his day; and how I rely on him in mine.

Listening, participating, and caring about each person's day at the dinner table each night has helped us recognize that we are a team. From youngest to oldest, each has his worth and his place in the family. Each child is listened to with respect as he relates his day. There is no dull household problem or minor school problem that isn't worthy of a hearing. Together, we can work it out and, hopefully, learn more about each other in the process. Hopefully, when our children reach maturity, they will be able to carry themselves into new roles with self-esteem, dignity, and flexibility.

Once more, we realized how utterly dependent the two of us were on communication. Without it, there could be very few smooth spots for our family unit. Without our willingness to share ourselves, our changing roles, our confusion over our images, there could be little hope of receiving understanding or help from each other. Instead of a partnership, we would continue as two individuals, struggling along. The concept of a full, honest partnership would be merely a vague idea, one to which we paid lip service.

Our lives are based strictly on love, and this opens the way to partnership and freedom at the same time. In the next three chapters, we'll try to show how it's worked in our marriage.

14.

Phantom Fatherhood

WHO IS THE PHANTOM Father? We think of him as the
man whose business, job, or community activities take
him out of his home to such an extent that his influence there is diminished. We mentioned briefly in the
last chapter that Dick, as a businessman, was often a
Phantom Father. But he is not alone, nor are businessmen and executives the exclusive Phantom Fathers in
our society. There are Phantom Fathers in all economic
brackets. More and more, through necessity, women
must cope with a dual role in the absence of their
men.

The Phantom Father who automatically comes to
mind is the traveling salesman. But what about the
insurance salesman who never leaves his hometown?
He often makes the bulk of his sales in the evening,
talking to couples. The painter, the carpenter, the con-
tractor, the architect—all these men do night estimat-
ing for new jobs because their daytime hours are spent
on current ones. Engineers who work on out-of-town
installations, pro football players, entertainers, doctors,
taxi drivers are all Phantom Fathers. Many times the
men who we envy because they have a nine-to-five
job, are the ones whose families suffer acutely from
their absences. These are the small, independent businessmen.

We begin to realize that the local druggist, shoe-
makers, morticians, and delicatessen or grocery-store
operators who dotted our neighborhood shopping
center were also Phantom Fathers. Their hours
were longer and harder than Dick's at times, and their

reward could be an early heart attack from the strain and worry involved.

Soon we became aware that any man who held down two jobs or a part-time job was a Phantom Father. Even those few men who did work a nine-to-five day but commuted to a major metropolis were Phantom Fathers. A friend of ours, who is a stockbroker in Chicago, worked normal hours, yet he saw his young children only on weekends. In order to commute to his nine-to-five job, he caught a 7 A.M. train before the children were awake and returned at 7:30 P.M. after they were in bed for the night. And that's a way of life for thousands of men who work in Chicago, New York, Los Angeles.

The factory worker, that stalwart of the home front, is in many cases a Phantom Father—while he sleeps. Until a friend related the lifestyle of the second and third shift worker, I had always assumed that the factory worker probably enjoyed the epitome of normal family life. Not by a long shot, according to his wife! When that father is working a second or third shift, he is home when the children are home, but he's sleeping. Keep the dog and the children quiet, don't vacuum, don't use the garbage disposal, catch the doorbell and the phone on the second ring, pick the baby up as soon as it starts to cry, and don't have friends visit during the day. Phantom Fatherhood's influence is as strong and as deep on those families as it is on the families whose fathers are actually out of town.

Why are Phantom Fathers so prevalent today? Why is the lifestyle so different from the one we, as children, saw in our own homes? Dick's job and all the jobs that we have mentioned require it. In order to provide for a family now, many men have no choice except to become Phantom Fathers. And they must risk frustrating or losing that same family because of it.

We will have four children (should they all choose to go) in college at the same time, at a projected cost of $64,000. How does a man earn enough to provide for such future expenses, yet still find time to "feed his soul?" In addition to college expenses, there's retirement to provide for and the staggering daily costs of a growing family. Dick says the whole thing scares the hell out of him at times!

There is another choice possible in Phantom Fatherhood—but it is one of degree. For the man who is already burdened with stacks of work, what about community involvement? Here we have some options, but they immediately become cloudy when you closely examine the choices. For Dick and many other men, their participation provides stimulation and relaxation of a different kind, much as a hobby does, but it also cuts into time with the family. Is a hard-working man entitled to recreation time? Can he play golf or tennis or fish or hunt, if that's the way he reduces some of his daily tensions and puts some fun into his life? Or, in the realm of community activities, who will work on the political campaigns, the community fundraising drives, the school boards, and the church groups if he doesn't? Let George do it, right? George who?

Some time ago when Dick and I were talking with a group of teen-agers, the problem of Phantom Fatherhood arose. Janice, a delightful high school senior, gave us some new insights into its effects in her home. "My dad tries hard," she said. "I know he wants to be a good father, but he's gone a lot, either working or raising money for a worthwhile charity. Sometimes he doesn't come home for three or four nights in a row, and then when he does spend a night at the house, he wants to be our buddy. He asks us to sit down and tell him about all our problems and interests so that he can catch up. Well, you just can't turn on and off like that. You're either involved or you're not. Maybe we have something to do that night, or we just don't feel like talking. Then he gets upset because he's home, and he thinks that we should spend the whole evening with him. Where was he last week when I wanted to talk to him and he wasn't there? Sure, I know why he's working hard, I want to live at college next year, and there's no way I can save up enough money to pay for it. He has to earn the money, and there's four more kids behind me. As for the volunteer work he does, I guess that's what I want him to do. We all complain because the older people aren't involved, but when they are, it's a problem, too. Some of my friends get disgusted and turned off by their parents who watch TV at home every night. All they hear their parents talk about is how awful everything is and how it ought to be changed. But there's their old man sitting in a chair, drinking. I don't know what I want, but it's not either one. I guess the whole thing is a mess. I just don't understand it." Janice managed to sum up well the problems Phantom Fatherhood presented in her life.

There are many ways that Phantom Fatherhood can create irritation. For instance, if we have planned a weekend away with the children, or a family outing, it invariably starts with a little flare of friction. Daddy said he would be home at 2:00 P.M., and then we'd go immediately. Youngsters take everything literally, and 2:00 P.M. means precisely that, not five minutes later. And anyone who has waited even five minutes with a bunch of wound-up children, who are waiting to do something exciting, knows that five minutes is a lifetime—for everyone. "What time is it now? Why isn't he here? Can I call him at the office? Can I stand outside and wait? What time is it now? I'll bet he had an accident." The time is now 2:05 P.M., and even if Dick walked through the door instantly (which is unlikely) my nerves are already so jangled, that I'm likely to jump all over him.

When he does walk in at 2:30 P.M., I grit my teeth, try to hold my tongue, and cheerfully say to the gang, "Daddy's home. Let's go." The car is already loaded, the youngsters are hanging out each window, and the poor dog has been jammed in waiting for a half hour, slobbering all over the seats. I look back over my shoulder and see Dick calmly reading the mail, to-day's paper, or turning on the sprinkler. There is no way that I can hold my tongue for one more second, and out flies the typical, bitchy wife crack. "For God's sake, why are you watering the lawn now! Can't you see we're all ready to go. We've been waiting around for an hour."

He looks annoyed and says, "What's the rush? I said I'd be home around 2:00 P.M. We're not late for anything. We have no special time to leave. What's the big problem?" Now both of us are irritated, and it's the most natural thing in the world under the circumstances. We've found that it's the same old problem—lack of understanding of what's really happening right here, right now. That friction can be eliminated easily, if we take the time to explain our day to each other.

Unless I know that Dick has been rushing to one meeting after another all morning, I can't possibly understand why he is taking another five minutes to read the mail or to water the lawn. For him, leaving instantly would be a switch from one high gear into another. He needs that five minutes to relax, to catch his breath, and then to shift gears downward for the weekend outing.

I was honestly surprised when Dick told me that many nights before he comes home, he parks around the corner from our house for five minutes. He sits there and smokes one cigarette before driving home. Why? Because when the children hit him at the door like a ton of bricks, it's too much. It's difficult to make the instant shift to "Look at my report card!" "Look at my scraped knee!" "I made the football team today!" "Suzie hit me at school!" "Mom said I should ask you if I can get a new bike!" He needs that quiet five minutes alone before walking in, to shift into their world and enjoy it. By the same token, he has no idea why I am so annoyed just before our weekend outing. Unless I can bring him into my world of waiting with the children how can he understand the frustration of that eternal five minutes?

We have to communicate with each other, so that those same frictions don't recur, and so that every Saturday outing doesn't start off badly. If we both understand each other's role, the solutions are quite simple. In this particular case, the answer is so blindingly obvious that we felt like fools for not seeing it earlier. Set the deadline ahead an hour. Allow for some breathing room. Tell the youngsters that we're planning to go at three o'clock, when Dick and I are actually aiming for two o'clock.

That was only one example of the thousands of irritants and frustrations that crop up because of Phantom Fatherhood. We face them almost daily in our lives, and I know that our friends do, too. The two of us are determined, however, not to allow them to breed resentment, and the only way that we can prevent that is to create continued understanding through continued effort. The solutions are never difficult when two people put their heads together. Communications have to be a constant way of life, not an occasional disclosure. That's one of the prices to be paid for understanding and appreciation; the effort never fails to bring rewards.

Friction can occur when Dick has to miss the school play, or our son's first track meet, or the Father-Daughter Girl Scout Tea. It can be avoided if I believe he is being honest when he tells me that he would rather be there than in Shreveport, or at an evening meeting with a client. I have to trust him to decide which is more important, or believe him when he says he has no choice. I have to believe that he loves his family and wants to be involved with them. That takes care of friction number one.

Friction number two is the children themselves. The person who can best convey to them why their father missed a play or a game, is Dick. By giving them as much of an insight as possible into the why he can help them to gain a realistic view of his options. And if I have full understanding of his choices and his role, I can help them understand that his absence in no way means that he doesn't love or care about them. We both can help them see that sometimes it's necessary for their father to be a part of their lives in a different way from other fathers. We've found that our children are most understanding when we've

169

shared our difficulties with them and allowed them to understand. They can be very big little people given the chance.

We've often seen how Phantom Fatherhood causes friction when the subject of discipline arises. A woman frequently has a softer approach; she doesn't inform her husband of mounting problems unless they get out of hand. At this point, we've seen many men lose their temper. Frequently, the husband doesn't find out that there's been a problem with Johnny until school calls to say he's been suspended. The father is involved, but uninformed. "What the hell's going on?" He assumed that things were going along normally, he was never made aware of the problem as it grew, and suddenly he's faced with a crisis. He really has very little understanding of Johnny, and in many cases, he will overreact rather than try to reconstruct the situation.

Actually, both parents are at fault. He left the complete handling of discipline to his wife, which he never should have done, and which she should never have allowed to happen. Nor should she have let problems develop without telling him. He can't be expected to understand now at the crisis level. The only way he can save face is to overreact, which drives Johnny and the rest of the family further away.

There is another area in which the handling of discipline can cause overreaction and breed resentment. Both can occur when a wife has little understanding of her husband's role and consequently feels unjustly overburdened and unappreciated. For instance, the husband has been away for a week and is greeted at the door with, "Here, take your children for awhile. They're driving me nuts! I can't stand them another minute! They're your problem now." With that outburst, she abdicates her responsibility. The husband walked into what he thought was his tranquil home, and he finds that he has to spank his youngsters before he gets his coat off. Mom said they were terrible, so they must be. He doesn't know

170

what the curcumstances are, but after a week's absence, it's his job to shape them up.

The situation is unfair to everyone. Because of her inability to handle or accept the responsibility for discipline, the mother throws up her hands in despair. In her eyes, her husband is the villain because he has left her with all the problems. On the other hand, she shows no understanding or appreciation of his position. In the children's eyes, he is the villain because every time he comes home he beats the hell out of them. What did they do that was so bad? Nobody ever asked, it was simply, "Mom said."

In our own family we've seen that this approach could never work. And we've seen its consequences in other families. Dick and I came to the conclusion that a joint effort is required to successfully raise and discipline our children. We recognized that we had to have a mutual agreement about such areas as: behavior, grades, hairstyles, smoking, drinking, stealing. Did we stand together, and did the children know where we stood? We had to, or chaos and overreaction would rule our lives.

Since we made that decision, we have been able to handle situations better as they arise. Often there isn't time to have hurried consultations in this busy world. When the principal phones and says that your sixteen-year-old has marijuana in his possession, and your husband is away on a sales trip, it's more comforting to be able to react as you know he would.

Please understand that we're not suggesting that you try to consider every possible situation or problem that could arise, but only general areas and your feelings about them. For example, if any of our children were to have a run-in with the law, do we back the authorities or say, "Not my child—there must be some mistake"? We've discussed the subject and decided we would support the law, follow due procedure, and work from that base. If the situation ever arises, I'm capable of handling it in Dick's absence.

Equally important, our youngsters need a balance of both of us in their lives to become complete people

171

themselves. Dick and I began to notice that while we agreed on philosophy, we often had two totally different ways of approaching situations and problems. Both were right, but there were times when the boys or the girls needed a masculine approach to broaden their horizons.

When our oldest boy was in second grade, he ran up against the class bully for the first time. For three days he came home crying, as the bigger boy gloried in pushing his face in the mud, or tripping him every third step, or throwing his hat into a tree. Life was miserable for him and for me, because I agonized with him. Normally, Dick and I prefer to see the children handle their own problems. If the children can work out their own solutions, they are usually more lasting. Only as a last resort will we call other parents, and then we try to speak to the father, because we've found that most mothers can't accept that their Billy is capable of being the neighborhood terror.

If one of the youngsters can't handle a problem, I use a sneaky approach before we consider calling. I corner the bully alone on the way home from school, I tell him who I am, and what I intend to do to him if I ever hear that he's been harassing our children again. It's a good scare, and he's never going to tell his mother that the bad lady down the street threatened to put him up on the telephone pole and leave him there overnight. He knows he's done wrong, and he'd have to squeal on himself at the same time. Usually the problem disappears overnight, if I have to step in.

Our son's situation hadn't progressed that far yet, and I was still hopeful that he could cope with this bully himself. On the fourth day, however, when he came home crying because that brute had chased him home, urinating all over him. I blew my stack. "You are going to learn to fight! You are going to school tomorrow and knock that kid's block off! You are going to finish him off once and for all!" Sob, sob. "But Mom, he's bigger than I am." "That's O.K., I'll teach you how to lick him."

172

Dick was out of town during this whole adventure, so I proceeded to teach my son to fight—my way. "Just walk up to him like this tomorrow and punch him. Hard as you can! But don't hit him in the mouth because you might break his teeth, and then his parents will have dental bills." We practiced for a while and the next day our son went off to school to conquer the bully. You guessed it already? He got wiped all over the playground. He was so concerned about not hitting the bully's teeth, that his first punch was a miss and he never got a second chance.

Fortunately, Dick came home that night. Daddy heard the story and immediately took over the fighting lessons. I was amazed by the difference between a woman's and a man's approach. "Who cares about his teeth? If he's a bully, he deserves what he gets. And don't worry if you knock out a few. I'll handle his parents when they call. You have to shake him up before he knows what's happened. If you hit hard first, you'll surprise him and put him on the defensive right away. Start slugging any place you can reach, and don't stop till you get him down. Remember he's bigger and once he lands that first good punch, you've had it. If he grabs you from behind and pins you, go back with your elbow and whack him in the stomach. No, not like that. You look like you're hitting a powder puff. That's it, harder! You've got to win this one tomorrow, or he'll hound you for the next five years. Now, let's try it again. Start off slugging and don't worry about where they land."

So they practiced and practiced that night. The next morning we watched our tiny gladiator go off to school with fists clenched and a tight smile on his face. It seemed like a lifetime until he burst through the door at lunch hour, grinning from ear to ear. "I licked him! I did it! You should have seen it, Mom! I got him down right away, and I kept punching him till he gave up. Then he ran home crying. All the guys said I was great. Can I call Dad?"

It's been six years since that fight, but we've had to teach all our children to defend themselves from some neighborhood terror. In each case, it's taken both of us to help them over the rough spots. They've needed the firmer attitude of their father, and at times the gentler approach of their mother. And they've needed Dick to instill the concept of fair play. "Now that you know you can lick the toughest person in your class, watch out that you don't become the class bully. You have to remember how terrible it was for you, when you were the one being chased home everyday. Always try to discuss your problems first, rather than fight." My sympathy and approach has been equally necessary when the bully is a taunter only.

Perhaps our son doesn't make the basketball team, or one of the girls can't understand why the teacher picks on her all the time. Whatever the problem, and there seems to be a new one each day, our children need both of us as an influence in their lives. If it's a necessity that Dick be a Phantom Father, then we both have to work harder to keep that balance present in our home. I have to keep him informed of problems as they arise and of progress—not only to keep him a vital part of the family, but also to learn what his perspective is on the problem. And when he's absent, I have to to try my best to impart both viewpoints to the children.

We both have to help our children learn what it means to be a mother, a father, a husband, and a wife. We have to show them that marriage is a partnership, and that we are not competing with each other for dominance. Instead, we're supporting each other and working together. With Dick's assistance, I have to convey what his work entails, why it is important, and the toll that it will take, so that they don't harbor any resentment.

And Dick, because he wants to remain a vital force in our home, has to devise new ways to reach his children. We've found that even though the actual time he spends with them may be less than other fathers put in, it's better utilized. During the nights that he's home, he spends time with each child, pri-

174

vately, at bedtime. It may range from five minutes to an hour, depending on the child's needs. But the youngsters know he tries. They do understand him, they do appreciate his role and his frequent absences, because they are included in the whys.

Whenever possible, Dick tries to involve them in any part of his business that he thinks might be interesting to them, so that they can follow along and understand better what he is doing and why he is frequently not home in the evening. Often, they'll wake up Dick to find out how a project came out, or call him at the office to see what happened. Whether or not he's physically at home, his invisible presence is felt in every aspect of our lives.

Dick has also tried to portray the partnership concept to them. He's found the time to convey to the children how much he needs me—what I mean to him in his life, and what it means to be a wife and mother in our home. They can see us working together in daily life, but we also have tried to share with them the way that we felt about each other's help and understanding.

How can we help the Phantom Father? By communicating. How can he help his wife and family? By allowing them to understand his day, his life, and his lack of choices. Thoreau said that man is the one who is truly housebound. He is the one who labors all his life pushing a mortgage uphill. What Thoreau forgot to mention, and we often fail to acknowledge, is that he's also pushing the doctor bills, the baby shoes, and the college educations uphill at the same time. His choices and our choices were often made for him years ago, and those determine a lifestyle today that he may not be able to change because of those obligations.

If Dick can honestly communicate his role, then I can understand his physical and mental exhaustion when he comes home each night. When he says, "Can you hold dinner for fifteen minutes while I catch my breath?" I can say, "Sure," and feed the starving mob some carrot sticks to tide them over. I can try to remind the children not to bother their father with their problems before he gets his coat off, but to wait until he's halfway through his dinner and has had a chance to relax. It'll never work completely because youngsters are human and they want their time with him, but the understanding is slowly sinking in and some progress is being made.

There are many ways that we, as a family, can make Dick aware of our appreciation for his role as a provider. If I know that an important deal is being closed on a particular day, I can bake his favorite cake that night, and let the children draw the picture of Dad in the frosting. A hero cake that says, "Win or lose, we love you."

15.
The Job: Bogie Man or Blessing?

WHY SHOULD A MAN'S job cause any friction within his home? Theoretically, the family should support that job in every way possible. After all, it provides the money for the bikes, the dishwashers, the vacations, the new carpeting, and the second car.

But often, far from joyous support, the job breeds friction, discontent, and resentment in the family. Women want both the dishwasher and the nine-to-five husband. The job has changed. It isn't what we thought it would be, any more than marriage is what we thought it would be when we stood at that altar. Both of them take far more work, time, and effort than we could have ever envisioned. Money goes faster and buys less today. Moreover, it is spent on articles that didn't exist twenty years ago. Last year's luxury becomes this year's necessity. Next year's vacation becomes this year's leaky roof repair. Basically, we know that we need that job more than it needs us, but its daily demands prove difficult. We're perfectly willing to take our husband's earnings to buy that new winter coat or the fiberglass skis, but we resent it when he has to work Saturday morning instead of putting in the new lawn.

We've talked about Phantom Fatherhood and we tacitly agree that it's frequently necessary for one's husband to go on that business trip. Otherwise someone who is willing to travel will replace him eventually. Without the nights and weekends spent catching up on reports and attending refresher courses, your man can be bypassed by younger or brighter men. The price of expertise is higher than we anticipated. And yet, how could we know what to expect? Our fathers didn't have these problems.

Time is our biggest problem—the lack of it spent together as husband and wife, and family. Money is another. There is never enough to meet the demands, and the only way to make more is to become better at your full-time job or take a second job. But either solution often takes the man away from his home. Many times community involvement is necessary as a means to advance the job. "Become better known. Make connections." Again, time away from home. Traveling, refresher courses, competition, financial needs, business appearances, all eat away at the lifestyle we desire and create resentment on the home front.

However, the time factor is not the only area that causes resentment. The entire lifestyle of the working man is changing, and the ramifications are felt at home. The salesman who has been on the road all week comes home Friday night exhausted and wants to relay. Maybe he would like to watch TV and forget work until Monday morning. But his wife has been at home all week with the children and would love to go to a movie or dancing at a discotheque. She needs an outlet, but one with loud music is the last thing he needs now. She's about to go stir-crazy, and he can barely stir his martini, let alone stir himself to swing tonight. Which set of needs gets satisfied? Who compromises? And who resents it?

Dick had observed another factor growing out of today's job scene that is affecting the marital front. The increase in alcohol consumption during the work-day is a new phenomenon which many men and their wives are having trouble coping with. The martini at lunch that's taken for granted today would have raised eyebrows in our father's day. And, Dick says, it's given way to the breakfast drink! Many businessmen's schedules are becoming so crowded, they frequently start the day with breakfast meetings, and one of the first questions asked is, "Who wants a Bloody Mary?" At 7:30 in the morning? Yes. And that stop-off after work for a drink with the boys? Dick explains that it, too, is not as much a social hour, as it is a means to extend the business day in a more relaxed atmosphere. There's very little baseball talked in busi-nessmen's bars at 5:00 P.M.

When the man of the house comes home drunk at 7:00 P.M., late for his dinner, is his wife angry? Yes. Does she resent him and that job more? Yes. Does she understand what's happening? No. She has no idea of the pressure that may be applied by associates to stop for that one drink, or how hard it may be to walk out after only one. Good old Gertie waits with the mental rolling pin to clobber him as he walks through the door. He's a bastard because dinner is spoiled, he didn't call, and now he's half bombed. She's a bitch when she lets him have it, because she assumes that he wanted to be with the boys in-stead of with her.

The difference between two people's conception of "the good life" on the road often breeds resentment, too. Gertie may see it as exciting and luxurious. There's nothing she'd like better than to go to San Francisco for a week and eat in all those marvelous restaurants. And someone else would straighten up the room every day. But poor Gertie is at home with the children, eating hash and watching the re-runs of "Bonanza," while he's having his kebab and watching a floor show at the Blue Fox. How could she know that he'd prefer to be in his own living room, with his shoes and tie off, watching "Bonanza"? The last thing he wants is one more trip to San Francisco this month, one more dinner with Mr. Glotz, and one more round of air terminals, baggage, and cabs. But Gertie couldn't possibly realize that, so she releases all her pentup resentment and frustration as soon as he walks in the door. "Here, playboy, take over for a while." During the entire weekend, she sulks and leaves him in charge of the children, the dog, the yardwork, and the garbage. He doesn't know why she's so crabby, but she is always like this when he comes home from a trip. That relaxing home is starting to look less and less inviting, while Mr. Glotz is beginning to look better by the minute.

Gertie's turning into a bitch. She constantly nags him to earn more money, yet to do so means more time spent away and more work. "What does she want from me? Doesn't she see that I'm already killing myself? I can't do much more and still take the pressure at home. Nobody understands."

No, nobody does understand. Gertie didn't expect this kind of life nor did the rest of us. We weren't prepared for it. But there we are. We're faced with the choices of getting out, giving up the dishwashers and the swim clubs, and buying a farm or joining a commune. Or we can continue to bitch at each other, ruin our marriages, and give our men ulcers and early heart attacks.

But there is one more choice. We can try to understand today's job and support it. It wasn't our fault that we weren't prepared for the job demands that we face today, but it is our fault if we don't make every effort to cope with life and make it as happy as possible. Once again, communication, understanding, appreciation are necessary for the job that feeds us all, the man who holds it, and the woman who stands beside him.

I consider myself and most of my friends home managers, not housewives. Frequently, we have the responsibility for the yard, the car repairs, home maintenance such as painting and carpentry, and finances. We run the family with an absentee head of the household much of the time. And many women resent this. They feel that their husband has dumped everything on them, to free himself to do more exciting things. They are the drudges. They feel their men have become successful at their expense, ignoring the man's valid view that the whole family is becoming successful at the expense of his leisure time. That growing resentment in wives makes fertile ground for the women libbers. As a good friend kiddingly stated years ago, "Who wants a live-in girl to help? I need a live-in boy with a tool box."

The absentee husband takes on the role of a guest in the house—almost a passing tourist at the local motel. The schedules, the routines, and the lifestyles often evolve without him. When he does appear on the scene and naturally wants to inject himself into family life, friction results. Or the wife may feel that she's finally managed to get things running smoothly and now here he is meddling in her world. Thus one of the greatest dangers of Phantom Fatherhood, as we see it, is the dominance of the woman and the "Who-needs-you" attitude that can naturally develop from it. She begins to think of it as her world, her children, her home—not theirs.

Again, this is a problem of a lack of communication, combined with the incorrect assumption that the man is enjoying the absentee role. Dick says that nothing could be further from the truth. The majority of men that he knows love their families. Certainly, they would prefer to relax at home with their wives and children rather than attend one more business meeting at the end of an already endless day. But the realization that he has no choice is seldom acknowledged. The wife resents him, his absences, and ultimately the big, bad giant itself—the job. She is cast in the role of heroine and he of villain in the drama.

In addition to carrying what seems to be an unfair

double load, many women feel lonely as a result of Phantom Fatherhood. If a woman doesn't have her own absorbing interests, what does she do every night while her husband travels or has evening meetings? Boredom sets in and resentment grows. We wish that the men were stuck at home with the children and were experiencing our boredom.

Weekends, for those of us whose men have to be away or whose mates are shift workers, are especially lonely times. We seem to be out of kilter with the normal world, and Sundays are especially endless. These are family days for most of our friends, and we don't want to intrude. Our social life is often curtailed, and night life is nonexistent if the husband has to work on weekends. For the woman, this means more boredom and increasing resentment.

It is difficult for many women to visualize men in equally lonely situations during their time away. Dick points out that a weekend or Sunday on the road is a time of almost total isolation for him. He's plagued by the same loneliness that assails us at home, but to an even greater degree.

Several times over the years when Dick has been out of town over a weekend. I've gone to a party or get-together with a group of close friends because after days of unrelieved children's activities, I was in desperate need of some adult companionship. Knowing the situation well, having been through it often themselves, the other couples would say, "Come anyway. We'll pick you up." I would go and enjoy myself, but I did notice that even among close friends with whom I was relaxed, my conduct was slightly more reserved. With no man of my own present, I was more aware of what I said and did throughout the evening. The harmless kidding and flirting that occurs between couples who know each other well seemed a little out of line for me on those nights. If Dick had been sitting across the room talking to one of the other women, I would have given no thought to dancing with one of the other men. As long as Dick was absent, I was conscious of how the other wives might view this, and altered my behavior accordingly. The same applied to drinking. I found myself drinking very little in Dick's absence. The last thing I wanted was to inadvertently find myself bombed, with another couple taking me home and tucking me into bed. Although I needed those evenings out, they weren't the same as the evenings out with Dick.

We can usually do nothing about the time spent away from home, but it does help to continually remind yourself of why, how, and for whom it is spent. Dick and I usually try to discuss thoroughly any new commitment before he gets involved. By doing this, we can better understand what it's *likely* to mean to the family. But no matter how completely we talk about a new project, we generally underestimate the amount of time and the strain that it will require.

Once we both have a fairly realistic idea of the effort and the rewards involved, we can decide whether we want to make the commitment. And if we do, then no matter how much we underestimated or how bad it gets, we try to grin and bear it. Occasionally that plaintive cry is still heard, "But you said this would only take about three nights a week for a month. It has been five nights a week for a month, and you're still not finished." Dick has to remind me that we could only guess the time involved, and we guessed wrong. I have to remember that the goal is worthwhile. "Keep in mind that if we make this big sale, we can pay off the boat this year."

One aspect of Dick's job that I don't begrudge is the time spent traveling on the road. I've been with him often enough to see what it's really like. Generally, it's a hard-paced grind, without much fun or rest. If more men would take their wives on business trips (ordinary ones to Cincinnati or Portland), they might find that the amount of understanding gained was worth the expense. Except for coastal cities, one large city looks very much like another. Husbands *do* tend to work on a trip, so unless you're an avid window-shopper, Cincinnati's charms start to pall after a day on your own. Your husband will have little time to go sightseeing, whether he's alone or you're with him, and evenings often mean dinner with the Gumps—those same clients that make you groan when you learn that you have to invite them to dinner at home. With the exception of a trip to Hawaii or Europe, there's very little to resent or miss on those business trips.

What does the job itself entail? Without understanding it, I can't be completely close to Dick. If he spends ten to twelve hours a day working and excludes me from the knowledge of his livelihood, or I don't care enough to ask, how can we stay close? If we can't communicate about it, we're bound to drift apart. Or he's likely to find some other ear willing to listen to the trials and triumphs of his day.

Dick doesn't like to repeat his day's activities as soon as he gets home. It's too exhausting for him. We've found that the best time is after the children are in bed. In the meantime, I can tell him about my day, which provides a relaxing change for him. Later, when he tells me the highlights of his day, I'll be aware of what's happening to him, and what's about to happen. I'll be able to anticipate tension when I know there's a big deal in the making or a rough shakedown period going on at the office. Given this insight, I can minimize tensions at home during that period of time.

Many men work in such technical fields that it's almost impossible for them to share their work with their wives. But Dick says that even in scientific, legal, and technical areas, there are personalities involved. Those he can share with his wife without discussing the nitty-gritty of his job.

Every plant, office, and business has its internal power politics. And if the wife is made aware of the power plays, knows the game and the players involved, and what's at stake, she can avoid making that seemingly innocent remark that proves so damaging when she is entertaining her husband's clients or associates. When Dick and I are planning to spend time with his colleagues or customers, I usually ask him to fill me in beforehand. "Tell me where Mr. Gump fits into the picture, and is there any area that I shouldn't mention?" Awareness also gives me an insight into the toughness and competitiveness of his day.

Awareness works both ways. A man must be willing to share his day's activities with his wife, if he expects cooperation and understanding. Otherwise, she can't be expected to appreciate or participate in his world, and often it's impossible for her to keep up with her man as he progresses. Many times I can't help Dick solve a problem, but I can lend a sympathetic ear if he has a tension-filled day.

What about the people involved in his work? What if you honestly don't like some of the associates or the clients that you have to entertain occasionally? What do you do, if you can't stand Joe because he's loud and drinks too much and gets foul-mouthed at 11:00 P.M., or Mrs. Gump drives you right up the wall? Do you refuse to see Joe or the Gumps because you don't think anyone should be subjected to that kind of torture? You can't refuse if you're realistic. If Dick has to entertain the Gumps and I won't cooperate, I'm forcing him to make a choice between the job and me. I'm no longer a supporting partner but strictly a taker. If he's explained to me how important the Gumps are to his job, and I still refuse to participate, he has every right to begin to resent me.

We find as many ways as we can to rescue each other from long, painful evenings by devising new ways of entertaining. Before we join our company, Dick allows me to moan and groan. Once it's out of my system, I feel better and I can make it through the evening with a smile. We've both done our part with a minimum of pain and a maximum of understanding.

Do we women think that our men enjoy business entertaining any more than we do? We certainly make that assumption most of the time. Dick's question is, "What makes you think you're the only one who hates to go? Do you honestly think that this is the way I would choose to spend a Saturday night? I'd much rather take you to a movie or stay home and enjoy my family. While it may be unpleasant for you, it's one more night of work for me."

Occasionally, wives resent the secretaries and women associates who are important to their husband's work. To many wives, they're seen as a threat. An automatic hot button is pushed when Harry says that his secretary did a fantastic job today; she got the reports out on time, after he had given them to her late in the day. If he mentions that he bought her a box of candy to thank her, watch the fur fly at home.

When women associates at work become a taboo subject in many homes, the fault lies with both the husband and the wife. If a man is able to make his wife feel secure as a woman and as his partner, she won't feel threatened by his female colleagues. With that bond of recognition and understanding at home, a man can form natural, normal relationships with these women and feel no guilt.

The wife who takes only a token part in understanding how her husband's day functions, is bound to resent the efficient secretary or the bright, female personnel director. She has no way of knowing how necessary these women are to his overall productivity and effectiveness. Let him mention that he has to take his secretary to Cincinnati with him, and watch the green witch scurry through his house, a week before and after the trip. God help him if he says that he took her out to dinner and a floor show one night while they were gone!

If anything happens out of town, it's because of the wife's attitudes. Her husband and his secretary spend eight hours together daily, five days a week. If she suddenly becomes a threat in Cincinnati, then you'd better realize she's just as much a threat at her desk downtown. The problem lies with you, not her. The solution is in your understanding of his role and hers —and your own.

Sometimes Dick has to ask his secretary to work late evenings or on Saturdays to help him catch up. When she does, I'm grateful for two reasons. First, she often bails him out when he's swamped. He's able to do a better job because of her, and all three of us know it. Second, if she didn't work overtime occasionally, I'd be typing those reports at three in the morning, one finger at a time. And with my method of typing, Dick would lose his job in no time. While he stresses that I'm a damn good wife and a damn good mother, I'm a rotten secretary.

Many men resent their wives' inability to cope with changes in their jobs. None of us like change; it's frightening. But Dick points out that no man can predict the course his working life will take thirty years from now. For the last ten years, we've been happily adjusted to a certain routine. Tomorrow could mean a transfer to Amarillo. If husband and wife don't have a common understanding of what his job means to their lives, and what a transfer and promotion might entail, there will be friction and resistance. "Amarillo! How could I leave Mother? And all our friends? And how can we tear the children from their schools and friends? And what about *my* job?"

So what does the poor husband do? If he takes the transfer and promotion, he's faced with the threat of making his entire family psychotic. And he knows that he'll hear about it for years. Every problem that pops up will have been his fault.

The man is caught between his family and his job. His wife may not understand, but he knows that turning down that promotion in Amarillo stops him cold in his company from that day forth. He'll never be asked again.

Years ago my father had to transfer from our hometown when we were all in school. I'm sure my mother didn't want to leave relatives and friends, but she never showed it. She made it a great adventure for all of us. She and my father made some house-hunting trips, and she always came back with pictures, brochures, Chamber of Commerce information, anything she could find to make our new town seem an interesting, exciting place for us to live. She made Dad the adventurer, leading us into a new world. Once we got there, if the cheerleading team wasn't what it had been in our old high school, and we never did find a replacement for that bosom buddy that we'd had since kindergarten, it was our problem, not Dad's. That was life, and you learned to make the best of it. If we couldn't accept change, it wasn't Dad's fault.

Many men encounter such resistance, such resentment, and such lack of understanding of their role as the provider, that they begin to consider a choice between the family and the job. The pressure from work and the counter-pressure from home becomes too great. So they run away or become apathetic on either the home front or the job front. We've all seen the men who don't care anymore. Their motivation has been deadened and they spend their days shuffling papers at the office, waiting for retirement; or they've tuned out at home and become indifferent creatures who watch TV and take no part in family life. The body is there, but the spirit died long ago.

It doesn't have to be that way. The job, no matter what time and effort it demands from the family, can be coped with in a full partnership. As long as Dick shares with me his life away from us, I'll be able to understand all that that life means to him and to us. Then I can help him, myself, and our children by passing on that understanding to them.

If he can make me feel secure and respected in my role, there will be no cause for me to view his job, or any aspect of it, as a threat. The little things he does that say, "Thanks for holding up your end of the partnership," blot out the occasional rough spots. The rose that he stops to buy on the way home from the airport, erases the tension I felt yesterday when Junior broke his nose, and I was alone.

If we wives complain, resent, and refuse to assume our part of the responsibilities in our husbands' absence, they have a choice. "Would you like me to quit my job and become a shoe salesman? We'd have to move to a smaller house, and the children might not get a college education, but I would be home with you every night. Are you willing to make that sacrifice? For me, life would be great. I'd have no responsibilities after work, I could relax and watch TV, I could play cards with the boys, and I could do some fishing on weekends. Is that what is really most important to you?"

I can see all the women automatically wincing. That's not the choice that we had in mind. Most of us want to have it both ways, and sometimes we are unwilling to be honest or realistic. It's easier to resent, to complain, to create a villain, than it is to understand. And even if we do understand, it's easy to have temporary lapses of resentment when our side of the partnership gets heavy. As much as Dick and I have talked, as well as we try to understand each other, there are still occasional flares of annoyance. "He's late for dinner again," or "You have to be out again, tonight?" Usually this happens when I've had a bad day, too. I've temporarily forgotten that we made a joint commitment to work out this way of life as best we can. I've forgotten that he's not stopping for a drink somewhere, but working for us. I've forgotten because I'm human.

But we don't despair at that point and dump the commitment. We reconsider our pledge and see if it has to be changed somewhat again, or whether I am actually reacting to the day's events—the dog biting the mailman and one of the children spilling ink on the rug. We may have to modify our areas of responsibility, or it may simply be the case of one incident in the day throwing my understanding out of kilter for the moment. If the latter is true, life can go on as usual tomorrow.

If there are things that I can't handle, work that requires a man, then it should be done when he wants, his way. It doesn't have to be done my way—now. We've evolved a system for chores that works most of the time. I make a list of what has to be done, and set a time limit with a wide range. If it's the storm windows or the rain gutters, I suggest anytime in the next two weeks before the weather changes. And the job always gets done. We've found that a great deal of friction can be avoided if I state my needs and then look the other way without nagging.

Only through deep and continual communication, can we hope to make our marriage work. With it, we can understand and appreciate how great the need is for each of us to commit ourselves to our partnership without resentment. And only through that understanding, can we clearly see the value of each other's roles and thus offer the support, respect, and dignity that each deserves.

16.

Identity Crisis for the Woman Who Hates to Clean the Oven

HAVE YOU WOMEN EVER asked yourself the basic question, "Who am I? Where do I really belong today? Where's my place, and what is my role?" If so, you have experienced the mental tug-of-war common to many women across our nation. The answers to those questions seem to produce a blurred image of overlapping or conflicting roles, and because there is no easy solution, the frustration mounts. The Now Woman, the Modern Woman, the Woman of Today —we would all like to think of ourselves in those terms, but we don't really know who she is, and who we are ourselves.

There are times when I think of Gramma's role with envy and longing. If only my life could be as simple, uncomplicated, and tension free as hers was; if only I could see and accept my role as clearly as she saw hers. But her world will never be mine. It is only in remembering hers that mine seems so confused and chaotic. Gramma had very few choices in life open to her, I have too many.

Many new roles have only recently opened up to

us. We've now been emancipated in many ways, whether we want to be or not. By constitutional amendment we have been guaranteed equality in every respect. Because of the recognition of our capabilities during the past generation, we're recruited as free labor into everything from politics to remedial reading programs. "Get women volunteer workers—they have the time!" Today, men have accepted us in new roles even though they have rejected us in others. The women's lib movement came on with such force and vigor that it threatened many men and has totally confused many women. But because of it, life will never be the same again. Sexually, we've been freed from unwanted children by the pill and liberalized abortion. Now if we could only find a tiny pink pill to free us from our hang-ups.

For women like myself, who are happily married, the liberation movement takes on particularly poignant meaning. Yes, I agree that women should be paid equal pay for equal work. Yes, I agree that women should be given equal job and educational opportunities. My pride in myself and my fellow women compels me to agree. But is my husband a pig because he cares for me, provides for me, and lights cigarettes for me? Must I renounce him as a chauvinist if he worries about me traveling alone, or reminds me to lock the doors at night when he's out of town? Must I call myself Ms. to further prove my equality? My love for him and my respect and pride in men compel me to reject that extreme also. Somewhere in that hazy middle ground there must be a place for me—between fulfillment of myself as a person and complete rejection of my traditional role as home-maker and wife.

Why is it hazy? Because I still can't comfortably and completely discard the past. As with sex and the changing family role, I am caught with a foot in two worlds, the one I was raised in and the one I live in. Somehow, to survive my inner turmoil, I must manage to hold onto the best parts of the past while finding my place today. Not in a role that is foisted upon me by someone else, but one that I have created.

The women's liberation movement has shown the average woman that she is not alone in her struggle to find her identity. Across the country women are meeting over coffee, in their homes and in their offices, to exchange viewpoints. And these talks let the frustrated woman know that she is not a freak of nature because she hates scrubbing sinks; she is not the only woman who feels that her life is being shredded and thrown to the four winds by demands on time and energy that would leave the average Samurai wrestler reeling; she is not the only woman who feels guilty because she has a college education, but isn't using her knowledge to make a meaningful contribution to society; she is not alone in feeling that her day is filled with meaningless trivia that will be repeated tomorrow, and that neither fulfils her nor gives her a sense of identity; and she is not alone in being utterly and completely frustrated by her role at times.

This frustration didn't rear its ugly head in our marriage for several years. Before we had a chance to catch a breath, we had three tiny dynamos in the house. I had neither time nor energy to be frustrated. My role was clearly defined. Survival—at least until they were all toilet trained.

Eventually a period came when the children didn't take up every waking moment of my time and thoughts. I began to find myself with a few extra minutes each day and then a few extra hours. What should I do with my precious leisure time? The doubts began to poke up through the wall-to-wall carpeting and pop up with the toast. I am an intelligent woman. Shouldn't I begin to use those extra hours to make some sort of meaningful contribution? Am I being selfish if I choose to spend this rainy afternoon curled up with Shakespeare for my own enjoyment? Shouldn't I get involved?

On the other hand, if I get involved, what will happen to my husband and to my children? How much do they need me? How important is that homemade birthday cake with the witch's face and the licorice hair? How does spending the entire morning decorating the house for a Halloween party stack up against helping ghetto children in a reading program?

One look at my child's eyes as he walked into his birthday party told me immediately. My place is here. But the next morning's paper screamed something else. The ghetto child without a winter coat needed someone, too. Me? I began to feel guilty every time I stayed home because the world needed help, and guilty every time I walked out the door because my family obviously needed me.

The TV ads were hitting me with the image of Today's Woman. When I heard, "You've come a long way, baby," I'd say, "Yes!" "Should you offer a woman a Tiparillo?" Of course! And then there was that classic of discontent: the ad showing a woman in a bikini, standing in her immaculate kitchen, holding her surfboard upright. "For women who have better things to do than scrub their floors." Instant identification. That was me. There were hundreds of better things I had to do than scrub my floors.

Yet Dick needed me and the children needed me. He looked to me as a friend, as a confidante, as a woman, and as a lover. Could I risk diminishing those roles for the school board vacancy or the ghetto reading program?

The children were reaching ages at which they no longer required two hands to shovel in Pablum or to change diapers. They needed a mother who cared, who wanted to guide them through the year with the difficult second-grade teacher, and who could try to ease the heartache if they didn't make the intramural football team. These were precious relationships to me, and I feared losing or diminishing them by devoting too much time and energy elsewhere. Anyone could be hired to clean and cook, but who else would care enough to nurse the injured frog back to health? How thin could I spread myself? Could I be a good wife and mother, and smoke Tiparillos, too?

A new complication slowly entered my search for identity. My role in the home seemed to be expanding instead of diminishing with the last diaper and baby bottle. There was more to attend to, and more people relying on me in a new way. I was becoming a jack-of-all-trades through necessity. As Dick increasingly became a Phantom Father, I found myself picking up the added responsibilities and working them into the normal daily routine. Part-time carpenter? That's me. Full-time chauffeur? Right! Disciplinarian, haggler with tradesmen, yardmen, full-time advisor to broken hearts—all wrapped up in one neat little package labeled Mom.

Despite the numerous time- and labor-saving devices on the market, my leisure periods seemed to decrease. And now they were in fragments instead of blocks; a few minutes here, a half hour after dinner. The comparison between the necessary trivia of my day and the challenge of outside activities made it doubly hard to get a fair picture of my role at home. So many of the things that comprised my day seemed both endless and meaningless.

I was living a routine suburban life. Cooking, cleaning, washing dishes, and making beds—all these chores have to be done again in the same manner tomorrow and tomorrow and tomorrow. No progress is made—you simply hold the line for another day.

Take the shoes to the shoemaker, the clothes to the cleaners, and the children to band practice. Tomorrow go back and pick them all up again. (Whoops, I left the children at band practice overnight. No wonder it was so quiet at the dinner table.) Collect for Cancer, the Heart Fund, and the Cystic Fibrosis drive on the block. Next month, collect for the March of Dimes, Muscular Dystrophy, and our local political party. Squeeze in coffee for the school board candidate before it's time to take Johnny to the dentist. Stop at the supermarket and get the peanut butter that slipped your mind yesterday when the baby fell out of the basket. Dick's having a meeting at the house tonight. Get some cold beer. Don't forget the brown thread to sew up Randy's jacket pocket.

Busy, happy housewife? Yes, but deep down that nagging, yearning thought remains. "Who am I?"

There is no real me when I look into the mirror of my life. I'm Eric's mother, Dick's wife, leader of Kelly's Brownie Troop 438. Will the real me please stand up? And of the busy hectic day, not one thing stands out as significant. Necessary, yes. Part of my reponsibility, yes. But what single accomplishment in my day can I point to with pride?

Perhaps this is why many woman despise the term housewife. To them it is demeaning; it is an invalid role to play for a lifetime. It implies such a narrow image in today's world. The traditional homemaker role pales before our eyes when contrasted with the challenges and stimulation of the modern woman's image as depicted in advertisements. We're often ashamed to admit that we do "nothing." Why else is that automatic answer heard so often, "I'm just a housewife." We've been forced or have forced ourselves to become defensive about our role. And whether the role is valid or not, the nagging doubt remains.

Fifty years ago Gramma had the security of knowing that no one else could do a better job. Today's women don't have that security. Much of the creativity has been taken out of our role. Betty Crocker can bake a better cake than I and with far less mess and effort; iron-on patches can mend Eric's pants far better than I (thank God) and a ten-year-old can apply them as well. Convenience foods, can openers, frozen foods, and disposable everythings make my day easier. At the same time, they make me feel like a home mechanic who runs an efficient and tasty assembly line, direct from the pantry shelf to the table, with a quick pass over the stove.

Even in raising our children, the area where Gramma's common sense reigned supreme and unchallenged, we drift in self-doubt today. A mother's basic role is in question. Books and weekly magazines carry psychologists' opposing viewpoints on the proper discipline. Spank—don't spank. Breast feeding is in vogue this year, but by the time you have your next baby it will be passé. We listen to all of them while our heads bob up and down, and then we come home immersed in self-doubt.

There is another area of conflicting images, which makes us doubt ourselves. Be a wife, No, be a mistress to your man. For years I was haunted by a vision of a calm, serene woman advertising some brand of wine. At 6 P.M. she was dressed in her hostess skirt, lighting the candles on an elegant table set for two. I could almost hear the soft music playing in the background as she poured the wine, without a chip on her perfectly polished nails. The man who walked through her door a few minutes later could have no doubts as to her role.

And there I was in my kitchen at 6 P.M., the phone on my shoulder, stumbling over the puppy while I grabbed for the spaghetti which was bubbling over the side of the pot. If the puppy didn't wet, I just might have time to dab on lipstick before Dick walks in. That is, if I can get this infernal insurance salesman off the phone, and if the children don't have another donnybrook within the next five minutes.

That ad, that vision of wifehood, and others similar to it, kept reappearing in magazines and on commercials for years. Each time I saw them, I became increasingly frustrated. Why couldn't I be as gracious, as peaceful, and as serene when Dick walked into the house? Didn't he deserve as much? Six o'clock in the evening is the worst hour of the day for me as I try to tie together all the loose ends and hope that the hasty knot will hold until we've finished dinner. How could I possibly create that peaceful scene? I'd have to tear out the phone, barricade the doors, and put all the children in foster homes. I'd have to start dressing every day at one in the afternoon to make that radiant, calm vision come true by six. And yet, were there other women somewhere who could manage their lives that way? I told myself that they weren't real; that I had to forget that woman, because she was the product of some advertising man's vivid imagination. But unbidden, her image would dart into my mind as I pushed the tousled hair out of my eyes and leaned back from stirring the spaghetti pot long enough to kiss Dick as he came in. I was still wearing my mud-splattered jeans that I had put on for the "Save Our Swamp" walk, and the comparison smashed against my mind with full force.

As long as I could live my own life, I could survive. But introduce comparisons: the serene wife, the vital career girl, the volunteer working to clean up the slums, the mother who manages to get a master's degree on the side, and my world becomes shaky. My role loses dignity, and my respect and pride in my self diminish.

"Who am I? What am I worth? What value does my role have in this exciting world? Do I want to continue with the frustration and the endless trivia for a lifetime? Can I hope to keep up this frantic pace of going nowhere for much longer?" And then, the frustration often turns to resentment. "Nobody appreciates me around here. Nobody realizes what my day is like and how unrewarding it can be."

At this point, many of our friends have turned to outside jobs for stimulation and fulfillment, or for extra money to provide more luxuries. But we've noticed a new and sad development arising from the escape-to-the-job situation. Many of us who have been married at least ten years are not qualified for what we visualize as the challenging, exciting, career-girl jobs. We must rely on our former secretarial or teaching experiences. The stimulating jobs are being filled by younger, career-oriented women.

More commonly, we have seen our women friends escape the drudgery of the home for the drudgery of the store or office. They are assigned the insignificant detail work of someone else's day. And frequently, the financial rewards are not sufficient to pay for the child and home care that they want. These women have merely exchanged their role as mother for that of secretary.

The solution of today's identity crisis for married women will not be found by running away from or running to anything. We must realistically decide what we want and can be. We need to take a long, hard look at ourselves and ask the question, "What do I need—for me—for my situation—for my life?" For those answers, we need total honesty with ourselves, plus the support and understanding of the men who love us.

So far I've said very little about Dick in this chapter. The problem of identity was mine, just as the problems of Phantom Fatherhood were his. The solutions to both had to be made jointly. If I was going to work, I would need his full support. Otherwise, our family and our relationship would suffer tremendously. If I was going to fulfill my role within our home, only he could give that role dignity and make it seem worthwhile in my eyes. But first he needed to understand what I was feeling inside. I had to allow him into my mind and under my skin, so that he could see and feel the turmoil there.

Men are not as aware of a woman's needs for recognition as we would like them to be. At times their lack of perception causes us anger and frustration. Married men have a broader role than their mates, and they are able to express their individuality in their work. Unless we tell them differently, why wouldn't they assume that the same was true for us? We nag, we complain, but we don't really communicate our lack of fulfillment to them. In their eyes we become bitchy women instead of genuinely troubled people.

Many times we don't bother to communicate our shift in thinking. Instead we begin gradually to bury ourselves in outside activities until there is friction at home. Remarks such as the following reflect the situation, "Judy belongs to so many clubs that she stops by the house occasionally to dust." A friend mentioned to her husband that she was bored and was considering taking a course at the local university. He thought that was a fine idea until he woke up three years later to find her carrying a full course load day and evening as she worked toward a degree. What had started out, he thought, as a mild solution to temporary boredom, had evolved into a new lifestyle for the family. She had never communicated the full problem or given him the chance to understand. Having tasted fulfillment as a person, she plunged ahead toward a career for herself. He might have willingly agreed to this if they had worked it out together, but now he felt only growing resentment as his life was being drastically affected by his wife's new interests. He didn't understand why.

We can't assume that the other person understands our needs, and then get angry when he doesn't respond. We have to tell him what we are thinking, knowing that if we love each other, he will respond. Before I could expect more than token sympathy from Dick, I had to tell him about the serene woman in the hostess skirt who haunted me. I had to let him know that at times I felt utterly trapped by my role, by my children, and by him. And I had to trust him not to betray me. He never has.

There are men who will not or cannot free their women to grow. Because of their own insecurity, the idea of their wives developing away from, or beyond them, is frightening. It's a threat to their manhood. Dick and I have seen men who are masters at paying lip service to the idea of freedom for women while finding all the reasons why it won't work in their own homes. "We can't afford it," (your degree) or "I don't care to live this way," (picking up my side of the partnership if you need extra time). These men can usually find ways to weaken a woman's resolve or belittle her appeal for personal growth—at least temporarily. Fortunately, Dick is not like this.

Knowing that you are not alone—that there are thousands of other women who share your turmoil is important. It enables you to look at yourself each day without wondering if you're losing your mind. Knowing that you're not alone—that there is a man, your man, standing behind you is something quite different. It means that the partnership is healthy, with each side genuinely wanting to help the other. Knowing these facts, the solutions should be easier to find.

For Dick and me, the obstacles had to be removed first. The activities of my life had to be reduced to such a point that I could take an honest look at what I wanted. I wasn't sure I knew what the questions were, let alone the answers. And before questions could be clearly framed, the guilt and the tension had to be eradicated. I had to learn to say "No."

Together, we looked at the Swamp Lady and her kind, who filled a good part of my day, every day. Dick asked, "Do you want to work on this project?" "Does it really turn you on, or are you concerned with what 'they' will think or say?" Actually, I hated the Swamp Lady and the swamp, too. I had no interest in women's clubs, garden clubs, or any auxiliary groups; I had been sucked into 90 percent of their projects because I felt it was my duty. It was part of my role.

Dick convinced me to say "No." "Tell them you'd like to see a lovely high-rise apartment building in the midst of their swamp. They'll never call you again." So the Swamp Lady and her friends vanished. Together, Dick and I began peeling away the barnacles that weighed me down. I found I had leisure time each day. Life was not so hectic, and I could actually begin to sniff the wind for things that I wanted to do. Dick reiterated, "Without guilt. Your whole life is ahead of you. Don't try to make a decision today. Give yourself a chance, and it will emerge eventually. Then you can commit yourself, with my full support and without guilt to whatever you want to do."

So for a glorious year the wind was sniffed. I reread Shakespeare and Milton; I volunteered to work at a Headstart school in our ghetto; I took a night course in Prehistoric Man; and I still had time to bake birthday cakes with licorice-hair frosting. With the pressure off, I slowly found myself returning to the artwork that I had given up years ago as a lost dream. It became apparent that this was what I most wanted to do. A career? We didn't know, but we did know that I could happily work a half day and still be a good wife and mother.

The woman in the hostess skirt ceased to haunt me. And there were times that I could almost manage the hostess skirt routine. But there was also the discovery that Dick really loved the vision of the spaghetti-stirring woman in the paint-spattered jeans in his kitchen.

My role in our home had deep meaning for him, and by letting me know that, it became more fulfilling for me. When he asked about my day and the children's day at the dinner table, it was because he was really interested; he wanted to follow our lives because he thought they were important. He wasn't bored. He was intrigued by the daily drama of home, schools, personalities, and my work.

By helping me to feel like a vital and worthwhile individual, Dick made my role in the home seem more important. His attitude has manifested itself in many ways, especially with the children. Years ago he organized the Sunday night cleanup that has become a family institution. When he learned that I spent most of Monday trying to clear away the weekend rubble, he said, "That's ridiculous. I'll bet if everybody picked up his own stuff it wouldn't take twenty minutes." So he organized the troops after dinner one Sunday night, and they marched through the house, picking up the lone sock in the bedroom and the crayons from under the couch. They put back records in their proper jackets and undraped their clothes from chair backs. Then Daddy marched through to check. He was right; it didn't take more than twenty minutes. Since then Mondays are one of the best day of my week. Of greater importance was the message that came through loud and clear to the children, "Your mother is not a slave in this house who waits on you and picks up after you. Show her that you appreciate her role, and that you don't take it for granted."

You should see what happens when I'm sick! You'd think Cleopatra herself was on her death bed instead of Mom down with the flu. It takes me a long time to get well because I get so much attention that I never get any rest. Somebody runs to the store for chopped liver because I love chopped liver. Somebody else makes a milkshake at 9:30 in the morning because I love milkshakes. I gain five pounds and end up with indigestion every time I have a cold, but I wouldn't trade it for the world.

We discovered that Dick's emotional support also helped me crystalize my self-image. To allow me to pursue my own interests required trust and self-confidence on Dick's part; he knew that he wasn't being cast aside or abandoned for something else. And he exhibited this trust in many ways.

He has no interest in art, but he supports mine fully. He's the one who comes home with a new art book or discovers an interesting course at the university for me. And he's found many ways to free more of my time. "Why not hire the teen-ager next door during Easter vacation to run your errands and help around the house? Then you can get that project done, and she can earn some extra money."

What started out years ago as the resumption of a hobby has grown into a business, but one that does not interfere with our lifestyle or with my roles as wife and mother. I could never have done it without his understanding and support, and at times I really wonder who's more proud of the success—Dick or me. He has been my biggest critic and my most ardent supporter.

But his support takes other forms, too. Although our principal leisure interests differ, he manages to convey dignity to both. "I know you're dying to tackle that new idea for metal sculpture. Why don't you sit down after dinner with your plans? Don't worry about the children's homework. I'll see that it's done." Or I might suddenly find myself led to a steaming bubble bath, and find a book next to the tub.

Money has never been a problem between us. However, neither Dick nor I liked the idea of one person running the financial affairs and doling out an allowance to the other. It seemed demeaning to whomever was the recipient. Since banks, checkbooks, and I aren't the best of friends, there was never any hassle about who was going to pay the bills. But I was still getting an allowance until Dick had a better idea. He figured out how much was necessary for the house—mortgage payments, gas, telephone, electricity—and how much I needed for shoes, clothes, groceries, and personal items. We would split the difference if there was leftover money. He opened a separate checking account for me, and I operated independently. If I could save money on groceries, I could spend it any way I wished, knowing that the other areas were already covered. I learned to budget and work with my "salary," as he did with his. And he strong-armed me into opening my own savings account and depositing a fixed amount in it each month. No fair shirking or stealing to round out the grocery tab. That money was mine to invest in the stock market, or to splurge on a trip, or to buy an expensive piece of art-work. It was a great feeling knowing that I didn't have to answer to anyone if I wanted to visit my grandmother for a few days. The plane fare and the sitter could come out of my nest egg without depriving anyone else.

No longer do I envy anyone else's role, or wish that I could escape the confines of my own. There are no strings that bind me except love. I can be content knowing that I have a valuable place in the world —in my own eyes and in those of my family. Although it took some time, together we brought me to the realization of what was necessary for my fulfillment.

There is a place in this world for the crusader, for the career woman, for the volunteer, and for the woman who chooses her place exclusively in the home. All are valid roles and all can be equally fulfilling as long as they are the roles we freely choose.

Some time ago, a leading clergyman was addressing himself to the problem of the turmoil in the Catholic church since Vatican II. Liberals and conservatives seemed to be at each other's throats, fighting for the dominant view. For many, the changes in the Church were coming too fast; for others, far too slow. This bishop stated that there was room for everybody within the body of the Church—room for the guitar masses, for the Latin mass, for the old, and for the new. "Remember, though," he pleaded, "as far as you may go, don't take away the rosary from the little old lady in the back pew."

That same wisdom can be applied to our personal search for identity as women. There is a place for all of us.

17.

Me and You Against the World

IF YOU MISS THE Indian Guide Father and Son Campout, your child will undoubtedly grow up to be psychotic! Everybody knows that. The odds are 13.6 to 1. This highly publicized fact was established by the Concerned Citizens League for the Preservation of the American Way of Life—Surburban Branch #206 (better knows as DO IT OUR WAY). The League, in its wisdom, has compiled long lists of acceptable standards of behavior. These cover any aspect of your life in which you may have had hesitancy or doubt. Would you like to tear up all that rotten crabgrass and do over your lawn in shiny green asphalt, so that you can watch the golf tournaments every Saturday afternoon? Go ahead, but remember that the chances are 84.7 to 1 that you won't be invited to the neighborhood Eggnog party next Christmas.

Every area of our daily lives can be nicely patterned along League standards: from how to plan our children's birthday parties to what we will serve at dinner parties, from the amount of outspoken thoughts at the office to whether or not we will buy a power lawnmower. I do not know if the very rich and the very poor have their own League to help them, but we of the middle class can count ourselves truly blessed to have such an active, concerned force in our lives.

In their attempt to keep us on the straight and narrow path, nowhere is the League more active and more persuasive than in suburbia. When in doubt over anything, all we have to ask ourselves is, "What would THEY do and what would EVERYBODY say?" In a flash, the acceptable mode of behavior is clear.

For the rare rebel who refuses to be guided and helped by League advice, there are subtle pressures that can be applied to insure future conformity. There was that eccentric artist friend of mine who, despite Neighborhood Branch warnings, painted on her front lawn, without wearing a bra. She claimed that the undergarment made her hot. The League refused to invite her to any neighborhood coffees or teas, or to allow her to donate her hard-boiled eggs to the USO. Unfortunately, she was so engrossed in her misguided ways that she failed to notice, and she continued to paint, while other noble mothers marched past collecting for Muscular Dystrophy. Eventually she moved with her family to a foreign country and our block had the satisfaction of saying, "Everybody always knew she'd go off the deep end someday." I understand she's doing very well, but I haven't felt it proper to mention that around Suburban #206.

Dick and I feel the pressure to conform in every aspect of our lives. There is practically no new frontier where THEY have not been the first to set up standards for us to follow. At times we can laugh, at times the pressure becomes more of an actual pinch, and occasionally we hear someone burst out in rage, "Who the hell are they to tell me how to live my life?" Most often the conformity is in response to subtle pressure to do things that we might not choose to do. Or not to do things that we'd really enjoy, because nobody else is doing them.

It's very difficult to be an individual today—to live your life, to speak your mind, even to dress your body as you think best. The price of a small bit of freedom and of uniqueness is the raised eyebrow, the tight-lipped smile, the whispered comment behind your back. The price for a large chunk of individuality is proportionately higher! Exclusion, ostracism, outright hostility. The majority of us want to be accepted and liked. That's why many of us wear masks that read GOOD FATHER, or GOOD CITIZEN, or GOOD NEIGHBOR, and allow ourselves to be coerced into doing things that we might not choose to do if left alone.

We've lived closely with the subtle pressures to conform. Dick has gone to Father-Son Scout dinners, when he would have preferred to spend the evening doing something else, or he would have chosen a different way to express his closeness to our son. In our small suburban community, the Father-Son outings are an established way to bring the two generations together. It seems to be assumed that without these programmed gatherings, fathers would ignore their children entirely, or that they, individually, can't find ways to relate or play with their offspring. To be viewed as a GOOD FATHER by your friends and neighbors, you must participate in the planned activities of the community. Little League? If you miss two consecutive games because of business, you're the town rat. If you miss a third because you wanted to hear the President's speech on TV, your communal name is Mud or Selfish or Unconcerned. The guidelines are set down with little room for maneuvering; you either conform or accept the reputation that they will give you.

In a similar fashion, it is taken for granted that mothers are dying to support the local school regardless of its demands. Brownies for the Parent-Teachers' Tea, cupcakes for the Room Mothers' Coffee Hour, selling PTA memberships, and distributing the school calendar door to door.

I've often wondered what would happen if someone blurted out, "I don't want to join the PTA! I don't want to bake any more brownies for the privilege of donating them to the bake sale. All these activities just to buy a new piece of playground equipment! Have you looked at the playground lately? It is completely covered with towers and mazes. You need a map to make it to the school door. When I came to the school-board meeting last week, I was lost for an hour. If a first grader hadn't come along, I'd still be stuck out there!" But you can't say such things. You'll continue to bake brownies. Why? Not because your children want you to do it. They don't care whether or not there's a PTA that brings in speakers to expound on such topics as, "Understanding Your Fourth Grader." We reluctantly drag ourselves to meeting after meeting, contribute, bake, and collect for the other mothers and fathers. It seems to be more important to us to be good parents in the eyes of our fellow parents rather than in our own eyes, or in those of our youngsters. In accepting this belief, we conform to the standards of THEY and EVERYBODY.

We think these same standards apply to being a GOOD CITIZEN or GOOD NEIGHBOR. Do you really want to join the Hospital Auxiliary or the Women's Club or The Garden Club that's going to save our environment? Supposedly, if you refuse such an invitation you're in favor of pollution, and you are joyously awaiting the destruction of all the juniper trees on the face of the earth. But what if you'd rather spend your time working to save the environment in your own way? Perhaps by buying a piece of wilderness land for the purpose of conservation, or by switching to lead-free gasoline, while you devote your extra energy to a political candidate who believes in pollution control. Or writing letters to the editor or teaching your own children how they can do things to save the environment—picking up litter; buying only white tissues, toilet paper, and paper towels; reminding their friends to respect the small buds and tiny trees that will become the flowers and foliage of tomorrow. The time we spend educating our children and ourselves about the environment may be more effective, but attending the community forum or the garden-club-sponsored program is more acceptable.

Maybe you think we're exaggerating, but have you ever paused to consider how much of our lives are controlled by the opinions of others? How many things do we do in a day or a week that we honestly don't want to do, but wouldn't dare refuse? They might upset other people; they are not worth the upheaval that they may cause in our jobs, our neighborhoods, our social lives.

Have you ever joined a club, an organization, or a group because your friends urged you to, or your business associates or boss pressured you? I have. "Oh, Paula, you'll love the Garden Club. The girls are so nice, and we do such wonderful things. We need people like you." If I had told Millie that such clubs bore me to tears, and that I'd rather read Shakespeare, I'd be in trouble. I'm rejecting Millie's world. Not because it's a bad world, but because it's not my world. Millie will never understand that, however. She'll give me the tight-lipped smile the next time we meet, but what will she say to the other Garden Club members about me? Snob? Too good for us? Lazy? Uninvolved? I was being honest when I declined. But whatever Millie chooses to read into my refusal labels me, doesn't it?

It is not any easier for men to say "No." In addition to the community pressures, there are the office pressures to join. "Harry, it would be good to be seen on the Kidney Foundation Board. Get your name circulated. You'll make some great contacts, and you know those never hurt our business. And Harry, the Trade Association would be a great place for you to be active. We meet one night a month with all the other local members of the Corn Plaster Industry. Get to know them, find out what they're doing. Will I see you at the next meeting?" Of course, he'll there because he knows enough to bend to that kind of pressure. Maybe he'd prefer to work at the School for the Blind in his spare time instead of attending Kidney Board meetings. Perhaps he thinks trade associations are a waste of time, with everybody in the same industry patting each other on the back. He could do more for his own job by taking a course at night, but he knows it will be the Kidney Fund and the Corn Plaster Association. Conform, Harry, or you're dead in this company.

Let's take a look at the gentle little tugs to conform at home, or our block, and in our neighborhood. Did you ever wonder what to wear to a party? Did you ever worry that if you wore your new slit-to-the-navel dress, you'd spend the evening facing a row of tight-lipped smiles, all female? "Darling, that's such an unusual dress. We don't see many of those around here. Do you wear it often, dear?" When you hear that tone of voice, you know you have made a mistake, and the telephone wires will burn tomorrow morning. What about the man who would like to wear a sport shirt and slacks to the neighborhood dinner party, but he is afraid that the other men will be wearing suits. The hostess didn't say that it was a casual gathering, but it's only down the block, and it is 97° F. tonight. Should he put on his casual clothes? Be safe. Better wear the suit, and sweat. Who wants to look like a fool?

Dick has a fur hat and coat that he loves because they keep him so warm. However, the Man-of-the-World topcoat and the neat businessman's hat with its little pheasant feather are the acceptable mode of dress for executives of a certain standing and position in our city. Whenever he wore his fur coat and Cossack hat to work the comments flew. "Oh Dick, it's really you. I thought it was the delivery man," or "Dick, I've been meaning to talk to you. You have an important client meeting at lunch tomorrow. You weren't planning to wear that furry thing, were you? I'd hate to leave the impression with Mr. Bigbottom that we're a bunch of country boys around here." Conform or it might reflect on all of us.

Did you ever say to your mate, "We should have the Clancys, the Johnsons, and the Levines for dinner soon. We owe them invitations"? Maybe you can't stand the Clancys, perhaps the Levines bore you, but you do owe them a dinner. It's an unwritten law that you'll pay off your obligations. The cocktail party was invented so that we could invite all those people at one time and let them bore each other.

Dick told me that many men remember who picked up the tab for lunch last time, whose turn it is today, who asked whom last time, and who should be doing the inviting next time. They are critical of the man who doesn't pay off lunch debts. "Clyde never picks up the check, does he?" Poor Clyde may be supporting his one-hundred-year-old mother or paying his child's medical bills, and thus can't buy lunch. But neither reason is made known publicly.

Among our friends and neighbors, the pressure to conform is sometimes intense. At home, in your leisure time, you should be able to be yourself and live your own life. But it doesn't always work that way. Dinner parties? We pretty well know in advance what will be served and how. In the good old days when we and most of our friends were struggling, we got together often over a pot of spaghetti and a six-pack of beer. Today spaghetti and beer are family fare. We can imagine the lifted eyebrows if Dick and I invited ten people to dinner and served chili. That's fine for the after-the-football-game midnight supper, but the dinner party has it own built-in rules and regulations. Unfortunately, my past tastes have not kept pace with success. I still love beer.

Social drinking presented another problem for us. Dick had always been an average social drinker, but some years ago he decided to quit because he no longer enjoyed it. Our friends refused to accept him as a non-drinker. For months, people would try to talk him into just one drink. They felt uncomfortable knowing that there would always be one cold sober body in the room. What if everybody got bombed and made fools of themselves? What would Dick think of them? For several years he was pressured to resume drinking.

Occasionally, Dick still feels that pressure at business meetings, luncheons, and dinners. "Oh, you don't drink?" Immediate discomfort, then someone remarks, "I'd better watch what I say," or "He must be an alcoholic." Business associates often apply the same

209

kind of pressure to the practice of playing around on the road. If everybody plays, that's fine. No one is acting as a moral conscience for the group. But if someone doesn't want to play, it makes the other men squirm somewhat. "He's not one of us. We don't need any homebodies around here, holding up a mirror for our morals." Conform, Dick. You're making them uncomfortable.

Can we let our children wear jeans to school if everyone else's children wear dresses or slacks? No. We'll be labeled bad parents. Can we allow them to let their hair grow to whatever length they want, without pressure to conform to neighborhood standards? No. We'll quickly hear Grandpa say, "I can't tell whether Junior is a boy or girl anymore. Don't you think he's ready for a haircut?" It doesn't matter if that hairstyle is the most important thing in Junior's life right now, and that he'd rather die than cut it. He embarrasses us by being different. We have felt pressure from our peer group, and so we pass it on to Junior.

One of the most beautifully stated examples of this pressure to conform came from the teen-age son of one of our friends. "You're making me cut my hair and look bad with my friends, so that you can look good with yours!" Right, Junior! If we have to conform so do you. Otherwise we feel that uncomfortable pinch.

Sex education that differs from the League's norm has become another taboo subject, especially in the neighborhoods and in the schools. Every parent plans to have that little talk with their children when they're about twelve years old. But if you start an open, continuing dialogue with Junior at five, he's going to be saying and thinking things that his peers aren't ready for yet; or at least that their parents aren't ready for! What if Betsy asks him where babies come from, and he tells her? "We weren't going to tell her that for ten more years. Our youngsters aren't safe with yours anymore." The child who didn't have the one-shot birds-and-bees talk, or wasn't handed that detailed book to read, but who has a healthy, open attitude toward sex, is regarded as a threat to the other children around him. We're back to that same old hang-up. If we tell our children too much, if we teach them what we wish we had known, how can we stop them from doing it? Does Junior's sex education have the restrictions ours did?

In our neighborhood, most children feel parental pressure to take college preparatory subjects in high school, regardless of their ability or interests. The unfortunate teenager who would pefer to be an auto mechanic doesn't have a chance. He can't say that he wants to go to vocational school to learn about cars. He has to fail his college courses in order to be accepted as a future mechanic.

Every minute of the child's free time is devoted to lessons and to hobbies aimed at broadening him: tennis, ballet, drama, art, children's concerts, Little League, gymnastics, music, swim club. It doesn't matter if the child despises the piano and would love to play lead guitar in a rock group some day.

How many millions of us were forced to take piano lessons as children because our parents had made an investment in the piano? We practiced each day, but we really wanted to play baseball instead of Bach. Today we can barely remember how to pick out *Chopsticks*.

When I was a youngster, there were always a few minutes each day that I could lay on my back, look at the sky, and chew a blade of grass. Our neighborhood children will make perfect soldiers someday. They march into their houses carrying their little violin cases and march back out a few minutes later, holding their tennis rackets. An hour later they march past again, dressed for Little League, carrying their bats. And so go their afternoons and Saturdays. When do they play?

A former neighbor once suggested that we all adjust the blades or our lawn mowers to the same height and cut the grass on the same day, so that the lawns on our block would look even. Dick made the mistake of laughing because he honestly thought Sam was kidding. Not only was he reprimanded with the suitable tight-lipped smile, but the next day brought an even more subtle message. As Sam trimmed the grass on his side of our joint fence, he managed to snip off all our morning glory vines at the root. "Sorry about that, didn't see them there." They were four feet high, and bright blue, and he'd been trimming around them all summer!

In suburbia, your property isn't really yours. It's a community status symbol. If you don't believe me try leaving up your Christmas wreath all year long, as we did last year. Every day after January 15th, one of the neighbors found a way to point out that we had forgotten to take it down. "No," I explained, "I like it. I'm going to leave it up because every time I drive in the driveway it reminds me of Christmas, and it makes me feel good." In the spring I took off the pinecones and decorated the wreath with daffodils. I guess they understood that I was serious then, because a week later it was stolen.

Any man who's ever heard the cry from his wife that Gertie is getting a new dishwasher, or is taking a winter vacation, or is joining the new tennis and swim club, feels the powerful pressure exerted by money and status. Keeping up with the Joneses is more than a cliché, it becomes a lifestyle for many of us. Soon after the first power mower or snow blower appears on the block, that ear-splitting whir can be heard from every lawn. How many men have you heard complaining that tonight is the night they get dragged to the symphony or to the ballet. Or that their wives volunteered their services to the Art Festival?

We play the game, we conform, we bend. We wear our proper masks and dress in our proper clothes, and let someone else dictate in what style we will live our lives. We quickly find out that it's all right to talk about politics in this group, but don't mention abortion. We learn every trick to make ourselves acceptable to every group and what do we become? Invisible people who blend nicely into any milieu. Good solid citizens whom everyone thinks well of but whom no one thinks about much. Hard workers, good mothers, and good fathers who earn those cherished labels because they learned to conform.

What if you think you know a better way for you? What if you can envision a better lifestyle for your family? You're not interested in preaching on street corners or putting up billboards; you just want to be able to live your own life, to decide what you feel is important and what is immaterial. Is is possible to break out of your molds and live your lives without the pressures to conform?

We found that it is. But unless you are an exceptionally strong person you'll encounter pain, frustration, and self-doubt. We've been raised to conform; it's not a habit that is quickly changed. Growing into freedom is a slow process. It may be too difficult for one person to stand alone. It's infinitely easier for a united couple to say we no longer need your patterns; we haven't time for your games.

Two people standing against the world can draw strength from each other. Society does not find them as easy a target as one lone outline against the sky. Where does one leave off and the other begin? What if I hit one and the other hits back? People who apply pressure to conform back away from the united image. "Certainly you and your husband will come to the block meeting next Wednesday night to discuss having the expressway diverted." "No, both of us know how we stand on the issue and we would rather spend the evening alone with each other because our schedules are hectic and those hours that we spend together are important to us." "Yes, but don't you recognize that it's your duty to bt involved?" "I don't think you understand me. Our duty is to ourselves Wednesday night."

We found that we could strengthen and defend each other, and that joint laughter was the best antidote to the taciturn smile. "Did you see the look on Bob's face when I told him we were letting the lawn go back to its natural state?" or "You should have heard the silence when I said that I wasn't interested in diverting the expressway." If the expressway got my husband home ten minutes earlier, hurray for the expressway!

Before you can laugh and lick the system, two people have to be in accord in wanting a lifestyle of their own. Dick and I became aware of this many years ago as we tried to free ourselves individually from some of the restraints imposed by the community. When it became apparent that each of us was still being coerced into conformity, we knew that we needed one another's help. But first we had to understand the other's needs and desires, and make some joint plans for our family.

It was important for Dick to realize that I wanted to paint more than I wanted to bake brownies. And I had to understand his desire to show his closeness to our children in his own way, rather than by attending Cub Scouts or Little League. Only then could we support each other and have the extra strength to say "No." We could help each other not to feel guilty just because everybody was doing something in the prescribed way.

We had to allow our children the freedom to be individuals as much as we yearned for that freedom ourselves. If Eric wanted no part of the bassoon, the oboe, or the cello, why force him to take lessons? If Randy wanted to drop out of Girl Scouts after the first month, that was her privilege. It seemed more worthwhile to let her spend that afternoon at the library reading if that's what she preferred than to force her to continue so as not to offend the troop leader. If she took Randy's withdrawal as a personal affront that was her problem not ours.

The youngsters were eager to get out of many of the organized activities so that they could be free to build things, to concoct nauseating experiments, to listen to music (rock). These were not the activities which would get them into the best colleges, but these were the things they enjoyed and which made them interesting, exciting individuals.

As we watched them grow in their unique ways, we became convinced that this was the right path for them, and our determination to be a free family was reinforced. Once we had communicated our desires and needs to each other, we had the strength to face the outside pressures to conform. The children could understand why Dick might not attend the school open house if it meant that he had to come directly from the airport at a frantic pace to arrive on time. On the other hand, he'd move heaven and hell to make the school play because he wanted to see Kelly act.

If the teachers put pressure on the children to have their parents attend the open house, our youngsters could explain how we felt about Daddy's time. If the pressure got too heavy for them, I would speak to the teacher. There have only been a few incidents that the children were unable to handle well themselves.

We were developing a new lifestyle designed for us alone. Occasionally I'd find myself agreeing to something I didn't want to do. When I told Dick how disgusted I was with myself for buckling under, he'd get me back on my feet. "Call back tomorrow and say you've reconsidered chairing the clothing drive because you have a big art project planned, and it's more important at the moment. Make me the heavy if you need to, Tell her your husband won't support your involvement in the drive because he feels it's too much for you to undertake." Knowing that Dick supported my decision, I made the call, using my own reasons.

Dick and I started our own small counter-league with two little gnomes called US and WHY NOT. They burst out with their masks off during family discussions and around the dinner table every night. The voices were loud and they sometimes disagreed vehemently. We didn't care because we believe that each member of the family is entitled to express his thoughts and feelings. Dick and I often found that the children had a great deal to offer, expecially when it came to family plans and decisions.

Compulsory togetherness is another suburban pattern, but we don't have much togetherness by other people's standards. "Dick is practically never home. He's always running around to some community gathering, and there's poor Paula painting the bedroom walls by herself. He's really a rotten husband!" Maybe Dick's meetings could include me but they bore me. Perhaps I love painting walls. Does Dick have to stay home and help me when he would rather be at the conference that night? Do we both have to go to the meeting together on Monday and stay home together on Tuesday to paint?

Dick's not a rotten husband by my standards, and I'm not a rotten wife by his. The lights in our house burn much later than in any other on our block as we try to catch up on each other's day with genuine interest. I love my world and my projects, and Dick shares my enthusiasm for them. He loves his world and his interests, and I'm eager to share them. We don't feel that we have to do every activity together in order to be happy.

We don't have to share the same friends or like each other's friends. We're going to attract friends who share our individual interests. And if some of my friends are men and some of his are women there is no reason for jealousy or friction to ensue. Only those people who can't understand the freedom of our relationship would consider such friendships threats. If Dick wants to take a woman to lunch because he enjoys her company and he finds her a stimulating person, he should. If I'm secure in my relationship with him, why should that make me jealous or uneasy? If I have a male artist friend, why can't I go to a gallery showing with him some evening or consult with him in my home some afternoon? Dick understands; he feels it is right and it is natural. But the neighbors' and friends' tongues wag and start the rumors when they see one of us alone with another man or woman. Because our behavior doesn't conform to their standards, it must be wrong. The inference is always that we have something going on the side.

Eight years ago after much family discussion, we decided to buy a summer home far from the city. The traveling time involved made it impossible for Dick to commute each night; he would only be able to spend the weekends with us. Althought it meant many nights apart, it was the right choice for us. We found the ideal place and we were all excited about it. As summer approached we began to hear comments such as, "You're not going to stay up there alone for the whole summer. The children will miss Little League and tennis lessons. You'll be back in a month with cabin fever after spending all that time with young children. And how can you leave Dick alone in the city all that time. Aren't you worried, dear." Or to Dick, "Why would you allow your family to go? Who will cook for you? It certainly seems unfair to make you drive up every weekend!"

We went ahead despite the ominous warnings that this was not the way people lived, and immediately the rumor that we were getting a divorce began circulating. We loved that summer and the others that followed. It turned out to be the best thing that Dick and I have ever done as individuals and as a family. What happened to the rumor about our divorce, I wonder?

There have been many times throughout the years when we as a couple or we as a family have been misunderstood by friends, associates, or neighbors. We try as hard as we can to be honest and to explain why we don't do things that others might consider important, and why the things we do are important to us. Sometimes the honesty is construed as a criticism of another's lifestyle, but this is not so. We're not crusaders; we don't intend to pose a threat to anyone— as individuals or as a family. We want to be allowed to grow and flower in our own way. We want only the privilege to have crabgrass on our lawn, to dress, to act and to join as we desire, and to raise our children by standards we have set. If our lifestyle becomes a problem to someone else or is viewed as a threat, that is unfortunate. We didn't intend it to be that way; we have infringed on no one else's lifestyle. If there is such a problem, we feel it rests with the other party. As for us, we're happy—we have each other.

18.

Families, In-Laws, and Traditions—
Your Gravy and My Christmas Tree

TWO INTO ONE DOES go, but sometimes the coming together scrapes. Unless you and your mate happen to have met in kindergarten, courted throughout grade school, and lived next door to each other all your lives, there are bound to be some differences as two backgrounds and two sets of traditions try to blend into one marriage. We bring with us such habits as borrowing our husband's razor to shave our legs, or our husbands shove dirty socks under the bed and they expect the sock phantom to make them magically reappear in the drawer—clean. "That's the way it always worked at home. How come it makes you so mad? My mother never minded."

Communication helps us work out our peculiarities and quirks. When I shriek at the top of my voice, "You left a ring around the bathtub again!" I'm communicating. Dick is finally aware that I am not his mother or the phantom. I'm his wife, and I get angry if I step into a tub and find someone else's ring decorating it. When he passes up the gravy for two years in a row, I finally understand his message to me. Perhaps I should visit his mother and find out how she manages to make gravy without brown boulders in it.

We can iron out our habits, our flaws, and our shortcomings because we love each other and we don't want to do things which will become daily sources of irritation. Dick tries to remember to pick up his socks, not because I nag him, but because he loves me. I swallow my pride and finally ask his mother how she manages to make pork chops that don't taste like boiled horse hoof, because I love him, too. The trivial differences eventually resolve themselves because we care and we communicate.

But what about the family traditions that we bring to marriage which mean a great deal to us individually? The this-is-the-way-we-always-did-it customs that are a cherished part of our backgrounds and which we might feel uncomfortable changing. How do we compromise, and to which side of the family do we conform? How do we make a new life for ourselves without trampling each other's traditions into the dust?

For us, these problems didn't arise immediately. During the first year of our marriage we lived a thousand miles away from both sets of parents. We worked out the socks, the hair left in the sink, and the toothpaste caps on our own, with no mammas on either side to whom we could complain or to whom we could run home. But shortly before our first Christmas, we moved back to Dick's hometown, and then the friction started. "Christmas dinner? Why, we'll have it at my parents' house. We always do, and the whole family will be there." "But, Dick, this is our first Christmas dinner. Couldn't we have it alone and get together with the family later?" One of us had to compromise. So we decided not to hurt anyone's feelings and eat with the family.

Another problem presented itself. Traditionally, each woman brought some part of the meal to make it easier for Dick's Mom. Would I bring the suet pudding? What the hell was that? "Don't you people eat pumpkin pie on Christmas? What is Christmas morning without the smell of pumpkin pie baking in the oven while you open your presents? What do you mean you open your presents after midnight mass? What do you do Christmas morning—get up and eat suet pudding? I've married into a family of barbarians. You probably don't believe in Santa Claus either! It won't seem like Christmas without that divine odor mixing with the pine smell of the tree? Flocked tree? How can you string popcorn and cranberries on a flocked tree with pink balls? I'll bet you never heard of tinsel! Would you divorce me if I went home for Christmas?"

I didn't go home and we didn't get a divorce. We compromised again. A green tree with tinsel at our house, and dinner at theirs, where I dutifully admired the flocked tree. I brought the salad and ate the suet pudding that someone else brought. It wasn't bad, but it wasn't pumpkin pie. And during dinner I kept picking apart my stuffing, looking for the roast chestnuts that weren't there. We went to midnight mass and then to bed. We opened our presents in the morning. Christmas passed with a minimum of trampled traditions, and the problem seemed to be over for another year.

But then New Year's Day rolled around! Coming up for a breather during the Rose Bowl game, Dick asked what I was planned for dinner. "Why, pork of course. What else would you eat on New Year's Day?" "But I don't like pork, and what do you mean, 'What else would you eat on New Year's Day?'" I patiently explained how *everybody* always ate pork because the pig was the only animal that rooted forward. All the others scratched backward, so you ate pork to bring you luck and prosperity throughout the coming year. Dick began gaffawing and drowned out the Rose Bowl band. What kind of a heathen had I married?

As the years passed, I still missed the pumpkin pie and the chestnuts, and Dick never completely adjusted to Easter eggs dyed in onion skins to make them bronze and gold. We began to resent the fact that the traditional holidays had to be celebrated according to someone else's way. Granted, we lived in Dick's hometown, and it was probably logical to do things their way, but I often felt squelched, and Dick knew it. There were parts of my traditions that he thought were great, and parts of his that I wished we had done as children. We wanted to incorporate the best of both our backgrounds for ourselves and for our children. But how to do this without hurting the feelings of all our aunts and uncles, grandmas and grandpas, sisters and brothers?

The pressure to conform is harder to avoid with family than with friends or neighbors. You love these people, you don't want to hurt them, and you know that they are not trying to meddle, but rather include you in their lives with that same love. Dick and I might be able to agree on ntw traditions for us, but how would his mother feel when we told her we'd like to have Christmas dinner alone with our children next year? Would she be hurt if we preferred to get together with the family earlier in the day or on Christmas Eve? Even if she understood that we felt Christmas morning should be spent with our four young children, would the rest of the family be as sympathetic? Would they believe that we weren't rejecting them? We wanted to share some of our time with them, but our children were at an age when teaching the rules of the Monopoly game on Christmas morning was more important than getting the turkey in the oven on time.

Would my parents understand if we used our summer vacation to take the children camping this summer instead of spending those two weeks with them? We honestly felt it would be good for the youngsters and for us, but could they accept that explanation without reading more into it? Would my grandmother still love me if she found out that occasionally I fed my children frozen pizza?

How would Dick's father feel if he didn't bank where he had always banked? If we chose to reject the law firm and stockbroker he had used all his life? Would he think that we had no regard for his experience and judgment, or that we had little respect for the men he had dealt with for almost half a century? Or would he understand that we wanted younger men who might better relate to us and to our lifestyle to handle such matters? How would our older sisters and brothers feel if we didn't go to the pediatrician and the obstetrician they recommanded? When Aunt Minnie came to visit, would we hide the frogs, pet snakes, and lizards the children took to bed with them because she'd be horrified? Or would we say, "We're proud of our youngsters, and this is the way we choose to live." Did we have the guts to stand up to Aunt Minnie and hope she'd understand?

221

But what if she didn't understand or approve? What if none of them understood? We decided that we'd have to try to live our lives our way. We'd go as gently as we could, and tread as softly as possible through the areas that were dear to another member in the family, but go ahead we must. And there were some hurt feelings. There was the sister who never understood what we tried to say about Christmas dinner, and the brother who had a year-long feud with Dick over finances. There were the tight-lipped smiles and the raised eyebrows. There was the house guest who never came back after the snake accidentally got into her bed, and the maiden aunt who never accepted that the girls wore blue jeans on Easter Sunday afternoon. But there was a lot of understanding, too. Dick's mother, who I was convinced would be the most hurt by changes in family tradition, was the most understanding. "You're building something good, something worthwhile," she said, "with your own children. Don't worry about what anyone else thinks." More support came from the eighty-one-year-old Gramma who croaked, "Damn right you should live your own life. Wish I had!" She gave us breathing room and encouragement; she made us feel a little less like hopeless rebels and misfits. And from this same wise old woman came the revelation that you need not feel guilty if you don't like all your relatives. Aunt Minnie may be an armor-plated battle-axe who checks your corners for dust, sniffs at the frozen green beans, and badgers the children about their manners. Do you have to invite her to dinner once a month because the rest of the family does? We decided that we didn't.

Brothers and sisters? After a few years of marriage, we discovered that we had a great deal in common with some and enjoyed being with them. Others drifted apart as our families and theirs developed different interests. Did we have to give everybody equal time because all mothers want their children to stay close? No.

We slowly learned through the years to rely more on ourselves and on what we believed was right for us. If my experiment with Spanish cooking gave Dick diarrhea for four months that was our problem, not his mother's or his sister's. If we decided to invest our savings in a stock-market gamble and lost it, that was also our business, not my father's or his. If we chose to let the dust accumulate in the corners while we became interested in snowmobiling, Aunt Minnie could lift her eyebrows in vain. As we zipped past through the snow, we wouldn't notice.

Not only did we want to build our own lives, but also we wanted to make our own mistakes together. Could we take the best traditions from both worlds and a little common sense of our own and combine them? Could we create a new world that was comfortable for us to live in, and still be members of a family clan? We could and we did, and tried to step on a minimum of toes along the way. Surprisingly, after the initial shocks wore off, we found that they still loved us and we still loved them—even Aunt Minnie. I guess that's the beautiful thing about a family. Love goes deeper than money or lifestyles or traditions.

19.
Money: The Devil Made Me Do It

TAKE A WOMAN who is frugal by nature and mate her with a man who lets money burn a gaping hole in his pocket. Have them share the same paycheck, and watch the sparks fly! That was us twelve years ago. Take a young couple struggling to buy furniture and appliances, and also starting a family. Put them face to face with a monthly paycheck that never seems to stretch past the third week of the month, and watch the tension build! That was us, too. Picture the young bachelor who changed cars every two years suddenly trying to figure out where a woman managed to spend that vanishing money. Picture a girl who had earned a good salary before marriage having to ask her new husband for an allowance each week to buy groceries now that they were living on one paycheck. Was that sweet young lady who resented the dependence and the dole-out me? You bet it was!

There's no question that money can be a source of tension, even in the best of marriages. Surveys rank finances just below sex as one of the major marital problems, and anybody who's been married longer than one paycheck or one bill-paying day can tell you why. Who spends the money and how, who earns more if both work, and why there is never enough, are questions which often breed resentment between two otherwise happy people.

In a marriage, the sources of potential money problems are as endless as the personalities of the people involved. Not only did Dick and I have different spending habits (the tightwad vs. the "it's only money" man), but we also had conflicting attitudes concerning that too-tiny dollar. We responded differently to the fact that there was never enough money. Dick always had the ability to react very philosophically when we couldn't pay our bills on time. When the hot-water heater exploded and wiped out the money for the telephone and electric bill that month, he could shrug his shoulders and still smile. He was very comfortable playing that old game—Rob Peter to Pay Paul.

Not me! I'd get hives just thinking that the phone bill was a month overdue. A cold sweat would break out all over my body when the milkman brought more milk if last month's bill was still unpaid. I'd creep around the house on Monday, Wednesday, and Friday mornings until after the milkman had gone, hoping he'd think I'd been carried away on a stretcher, ill.

I decided that the credit people working for the utility companies are especially handpicked, from a group of former prison guards. No matter how you bare your soul or what sad story you tell them, they maintain that steely-voiced calm on the telephone. "We are shutting off your service tomorrow." Click! They'd never call at night when Dick was home. Always during the day when they knew I'd be left in terror for hours, visualizing the cut wires hanging from the side of our house tomorrow for all the world to see. Or they would wait until your afternoon bridge club arrived before calling. I wonder how many other women have become adept at the totally one-sided phone conversation. "Yes, I'm aware of that." (Sweet voice and smile.) "Oh, certainly, dear, we plan to. Yes, yes, soon. Oh, very soon. Bye-bye. You'll be hearing from me." (Like hell you will! As soon as this bridge game is over I'm taking the first plane to Fairbanks, Alaska!)

- By the time Dick got home at night after one of those phone calls, I had worked myself into a frenzy. "Pay them! What if my mother calls tomorrow, and they've shut off the phone?" When you're convinced that the world is collapsing there is nothing more frustrating than being faced with a calm husband. "Don't worry about it, honey. I'll send the phone company the money we have set aside for the gas bill, and the gas company will have to wait until next month."

We also disagreed about how our money was to be spent. Just what each of us thought was of primary importance proved to be very enlightening. When Dick felt that it was time to add to our insurance program, I invariably thought that a new living-room carpet was first on the list that year.

Since we had children quite early in our marriage, we were a one-paycheck family sooner than most. Initially, I found it difficult to adjust to being financially dependent. However, we did miss another type of problem which some of our friends had to tackle: The *my* money and *your* money attitude that often develops as a result of two paychecks.

It is not easy for some working wives to accept an *our* money concept. Many feel that they are working for the luxury money in the family, and therefore, they should make the decisions about how that money is spent. What the women hoarders seem to forget is that the man's income is still paying for the essentials. Without that income, there would be little *my* money left to buy bubble gum, let alone a color TV.

We're not attacking women only, when we talk about *my* money. Dick points out that there are just as many men who have the same attitude. Uusally these men are the sole providers of the family's income. They prefer that situation, but not always for the noblest of reasons.

"I'll make the money decisions in this family! I've earned this money, and it's mine! I kill myself working to give you all this! I gave you a second car!" Any of those lines sound familiar? They are the words of the dole-out husband. Dick doesn't believe this man approached marriage with the idea of sharing life with a wife and family. He bought a bunch of slaves to worship at the foot of his throne, and he never lets anyone forget that he's the provider. Don't expect him to loosen those decision-making reins for one minute. As long as he can manipulate the people in his family with money, he has power.

Since both he and the lady hoarder use money as a source of power, it's difficult to imagine any feeling of partnership in a marriage to either one. The *we* people that Dick and I know seem to be *we* in all aspects of their marriage. But the *me* and *mine* people on finances also appear to be the ones who don't communicate deeply, who don't perceive each other's needs, and who don't give very much in any area of marriage. We don't know which came first—the selfish attitudes or the marriage problems—but they seem to go hand in hand.

Another common money problem that Dick and I have encountered is the inability to understand how much each side of the partnership requires. What amount do I need to function? To maintain the house? How much does Dick need to operate as a businessman? Men have a difficult time understanding where the houshold money goes because they aren't spending it; women have an equally hard time understanding how a man can spend so much on lunches and gas.

Dick is usually appalled when he sees the astronomical amount listed in my miscellaneous column. "Surely you can't need that much for odds and ends." But I do. And it's almost impossible to itemize how that money dribbles away for school supplies, for flea powder for the dog, for Girl Scout cookies, for a ticket to the high-school band concert.

We've reshuffled our financial responsibilities so many times that it's frequently a chore to remember which of us pays what bills. We've started so many new budgets and budget books that singlehandedly we must be keeping both the accounting book industry and the pencil industry alive. No single method of money division seems to have worked for long, nor any single bookkeeper or bill payer. I've tried paying all the bills, but that's proved disastrous. We've attempted to divide them in half—Dick concentrating on intangibles such as mortgage and insurance, and I taking care of the household essentials such as groceries and clothing. But we are constantly borrowing from each other to make the budget work. At the end of the month, it would take an accountant to figure out who owes whom what. We've charged every item for several months so that we could see where the money was going. That was calamitous! We've paid cash for everything for the same amount of time, and as a result, we almost starved the last week of the month.

We concluded that there was no simple perfect way to run our family budget. Perhaps brighter people have devised one that works, but we can't seem to do so. Finally, one thing became blatantly clear to us. However we managed to run our financial affairs, money had to cease being a source of friction. Whether we had too little money, or too much (Ha, ha!) didn't really matter. What we needed was a common philosophy of what money meant in our lives. Once we had that, the spending would take care of itself.

Did money have to be a negative force in marriage? It didn't seem so. But if we believed that, how could we make it more of a positive element? We realized that each time money had become a problem, it was because one of us didn't understand *why* that money was spent. Every argument we had had boiled down to either lack of communication or a lack of joint goals.

Whenever Dick raised his eyebrows over the amount I spent at the beauty parlor or the art supply store, it was because I hadn't explained why I considered that money well-spent. And when I questioned the money we allowed in our budget for his lunches or pocket money, it was because I didn't know that frequently he had to take others to lunch or to buy drinks. It was just as important for him to be able to play poker with the boys and lose as it was for me to buy art supplies.

Yes, the cosmetic bills at the drugstore were high at times. But Dick wasn't aware that I was as uncomfortable outside our home wihout lipstick and with straggly hair as he would have been attending a meeting with frayed cuffs. Yes, the long-distance telephone bills were astronomical every so often. But it was important for Dick to be able to make those calls; he wasn't a letter writer. The telephone was a lifeline for him, and the money was well spent in his eyes. But I had to understand that before I could stop complaining about the phone bills. I had to recognize how much the recreation with the boys meant to him before I could stop fussing about the money he lost at poker. What a blow to a man's ego to admit to himself that he better not play tonight because he might lose, and then his wife would be furious.

We decided that before we had one more argument or misunderstanding we should thoroughly discuss what part money was to play in our lives, at present and in the future. How could we turn it into a positive force? We looked at some of the costly areas in our budget. Surprisingly, they weren't the utility bills, the groceries, or the mortgage. Those bills remained constant. Our budget problems usually were telephone (Dick), arts and craft supplies (me), cosmetics, beauty shops, etc. (me), gambling (Dick), records (me), and books (both of us).

How clear the pattern became all of a sudden. In each area of overspending that caused friction, one of us was fulfilling a need. I bought records for the same reason that some women buy new hats—to cheer myself up. Nothing seemed to pick me up faster when I was depressed, than coming home with an armful of new records and filling the house with music. For Dick, the telephone served the same function. Whenever the spirit moved him, loneliness or sharing a high, he phoned a friend or relative somewhere in the country. Gambling relaxed him; the stakes didn't matter. It was an important outlet to reduce tension, as art was for me.

Were these outlets wrong for either of us? No, of course not. They were only harmful when they caused friction between us. If Dick had been worrying about how to make the car payment this month, and I came home with five new stereo albums, there would be problems. And I could justifiably snap back, "Just take a look at the phone bill. I didn't make fourteen long-distance calls last month."

The problem wasn't the money itself, or even the way it was spent. It was that we had never explained to each other why we both consistently overspent on the same things. Neither of us had tried to understand that each of us had needs that had to be met in different ways and at separate times. Once this was understood, both of us were more than willing to let the other use any money available to fill those needs, to relax, and to grow. But where were we going to get the money without constantly living beyond our means? We had to look honestly at our priorities. Were we willing to cut down on other things so that we could follow some whims? Yes, we could eat hamburger three nights in a row if it meant I could paint in the afternoon, and Dick could play poker whenever he wanted. Did it matter if we kept up with the neighbors in regard to cars, clothes, and clubs, if we could indulge ourselves in those areas which really meant something to us? No, it didn't matter at all.

Dick's philosophy of money was based on the premise that it should be a life-giving force in marriage. It should be a vehicle to free us rather than to enslave us. Whatever money remained after the basic bills were paid should be spent to bring happiness to ourselves, to each other, and to others.

During the early years of our marriage when there was very little money, we still found ways to use it to feed our souls. Sometimes it meant cutting out a seeming necessity, but we learned that there were a minimum of real necessities in our lives. The extravagances of books, and music, and fun were gigantic by comparison, and their memories are still sweet. As our income grew through the years, our philosophy stayed constant. There was the mutual trust that neither of us would abuse the freedom to spend. Ours was and is a partnership based upon the thought "What can I do with this money to make the person I love happier and freer? What can I do with it to help myself grow?"

Dick would find ways to help me if he had leftover money at the end of the month. He'd suggest that I get a teen-ager to take the children to the park every day for a week after school. They loved it, and it enabled me to spend more time on some project about which I was very excited. If he was flying home from California, I might suggest that he stop off in Las Vegas for a day. One more day away wasn't going to hurt our marriage, and he'd come home happy and relaxed instead of beat and harried from the business trip.

We changed our whole system of bookkeeping for the 1000th and last time. We stopped the joint checking accounts and we opened separate accounts. Each of us had certain responsibilities, but once these were handled, any money that remained was considered play money. We could spend it as we chose or save it if we wanted. We didn't have to explain or justify the expenditures to each other. We trusted one another's judgment.

Both of us had independence, but we didn't use it to compete with each other. Sure, once in a while, I ran out of money before the end of the month. I probably always will. We still got fouled up by unexpected major expenses, and we had to borrow from each other's accounts. In many ways, our budget was as chaotic as it had always been, but we didn't care. The atmosphere had changed. No more allowances, no more my money, your money divisions. Only our money, with spending limited by the sole question, "Is it meaningful spending to one of us?"

We applied the same theory to the children's allowances. Since we took care of their basic needs, they could spend their small allowance as they wished. There were no forced programs of putting half in a savings or checking account. If our six-year-old wanted to spend his whole allowance on candy and to eat it at once, that was his privilege. It made him feel good. If he got a tummyache, he learned not to do it next time in a way that was more effective than our preaching. Saving is a habit that can be forced on a child, but the virtue of saving can come only from the child himself. We watched as the youngsters frittered away their allowances on cheap toys, which soon fell apart, causing them great disappointment. But we let them do things their own way, just as Dick and I let each other operate. Eventually, they began saving on their own for the things that they wanted badly. And they learned to supplement their allowances with outside jobs to save for the big items.

Bill-paying day became another day in our home. No one growled or groaned. We never got upset with each other. Dick can pay bills and enjoy it. Why? Because he views money as a life-giving force. He can sit back as he makes the mortgage payments and take a moment to reflect, "This is a nice house; I'm so glad we have it." Or think about how warm it is in the house during the winter as he pays the heating bill. As he runs down the list of long-distance calls, he can smile remembering each conversation and think that it was money well spent. Clothes, toys, car payments, even utility bills can be paid with joy if we remember the pleasure that all these things have given us. It's unfortunate that we often forget by month's end the enjoyment we had spending that money.

We need to make ourselves aware of the positive side of money in our daily lives to stop it from becoming a source of trouble in our marriages. It doesn't matter whether there is enough or too little. We have lived with both situations. Money could be, should be, and is a life-giver for two people and for a family.

20.

Sharing a Pregnancy—or the Baker, the Bleb, and the Beach Ball

THE PHONE RINGS. The sweet young girl in the new maternity dress starts to rise from her chair to answer it. At the same time, a nervous, high-pitched voice yells from the basement laundry room, "Don't move, honey! Don't get up! I'll get it!" Frantic feet bound up the stairs; he reaches the living room just in time to catch the final ring. "Hello. No, Marcia can't talk to you now, Millie. She's resting. I'll have her call you later." (Solicitous pats on his wife's shoulder as he is talking.) This is obviously Marcia and Bob's first pregnancy.

The same living room five years later. Bob is watching the ball game as Marcia (same maternity dress but slightly faded) struggles past, carrying the stepladder and a fifty pound drum of tar. "Bob, would you open the front door for me? I'm going to shingle the roof." As soon as the next play ends, Bob gets up and opens the door for Marcia. As she struggles to fit her equipment and her stomach through the door simultaneously, he again pats her solicitously on the shoulder.

"Be careful, honey. Don't fall off the roof." This is obviously Marcia and Bob's third pregnancy.

Although our story is exaggerated, it does underline the unique difference between the first pregnancy and all others. By the second or third time, the mystery, wonder, and fear surrounding pregnancy have disappeared, and both of you worry less.

The first pregnancy is one of the most beautiful times in a couple's married life. But in many ways, it's also the most insecure, upsetting, frightening, and longest nine months that a husband and wife will spend together. At least it was for us. Most couples enter pregnancy with little knowledge of what that nine months is likely to bring. Everything is new and different. Familiar daily routines become a source of uncertainty. "Should I vaccum? Can I still sleep on my stomach? If I have an alcoholic drink, will the baby get drunk? Will it hurt the baby if we make love?" All normal, natural questions and worries.

During this time, a husband is often torn between a tremendous feeling of pride because he has helped to create life, and the natural but frightening thought, "What if something happens? I did this to her." Dick has tried to explain the feelings of inadequacy and helplessness that a man experiences. He's ecstatic, he's worried, he's proud, he's concerned, and he's totally helpless. Dick believes that the nine-month wait can be compared to baking a loaf of bread in the oven. The oven and the bread are doing their job, and there's nothing for the baker to do except look at the oven door and wonder what's happening inside. He has no control over the situation, and he can't peek to see how it's coming along. The best thing he can do is to keep himself busy, tidying up the kitchen. And then the trouble starts.

There are the calm husbands who try to pitch in with the heavy chores only, and there are the hysterical helpers who think lifting a hairbrush might be too much of a strain for their wives. Most husbands are a combination. The maternal instinct in man comes out

233

for one of its rare appearances, and many women have a difficult time handling it.

Given a woman's natural worries and fears during the first pregnancy, this sudden surge of helpfulness tends to make her feel inadequate. She had little to do but have self-doubts, and worry about what's happening to her body and that baby. After all, she's only the oven—she can't peek either. So, she waits and wonders, while weird things begin to occur in that body that she thought she knew so well.

She begins to have cramps in her legs, and she wakes every morning with a charley horse. "Is that the pregnancy, or am I getting gangrene of the leg? Nobody ever mentioned that as a side effect." She's tired and she feels nauseated. Her hair doesn't shine any more; little red spots begin to erupt all over her body. Her back aches, and she spends half her waking life in the bathroom. And half her waking life seems to be about two hours a day! And why is she the only one wearing a sleeveless dress in the middle of winter? What's the matter with all those other people? Aren't they hot?

One glance downward convinces her that never again could she possibly feel or look the way she did before her pregnancy. Who is that matronly-looking creature with the fifteen-pound basketball tucked under her shirt, wearing her husband's bedroom slippers? (Not that it matters. Her feet are so swollen that she can't get them on anyway.) She's the same lady with the circles under her eyes and the food stains all over her stomach (because the napkin won't stay on her lap). The one who looks as though she needs a good shot of Geritol and five months at a reducing salon. And where is the girl who used to dance all night and still be able to get up for an exam at eight in the morning? Is she gone forever? Is that fun-to-be-with lady, who spends all her waking hours enroute to or from the bathroom, really the new me? Will I ever be the same again?

By the end of nine months it certainly doesn't seem so to any woman—or any man! She doesn't understand herself, and her poor husband doesn't understand her. "Why does she cry when I try to help her scrub the floors? Why does she burst into tears when I say she looks nice? What's happening to us?" Their sex life is not active. She thinks she's so ugly and undesirable that he doesn't want to make love to her; he thinks she's never looked more beautiful and radiant, but he is frightened that he may hurt the baby. She feels fat, ugly, tired, and sick; he adores her. She says, "Tell me that you love me," and then doesn't believe it when she hears it. Her husband is trying to truly cherish her as well as to make life easier, and she thinks it's because he feels sorry for her.

Both the expectant mother and the expectant father need more love, more patience, more understanding, and more communication than ever before in their lives together. Simultaneously, they both feel pride and anxiety, joy and inadequacy. Sharing those feelings is very important, expecially during the first pregnancy. The man can be more than an overly helpful partner to his wife; he can let her know his thoughts and fears; his uncertainty in meeting new financial responsibilities—the doctor bills, the larger apartment. In addition, he can share with her the shock and exultation of manhood, "I created a child," and the ensuing helplessness he feels while he waits for the birth.

Likewise, the woman can provide the man with a deeper understanding of the pregnancy itself, and she can allow him a deeper insight into herself as an unsure human being. She can share her wounded ego, her jealousies at seeing slim, young girls cavorting at the beach, while she sits on the sand like someone's forgotten beach ball. She can tell him that she worries about his love continuing when she feels so tired, crabby, and unattractive. She knows he didn't bargain for a wife who vomits first thing every morning and who falls asleep at 7:00 P.M. She can honestly tell him that she's terrified every time she looks into the mirror and sees those red spots on her nose. Then maybe he will understand why she cried when he says,

235

"You look beautiful." Why she craves his love and attention, yet says, "Leave me alone" at the same time.

During the first pregnancy a husband and wife come the closest to cracking open their shells, ripping off their masks, and crying out for help. With a little understanding and a little help from each other, two people can drop the blustery, self-confident images and reveal that they are afraid and that they do need each other desperately.

Even if a couple never reach that deep level of communication, it's still vital to share as much as possible of the pregnancy with one another. It makes the nine months go easier and enhances the partnership. Dick and I wanted to develop the attitude that the pregnancy was *ours*. Hopefully, later, it would lead to the concept of *our* baby. We tried to share that pregnancy as many ways as we could. Not only feeling life, when it first occurred, but also sharing worry over the blebs (red spots).

We asked our doctor if there were any restrictions on our normal activities. His attitude was great. "Do anything that you're used to doing, and that you feel like doing. And if you get a hangnail, don't call me at 5:06 A.M. and ask if it will affect the baby." Basically, he was saying, "Use your head," and we tried to follow his advice. We avoided most of the hysteria, except when I was in my ninth month and I fell on my stomach into a pen full of puppies. Even the doctor couldn't convince us that the baby wasn't going to be born flat as a pancake. But three weeks later our newborn child proved he was right.

We tried to continue most activities together unless I felt tired or sick, and then Dick always seemed to understand. Mainly, we made serious attempts to share our thoughts and fears. We discussed the whole misunderstanding about lovemaking. And Dick had a good talk with our doctor so that we weren't burdened by the old wives' tales on sex during pregnancy. We followed his common-sense approach—sex whenever we desired it, as long as it didn't become uncomfortable. Instead of Dick waiting for me to make a move because he wasn't sure how I felt, he'd approach me normally. If I was having a bad day, I could tell him so, knowing that he still desired me, even if I looked like a walrus. As soon as I felt better, I communicated my desire. We tried to share our thoughts and feelings, and keep the anxieties to a minimum. We were really pretty cool about everything until I went into labor. What a fiasco!

Baby number one had the gall to be born several weeks ahead of schedule, and this was one aspect of the pregnancy that we had not considered. If the doctor said March 26 why, naturally, it would be March 26. As a result, when I suddenly went into hard labor one night, neither of us believed it. "Gas pains," we said to each other, knowingly. I shouldn't have eaten so much at that party last night. The two hours that followed that sage diagnosis at 5:20 A.M. were similar to a scene from the Keystone Cops.

Dick began to get concerned a few minutes later when I could no longer stand up. He wanted to call the doctor but I insisted that it was only a little gas, which would pass soon. After another miserable fifteen minutes, Dick took one look at me and called anyhow. Since the doctor must have been convinced by my yelling in the background, "It's only gas pains," he told Dick to give me an enema and call him back in several hours. An enema! Nobody's given me an enema since I was six, and *then* they had to strap me down!

My refusal was to no avail. That's what the doctor had said, and that's what Dick was going to do if he had to sit on me. Out he flew to find an all-night drugstore, and he was back in fifteen minutes with two Fleet's emergency bottles. But the enema didn't work. A half hour later it had done its job, and my gas pains were the worst yet. Dick, in his calm, man-of-the-house voice, said, "We're going to the hospital." Well, I wasn't going to the hospital to be told I was there too soon and have to be sent back home. No! I and my gas pains weren't budging! Besides, my suitcase wasn't packed. I had to iron a dress, and shave my legs. That manly voice again. "Do you want to get dressed, or shall I carry you to the car in your nightgown? Either way, you are going now."

Somehow, we stuffed me into some clothes (because I could no longer stand up), and Dick carried me to the car. It was 7:30 A.M., and the morning rush hour was in full swing. Between moans and groans in the back seat, I made it very clear just how embarrassed we'd both be when the hospital gave me an Alka Seltzer and sent me home in another hour.

Then it happened. The ultimate mortification! My water broke, and I thought I had wet my pants. "Dick, you've got to turn around and go home. I can't go in there with wet pants. I'll just die!" But he whipped the car into the hospital emergency lot at that moment, and in seconds he was up the ramp and back with a wheelchair and two attendants, who bodily dragged me out of the back seat.

From that point on, things became a frantic blur of masks and gowns. I don't recall how I got my clothes off; the only thing I remember noticing was that the doctors were in green. I thought doctors always wore white. The baby was born ten minutes after we pulled into the parking lot. I had gas pains for a grand total of two and a half hours!

Dick was lucky that first time to miss the whole labor and delivery-room scene, the one that sends the calmest of husbands into a state of shock. Before he had finished signing me in at the desk, the nurse appeared to announce that he was the proud father of a male gas bubble.

Despite all the jokes that have been made about the nervous husband, it is a traumatic experience for any man to watch the woman he loves in pain for hours, and to be totally helpless. What can a man do except pace the floor and chain smoke? One of the things that infuriates a man during his wife's labor is the seeming callousness of the hospital staff. He forgets that although this is his wife's first delivery, the doctor and nurses manage to perform or assist at a dozen or so each day. There they are, bustling in and out of the labor room, calmly ignoring that dearly-beloved figure, writhing on the bed. "What's happening?" he asks frantically each time they enter to take blood pressure. "Nothing!" is the response. From their point of view, nothing is happening; but from his, the world is obviously coming to an end.

You would have been proud to see how wise and how calm we both were for the next birth, fourteen months later. We like to think we had learned something but it was the doctor who changed the routine for us. Because my first delivery had been so fast, he decided that our future children should be induced. I don't think he trusted our judgment after the first birth, and was afraid we'd have the baby on the freeway while I was busy in the back seat shaving my legs.

I was so calm for the second child that I told Dick there was no reason for him to come to the hospital with me in the middle of a workday. I drove to the sitter's house and dropped off baby number one, and then drove myself to the hospital to have baby number two. There I promptly managed to fall up the steps and gash open my leg. After a short stop in the emergency ward for stitches, I was carried upstairs to have my baby.

For the third birth, fourteen months later, Dick brought me to the hospital by appointment early in the morning. The staff said it would be hours before anything happened, so he might as well go to the office and get some work done. They would call him when I was in labor.

However, everyone misjudged my single-mindedness. If I was coming in to have a baby, I wasn't going to fool around all day! The injections and routine took about an hour before labor actually started, and then I delivered within fifteen minutes. Actually, I almost missed that birth, myself. I had strolled out of the labor room and into a phone booth in the hall to call a friend. We were chatting away, when a sudden panicky sensation hit. "Sorry, Suzie, gotta go. I think I'm about to have the baby." Once again, I just made it to the delivery room.

After the birth of a baby, Dick is at his best. I've never met any man who is more attuned to a woman's needs during that adjustment period in the hospital or at home with the new baby. He always sensed that the worst thing he could do was to bustle into the room telling jokes to cheer me up. In the first place, I didn't need cheering up now that delivery was over. In the second place, did you ever try to laugh with a bottom full of stitches! He even found one of those child-size inner tubes for me to sit on for those first few days at home.

His most thoughtful gesture was the after-baby present, which he gave me while I was in the hospital. Knowing how I felt during those last few months of each pregnancy—that I would never look like my old self again—he devised the world's greated morale builder. For one baby, it was sexy, black, lacy underwear, in the smallest size available. After another birth, it was black stretch pants in such a small size they would have looked painted on Twiggy. About the time I became aware that there were still eight more pounds to lose, he would give me a beautifully wrapped incentive. This was his way of communicating, "I love you. And I think you're sexy, stitches and all." Somehow, he recognized that it is important to make a woman feel that she is her old self as soon as possible after the baby is born.

Moreover, Dick very capably handled that period known as the Baby Blues. When our first child was born, I had no idea that such a thing existed, and I was unprepared for the sudden reversal in my termperament. We don't know what causes this, but most women seem to go through a period of sudden depression about two or three weeks after the birth. Suddenly, you're as sensitive and teary as you were during pregnancy. A compliment from your husband brings on a sudden burst of tears, and the whole world looks black. You can't seem to cope with things. Fortunately, it only lasts a short time, but if you don't expect it, both of you can really be thrown for a loop.

Our doctor assured Dick that this was a natural occurrence. He was never more patient and understanding than during that week. When I felt like crying, he let me cry and tried to make me feel that tomorrow the sun would be shining again. He helped create a relaxed atmosphere at home while we both adjusted to the new baby. And it was he who insisted that we shouldn't let anyone pressure us into resuming our hectic pace until we had the situation at home firmly in hand.

Many husbands and some wives get bored and become discontented during those first few weeks at home. As a consequence, they try to do too much, too soon. This restlessness places an unnecessary burden on a woman when she should be concentrating on working that baby into a routine that is acceptable for both her and her husband. Many men sometimes feel excluded because of the time and attention a new baby demands. That was time and attention that used to be theirs. It will be again, if they can help their wives establish a workable routine with the baby from the start and be patient enough to give everyone a chance to adjust to it.

That first month is vital to the communications between husband and wife. Naturally, life is different. Now you're trying to live with an eight-pound illiterate, who has no respect for the fact that you used to enjoy sleeping late on Sunday mornings and having a leisurely breakfast in bed. Never again will life be the same as it was for just the two of you. But with a little communicating and a lot of understanding, the new routine can become a pleasant substitute for the old one. It doesn't have to be a source of resentment for a man who feels he's being replaced as number one by this tiny intruder. It doesn't have to be a source of frustration for a woman who tries to make both papa and baby, number one at the same time. That's an impossible expectation, which can only lead to increasing tension for her, at a time when she needs a relaxed atmosphere.

It's difficult for a man to understand why a woman suddenly loses all desire for sex when she hears the baby start to cry. Frequently, the husband fails to recognize how torn a woman is in this position. Yes, she loves him. Yes, she wants to make love. But the baby's crying, and all her built-in motherly antennas immediately are alerted. She won't be able to enjoy sex until that crying stops in the next room. A man has to understand that his wife isn't rejecting him. Two instincts are battling within her, and she can't relax with that conflict.

A similar situation can arise while the wife is frying eggs for her husband's breakfast on a morning when he's late for work; or while they are in the middle of a conversation. If her baby cries she's going to be torn. If a man can try to understand, if a woman can communicate the tension of that pull, then the adjustment to a baby can be made with a minimum of frustration and resentment. Without that communication, a man needs an incredible, innate understanding of a woman to survive this period without feeling resentment and exclusion. Most men don't have it, so it's the woman's responsibility to share these new feelings with her husband.

We were fortunate to have a fantastically wise pediatrician for our first child. Before we took the baby home from the hospital, he paid us both a visit, which has had a tremendous effect on our lives together. "You're going home," he said, "and you can make life miserable for yourselves once you get there, or you can try to be sensible. You have two choices. You can either make you whole life revolve around that baby, or you can make the baby fit into your lives as best you can. Babies cry, and always at the wrong time. I usually recommend that people let their children cry. If the baby's been fed and changed, and there isn't a pin sticking in him, let him cry. It's good exercise for his lungs. If you can't ignore it, move him to some part of the house where you can't hear him. If you live in a small apartment, turn on some music and drown him out. Try to continue life with him as a new addition, not as the center of that life. Remember, from the moment you leave this hospital, that baby is either going to be running you, or you're going to be running him."

Well, we listened, although it was hard to follow his advice at times. Since both of us had been there to hear it, and we both agreed that he made sense, we attempted to shore up each other whenever one of us forgot. For the first few minutes, it was difficult to ignore that helpless, screaming little bundle, but we soon learned that the pediatrician was right.

The first baby and subsequent babies became a part of our total family, rather than a wedge between Dick and me. We didn't grow apart. We stayed as close and as intimate as when there were only two of us.

We learned that pregnancy and the coming of children don't have to change a relationship. Despite rough spots, if that vital communication can be maintained, the relationship will be preserved. If two people can open themselves and understand each other's needs through those difficult adjustments, the partnership will remain precisely that—a partnership.

21.
Creative Communicating . . .
What Really Works

WE'VE SAID MANY TIMES in this book that communication is the lifeblood of any relationship. How do you open up? How do you help your mate laugh, cry, and pour out his thoughts, his feelings, his yearnings, and his fears? It's not easy, but we believe it's worth the time, the effort, or even the heartache that it might require to start the exchange.

We're all tired of hearing doctors, psychologists, and the monthly women's magazines tell us how important it is for two people to have full communication, and then never give us a clue as to how this elusive goal can

243

be attained. We can't guarantee that what's worked for us can work for someone else. But we can share with you the ways that have helped us to be free with each other. Let's discuss some of our general concepts first, then we'll attempt to fit them into specific ideas for daily living.

In any intimate, long-term relationship between a man and a woman, goals have to be defined: Who are we? What do we stand for? What kind of a life are we building together? Are we going to live together or marry? Is this temporary or permanent? Do we want children? How many? As a woman, do I want to continue to pursue a career or my schooling, or devote my time solely to raising a family? Do I plan to return to my career after my family is grown? As a man, what do I want my work to mean to me? Is it to be a fulfilling end in itself, or a means of support, which will enable me to devote more of my time and energies to outside interests and hobbies? What are my priorities?

Both parties should know where they are going, and how they are going to get there. Goals will probably change as time passes and new circumstances and opportunities arise, but it's reassuring to have a frame of reference from which to work.

Individual thoughts, feelings, and views on all subjects should be discussed frequently because they are constantly evolving. Of course, you can't enter into an intimate, enduring relationship with someone else unless you understand what makes that person tick. You may not always agree, but at least you know your mate's position and where you stand in respect to it. Dick and I have different opinions about a variety of things—politics, our social life, entertaining, music, and food. We have no desire to be carbon copies of each other, but we do want to understand each other. We've argued about and laughed at our areas of disagreement, and we finally reached an honest understanding and respect for our differences. This gives us the security of knowing which are the "hot buttons" and how to avoid pushing them on a blue Monday. I can predict pretty accurately that if I invite two hard-drinking friends for dinner after Dick's favorite team has lost the Super Bowl, and then serve Mexican food, it's going to be a bad scene.

Our thoughts, our feelings, our positions have changed throughout our marriage, but we've tried to keep each other aware of them through frequent sharing. In this way, we can react to one another without fear of rejection or ridicule.

However, we believe that financial goals, be they high, low, or nonexistent, should be one area upon which both partners agree. Otherwise, there will be trouble. A philosophy of money has to remain somewhat flexible, and the communication lines have to remain open because our financial situation and circumstances change over the years. New facets of spending continually emerge and we have to be prepared to deal with varying conditions. For example, Dick is a gambler by nature—I'm not. He loves the crap table almost as much as he loves me (although he denies it). Fortunately, we don't live in a state where gambling is legal, but we manage to vacation in one occasionally. The first minor crisis occurred the year we bought a new dining room set and vacationed in Las Vegas almost simultaneously. Within a few hours of our arrival, Dick had won enough to pay for the dining-room furniture, plus a good deal more. I was thrilled! An hour later he has lost all the money, and I was furious. Why couldn't he have walked away from that table while he was ahead? Primarily, because he was having fun—win or lose. But it was impossible for me to understand this attitude. To me, gambling meant either winning or losing money.

Since that time, we have discussed gambling money and the gambling spirit often until I finally grasped his feelings. I'll never be able to treat vanished money with the same degree of casualness that Dick does, but I do recognize that gambling is a means of recreation for him. He doesn't care whether he wins or loses—it's the game and the excitement that's exhilarating. Now, whenever we are on a trip, we put aside a certain amount of money for the crap table. If he loses the money, it's not begrudged. If he wins, that's fun money to be splurged on some extravagance that can serve as a remembrance of the trip. Winnings are not used to pay for dining-room sets or doctor bills.

It has become much easier for me to avoid playing the bitchy wife who frequents every crap table and poker game in the world. "How much have you lost, dear?" "Don't you think it's time to quit now?" I wait until the end of a trip before asking Dick if we're ahead or behind, and the only reason I ask then is that my curiosity is killing me. I have no idea of the amount set aside for gambling. But my confidence in Dick assures me that it is reasonable, and we won't come home someday to find our house gone. The point of this story is that problems arise constantly when two people set a life course together. They cannot be buried to fester. Gambling was one problem which we discussed the first time it reared its head. We stayed with it until we reached a comfortable way of handling the situation, and thus we avoided years of friction and spoiled vacations.

The ideal situation is to be completely open with one another at the start of your marriage, or better still, before. Dick and I made a pact the night we got engaged on the shores of a lake, that we would never shut each other out. If something was bothering one of us, we would discuss the situation, no matter how unpleasant, and we would not drop the matter until we were satisfied that our partner understood. Agreement didn't necessarily follow, but we made an effort to share our viewpoint. In the "Lake Shore Pact" we also agreed that we'd never go to bed angry with each other. When you are mad or hurt, it is so easy to hop into bed and turn your back, but that behavior closes doors and creates frustration. It is not loving, it certainly is not mature, it wrecks marriages, and it spoils lovemaking. Some of our tenderest sex has taken place after we have attempted to straighten out a misunderstanding. We may not always get things

246

cleared up in one night. We may decide to sleep on the problem, but we know we'll work out the solution together. This approach is so much more sensible than lying in the dark seething, thinking of every nasty thing your mate has said during the past ten years, and waking up feeling just as nasty.

Dick and I have invoked the "Lake Shore Pact" hundreds of times in our marriage. Why couldn't such an agreement be started at any time in a relationship, similar to the signal system in sex. Use a simple word or phrase, that is mutually understood and that says, "You're shutting me out." "This argument is getting out of hand." "Don't say there's nothing wrong: I know you're mad at me." You have to be sincere or the pact will fall apart the first time you try to use it.

Another great help in daily communication is a third party, preferably of the opposite sex. Men and women don't think or operate on the same emotional level. Sometimes in the midst of anger or of a crisis, it is difficult to put yourself in the other person's shoes. No one can completely see things the same way that another does, no matter how close they are, or how much they've shared. Often, a good male friend can help a woman understand how her husband feels as a provider when his job situation is rocky. Likewise, another woman can help a man appreciate the feelings of insecurity his wife may have during her first pregnancy. We've both had friends whom we have sought out as sounding boards and sources of strength. It is important, however, that each trusts the third person and that each knows when that party's advice is being asked for.

Often, when I'm floundering with something that's out of my experience, I call a friend of ours who knows and understands us both. He can say, "This is what Dick's going through at the office," or "Men don't see things that way, Paula. This is how we feel about such and such." It's more than helpful to have another man's or woman's filter to see through occasionally. Sometimes it's vital to regain a true perspective.

247

If you haven't had good communications in the past, how can you initiate your first intimate discussion about each other and your feelings? A friend shared this idea with us, and we think it's an exciting one. Are you familiar with those quizzes that appear in the supplement section of the Sunday newspaper? They include such questions as: "How good a father are you?" or "How do you stack up against the great lovers of all time?" Our friends made up his own, one rainy Saturday afternoon when his children were at the movies. It was short and simple. "What are the three things you like most about me? What are the three things you like least about me?"

He didn't have as much trouble talking his wife into answering the questions as he had anticipated. She was as curious as he; they separated for an hour and wrote down their thoughts. The discussion that developed lasted long after the children returned home from the movie. Our friends decided to go out for a hamburger dinner alone so that they could continue their talk. They returned after the children were in bed and talked all night. Misunderstandings and petty habits that had been sources of irritation for years were voiced and cleared-up. But most important, they had found a vehicle for opening the lines of communication. Each other's flaws were cushioned by virtues so that neither party was left shattered or hurt.

So many times when we're upset about an irritating characteristic of our mate, we attack. A verbal fight ensues, which revolves around the flaws. It becomes a game of one-upsmanship to see who can hurt the other more. How much better to counter the bad points with those qualities which make you love your partner. That simple quiz has changed our friend's whole marriage. He and his wife are excited about talking to each other and about each other for the first time in years. Why? Because each found he could expose his vulnerable spots and the other wouldn't lash out at those weaknesses.

Since talking to him, we've thought a great deal about his idea and its many implications and variations. It can be expanded or altered to fit anyone's relationship. "What is the one thing you do for me that I find most supportive?" "What is the one thing you could do in our marriage that would make me happier?" It could also be adapted to relationships with children, particularly teen-agers. What a fantastic way to initiate communications between a boy and his father—a discussion of the three things they like most and least about each other. A word of warning, however. Children can often be more honest and direct than adults, so prepare yourself for some stinging, yet honest criticism.

Once communication is begun between two people, they must work constantly to keep the exchange flowing. And this isn't as difficult or time consuming as it sounds. It's simply a matter of forming the habit.

We would like to talk about some of the things that make our marriage run smoothly, First, we make certain that we have time together *alone*. Vacations without the children are a luxury, but one that every couple should make an effort to afford. Every so often, the two of us need to go off together to recapture that special "us" feeling that came before the children and, hopefully, will endure after they've grown up and left our home. Our time is stretched so thin that a man-woman relationship can drown easily in the whirlpool of family life. The excuse many of our friends use is, "It wouldn't be good for the children." We disagree. They know how excited Dick and I get as we plan our time alone, and they can see our love for each other. And we hope that it's an attitude they will carry into their own marriages.

What if you're on a strict budget? You don't have to fly thousands of miles to get away together. We've taken care of friends' children when money was tight. "If you take care of our youngsters this weekend, we'll take care of yours some weekend next month." Staying at a nice, local motel for a few days can give you as much relaxation and uninterrupted time together as many hectic two-week vacations do. And if you're in your home-town, you won't feel obligated to rush around sightseeing. Pick a motel with an indoor pool, sleep late, have breakfast in bed in the morning, and eat your meals whenever you feel like it. Make love in the morning, noon, or night as the mood and closeness moves you. Soon you'll both recapture the desire to be intimate in mind and body. If you can't afford the motel, go back-packing or camping together for a few days—alone. It's the frenzied time schedule and the constant interruptions of family life that you're trying to escape. Remember what it was like before you had children? Both of you could walk out of the house for a day and not have to account to anyone. The two of you could pick up and go, wherever and whenever you felt like it. That's what you're trying to, and can, recapture.

Have dinner out together as often as you can afford it, expecially if you have something to discuss. Remember the man who tried the quiz on his wife? If they had stayed home for dinner that night and had let several hours lapse before resuming their discussion, they might not have been able to recapture the initial mood.

Quality time is important when you have something to discuss, so don't start when it's late and you're tired. Dick sometimes calls from the office and asks me to meet him for dinner. It's usually when he's had a bad day or he knows I've had one. We can still be home in time to say goodnight to the children and spend a little time with them, but it's given us a respite in between to collect ourselves and visit leisurely with each other.

One of the most neglected forms of communication in marriage is the "bad-day signal," and it's unfair to your partner not to use it. We all have times when we're ready to throw in the towel, but why should a loved one have to suffer if he's not at fault? If something goes wrong at work and Dick is in a foul mood, he calls me to tell me so. The problem and the mood have nothing to do with me, but I have advance notice that they are present and can act accordingly. I can act as a buffer between Dick and four noisy children.

If a woman is wise, that's the night she might pamper her man and have a drink waiting for him. She can suggest a short nap while she feeds the youngsters, and later they can have dinner alone.

The same principle should apply to a woman's bad days. Why not call your husband at work and say, "I feel rotten. The children have been awful. My head is splitting. If I bite your head off when you walk in the door, it's not because of anything you did." Forewarned is forearmed. He knows he's married to a normal human being whose life is temporarily out of kilter. If he's smart, he'll stop on the way home, buy some flowers, walk in the house, and say, "I love you." Then he'll suggest seeing that syrupy love story at the local movie house that he's been avoiding for two weeks. Total amount of money spent is about $4.00. Result—one very happy woman who's convinced she married the most understanding man in the world.

Another signal that's sadly overlooked is the telephone call from the office saying, "I'm going to be late for dinner." Most women I know become furious when their husbands arrive home an hour late for dinner without warning. Dick and I are convinced that it's a lack of understanding on both sides as to what's involved, but that's still no excuse for allowing any source of irritation to remain in your lives. Dick feels many men don't understand that dinner is the focal point of a homemaker's day. It takes time, thought, and effort to prepare a meal, and a woman rightfully feels abused and belittled that her man could cast aside her efforts to please with seeming thoughtlessness.

On the other hand, women frequently don't understand that a man cannot always call. He may be tied up in a conference with his boss, and doesn't want to look henpecked in front of him or any other associates by saying, "Excuse me, I have to call my wife." Or he may be in the midst of an important discussion, and he may not want to break the train of thought. Or he may be engrossed in his work and honestly lose track of time. In any case, if you don't work out a solution there are liable to be two very unhappy people when the roast becomes a cinder. It took Dick and me almost eight years to find a method that works for us. Our standard operating policy boils down to this: If it is humanly possible, Dick will call me if he's going to be late. If he's not home by 6:30 P.M., the children and I start dinner, and he makes the best of whatever is left when he gets home.

As we mentioned not too long ago, the busyness of our daily lives does not encourage good communications. You have to consciously set out to create the times and the mood to talk. You may have to take a long look at your living patterns and possibly consider making some changes. Dick and I hardly watch television because we believe that it has been primarily responsible for destroying communications in family life. In general, you only converse during commericals and station breaks, and how deeply can you discuss anything during a one-minute soap ad? Turn off the set for a whole night once in a while and do something that involves both of you. Paint a bedroom, play cards, or go for a bike ride. You'll be surprised by how much you have to say to each other.

We love to go for long walks or bike rides late in the evening when the children are asleep. It never fails to put us in the mood to talk. Some time ago, we saw *Little Big Man*. Dick suggested we go for a walk and soon we were discussing the movie and its political implications. As we mentioned earlier, politics had become a "hot button" for me. It was a subject I had been avoiding discussing in depth as I had found my views changing, my thoughts confused. I hadn't been ready to share my new muddled feelings or been sure of what their reception would be. This was during the time that I felt Dick was lecturing me. That night the mood and the time were right to get it all out.

We talked until three o'clock in the morning, knowing that the next day we would feel ghastly, but we learned so much about each other that night that we would have been fools to let that moment pass by.

We briefly mentioned in a previous chapter that a

built-in atmosphere for intimate communications is present after we make love. Don't ever roll over and go to sleep no matter how tired you are, without savoring at least a few of those precious minutes. It is one of the most intimate and secure times. In each other's arms, a man can cry, pour out worries, and talk of being frightened: a woman can share her anxieties and tensions. In a mood of receptiveness and love, problems can be heard and understood.

Dick and I speak to each other of our love in many ways. Occasionally, Dick writes me short love letters from the office. Women need to be shown and told that they're loved in order to feel secure. Men do, too, but I think women need the outward signs more than men. You don't have to be maudlin to communicate your love. There are many beautiful cards on the market today that say it for you. Frequently, we send these back and forth from home to office. I know it means a lot to Dick when he opens a card or letter from me in the middle of the day that says, "I'm thinking of you."

Telegrams are also fun. They're inexpensive and fast. You have no idea what a thrill it is for a woman who is in the middle of making peanut butter and jelly sandwiches, to have the phone ring and a telegram read saying, "I love you" especially when her husband is only five miles away at work.

There are so many ways to say, "I love you" without words. It can be that special look across a crowded room that means, "Let's get out of here and go make love." It can be a squeeze on the back of the neck as Dick walks past my chair after dinner, telling me thanks for another good meal, or a pat on the behind as I go up the stairs that says, "You've got a nice little ass." It's a touch, a tone of voice, a little extra money at the end of the month without a lecture when I'm overdrawn. It's occasionally buying clothes for me that says, "I like the way you look." It's making his favortie chocolate chip cookies on the day of an important business deal that lets him know, "Win or lose, you're important to me." It's taking a bath and putting on fresh clothes before he comes home for dinner that tells him, "I want to look good for you." It's never going to bed with curlers in my hair so he can always reach over and put his arms around me. It's being the only man at "Breakfast with Santa" that shows how much he supports the children and me.

All those many little gestures in our life communicate love. It's the hostess at a dinner party saying, "You're not going to sit next to your own wife?" and Dick answering quietly, "Yes, I am."

As a friend wryly commented to Dick, "You sure are making it tough on the rest of us!" But why can't any man and woman be creative in expressing love? For each couple the silent signposts on the road are unique. They can be as many and varied as their love and creativity will allow, or as simple as a squeeze of the hand.

For us, there is one sign above all others. It is the single red rose that arrives at odd times for no reason, and only we two fully know its meaning: "I love you. I cherish you." Wasn't that what we promised years ago, standing together at an altar? Yesterday in a car marked "Just married," today with runny noses to wipe, tomorrow through old age when it will be just the two of us again. Through pregnancies and births, through measles and monkey business, we said we would love and cherish each other. We can only fully live that promise through communication.

Life Through Love— To Love and Cherish

22.
Life-Giving Qualities

At the time of our marriage, Dick and I didn't know each other very well. At least that's the way it seems in retrospect. We were young and in love, and we thought we knew everything about making a good life together. Today, we wonder how we survived. We knew so little then about life and about each other.

But we had made a commitment that was strong and deep enough to carry us through that early period of ignorance. It said, "Someone you can count on, no matter what," and that was how we wanted to live. Spiritually, we believed in the depth of that promise. Without strings or qualifications we had said to each other, "I will love you, I will trust you, and together we'll try."

It was not until five years later that we heard someone explain what that *try* actually meant. We were talking to a friend who had been married for twenty years, and she expressed concern about the rising divorce rate. She was distressed that so few couples seemed to be prepared for what marriage demanded.

"There's so much to give and to share," she remarked "and they don't seem to realize that. We marry because we love each other, and we think everything else will take care of itself. But that's not true. To have a good marriage, you have to work at it every day of your life." She was right. She and her husband after twenty years, and Dick and I after only five, were still learning how much there was for each of us to give.

There were life-giving qualities that were necessary to keep our relationship growing: sensitivity and honesty toward each other; understanding and acceptance of both of our strengths and weaknesses; dignity and respect for each other; and affection and thoughtfulness. For our love to be lasting, Dick and I had to learn how to bring those life-givers into our daily lives.

Sensitivity and understanding of another person's strengths and weaknesses can be used to build a relationship. With equal effectiveness, they can be used to destroy the people involved. A married couple learns very quickly to sense each other's weaknesses, needs, or vulnerable areas. What do we do with that knowledge? Use it to drag down our mate or to build him up? Look at your friends to see how well it is used both ways.

Most people have encountered the "waiting-to-pounce" couples. They have each other's flaws—those things which can be held up to ridicule—written across the inside of their eyelids. And these are commonly verbalized at social gatherings. After a few drinks, one partner begins telling a supposedly funny story at the expense of the other.

Harry's inability to drive home from last Saturday's party because he was so bombed is a hilarious story —to everybody except Harry. He's embarrassed, he doesn't need to be reminded in front of his friends. But his wife Edith tells the story with relish. She relates every funny detail of putting Harry to bed and of the children asking why Daddy is always sick on Sunday mornings. Everybody has a good laugh at Harry's expense except Harry and Edith. They seem to be enjoying her tale, but inside each one is seething. Edith is telling the story because she knows Harry doesn't want it told, but she wants to hurt him. In a socially acceptable way, she can ridicule him, yet be the life of the party. During the week, she can dig at that same vulnerable spot by casually remarking, "The yard is a mess. If you weren't so hung over every weekend, maybe it would look as nice as the neighbors'."

After Edith has gotten her chuckles from everybody at the party, it's Harry's turn. Smiling and with perfect innocence, he launches into the story of Edith's unsuccessful battle with the bulge. His accounts of Edith's adventures at the reducing salon, of Edith in her grey sweatsuit jogging, of Edith's wheat-germ and mango-juice diets have everyone guffawing. Edith endures the story with a frosty smile. Yes, she is twenty pounds overweight, but she certainly doesn't want her reducing efforts to be highlighted. And Harry knows that. He's only evening the score.

It's easy to be funny at someone else's expense. We know exactly how to put the other person down, but if we love each other, why should we want to do this? If we're insecure, jealous, or frightened of our own weaknesses, we can belittle and demean our mate to make ourselves seem bigger, or to keep the other person from growing. But no one of us is perfect. Our intimate knowledge of our partner's vulnerabilities should be used to help that loved one.

During the week following our honeymoon, Dick and I had our first learning experience about handling weaknesses. I asked him to put up a wall can opener in the kitchen. I was busy doing other things at the time, and he had a minute free. He had told me once that he was the most unmechanically minded man in the world, but I guess I had forgotten. Soon I heard faint mutterings and then curses, as the screws were put in crooked, and as each effort knocked off another hunk of plaster. After a few minutes, he stomped out of the kitchen and returned with a hammer and nails. Was he actually going to use the hammer? Just as I was about to ask, he struck the first blow—right on his finger. With a deafening roar, he ripped the can opener (hanging crookedly by one screw) off the wall and threw it across the room.

I couldn't believe what I was seeing. Who was this red-faced, swearing stranger? I didn't know that Dick had a temper. Naturally, I remarked, "That was the most ridiculous, childish thing I've ever seen." Clever of me, wasn't it? At that point, he uttered a few more four-letter words, banged the hammer on the counter, then slammed the kitchen, bedroom, and hall doors on his way out. I was paralyzed! How could one can opener make someone so angry? And why did I make things worse by saying the obvious? I didn't know what to do—put up the can opener myself, leave it on the floor, or sit down and cry. Fortunately, I was still pondering my next step when Dick quietly came back five minutes later. He was whitefaced and very sorry about the whole thing. He wanted to talk.

"I knew that would happen before I went into the kitchen," he said. "It always does. I told you I can't work with my hands, and I wasn't kidding. Everytime I look at a hammer, it hits me on the finger. Everytime I touch a screw, the plaster breaks. It's been that way all my life. The harder I try, the worse it gets; and the madder I get at myself. There was no reason to take it out on you. I'm sorry."

I felt sorry, too. For not listening or believing him when he told me that mechanical ability was not his strong point, and for making a stupid and unnecessary remark. I recognized that not only did he consider this a real weakness, but also it bothered him. Now what were we going to do? How were we going to resolve the situation without stepping on Dick's pride or without having a hammer-throwing, swearing session whenever a picture needed hanging?

"Tell me honestly," I asked, "would it bother you if I did it?" No, it wouldn't. He knew his limitations and he knew his strengths. He would rather devote his time to the latter. Great! I grew up as a tomboy, with a father who could and who did fix everything—and who had taught me how. I enjoyed puttering around fixing things, as long as Dick didn't object to his wife doing it.

After that first thoughtless remark, I never used the can-opener incident as a source of ridicule. I didn't mention it at parties to entertain my friends nor did I laugh with my Dad about Dick's mechanical ineptitude. I had shortcomings too, and Dick had never used them to belittle me.

For example, the telephone has always been one of my pet bugaboos. There are times when I actually hate that black monster, especially when I am asked to solicit for some charity. Perhaps it's because I consider the phone approach so impersonal, or because I know I'm not good at conning people into things that they really don't want to do. In any case, it's my least favorite job, and I've always shuddered and procrastinated when faced with a long list of telephone numbers to call. Dick learned this very quickly. Instead of ridiculing me, he often volunteered to make the calls. That was his forte; he did it well and with ease.

Dick and I try to blend our individual strong points rather than pick apart each other's weaknesses. Dick can be oversensitive in his relationships with others; I can be much more philosophical. No approach is simply, "Nobody is ever going to love you all the time, not even me." I could make Dick feel foolish when he reacts too sensitively to a situation. But that would hurt him, and why should I want to do that? Instead, I tell him how I see the situation from my perspective— why the person in question acted the way he did, or why he may have said what he did. Usually Dick can reappraise the situation from a broader perspective and recognize that there was probably no harm meant or done. He may have misread the intent.

My biggest weakness is that I take on too much; I always have. There's a nitwit that lives inside me, who thinks that she can do twenty-five jobs at once, and who won't settle for less than perfection in each of them. About every six months I find myself drowning in my own projects, and I have to be bailed out. Dick usually notices the signs before I do and moves in to alleviate the situation before it reaches crisis proportions. In a very short time, Dick can figure out exactly what can be eliminated or curtailed to allow me some breathing room. And that's precisely what I usually need, not a lecture.

As adults we don't want to be reminded of shortcomings. The riding and the needling make us feel like naughty children being reprimanded, and we become defensive. Have you ever scraped the car against the side of the garage? Do you need a sermon or a lecture to tell you that it was a stupid thing to do? Of course not. You're already feeling dumb and defensive. But for some reason, it's very hard for the other person not to say, "You did it again, stupid."

Dick and I have been working for a long time to break that almost automatic impulse to comment. We recognized that it didn't make things any better, it only made them worse. Both of us have enough bad habits and faults to spend a lifetime bickering about them and building fuel for resentment. But we choose not to live that way.

I'm a table burner. Eventually, I manage to brand every piece of furniture in the house with a careless cigarette. Why? Because I get too engrossed in what I'm doing. I forget that I laid a cigarette on the edge of the stereo ten minutes ago. I'm sure Dick doesn't enjoy seeing that month-old stereo with an inch-long burn, but he doesn't use that as an excuse to belittle me. He knows that I didn't purposely set out to burn our furniture and that I'm embarrassed each time it happens.

Dick is a coffeepot burner. About once every six weeks, he burns the bottom of our coffeepot. He becomes so involved in whatever he is doing, that he forgets he turned the burner too high. Not until we smell melting metal will he remember the cup of coffee that he was going to have. Does he feel sheepish? Certainly. Does he need the extra dig from me? Of course not. I keep a wary eye on his coffee perking, because I know his habits. When he sees me camped in the middle of the living-room floor with a book that I was returning to the bookcase, he looks around for the cigarette.

Dick and I can discuss our shortcomings honestly and accept criticism because neither of us has felt that our weak spots were going to be the object of ridicule. For example, several weeks ago we were absorbed in conversation as Dick drove down the expressway. Suddenly, he saw that he was about to miss a turnoff, so he swerved to get into the correct lane. Both of us experienced that heart-thumping feeling that frequently accompanies a scare. For a minute or two we rode in silence. Then I remembered something that I had been wanting to mention for a long time. "Dick, you're a good driver, generally. But during the last year, we've had a couple of close calls, and I think I know why. I've noticed that you get totally involved in our discussions and keep looking over at me while you drive. You're dividing your attention between the road and me. That's okay if you're going 25 m.p.h. in the suburbs, but at 65 m.p.h. in heavy traffic, it's a different situation. I've been meaning to tell you before, but either I forgot or someone else has been in the car."

That's all I needed to say. Dick hadn't realized a new habit was forming; he appreciated my honesty. "I'm glad you told me, but you're going to have to help me break this habit because I am not aware that I'm doing it. And it's too dangerous to let it continue. When you notice me looking over, just remind me." Within a month, he stopped doing it.

Knowing that we can be honest with each other about flaws, faults, and habits is a tremendous boost to our freedom with each other. We both are aware that whatever comes up, it will not be used as a dig. We know, too, that after it's discussed, there won't be any grudges harbored. We honestly want to help each other, not tear each other down. I can kiddingly give Dick a case of coffeepots for his birthday knowing that he'll think it's just as funny as I do. He can notice a burn on the new end table and say, "It's finally ours! I never really feel like we own something until you've

261

put our brand on it." They aren't digs at each other. They're smiling acknowledgments that both of us are very human—and glad that we are. Wouldn't you hate to live with a perfect person?

We try hard to maintain an atmosphere of freedom with each other. "What kind of a climate can I make for you to grow in?" is the unsaid thought. When we plant a flower seed, we take care to give it proper soil, sunlight, and water. We want it to be what it was intended to be—a beautiful flower. With neglect, it could be a straggly weed.

And like a flower seed, both of us need constant watering, sunlight, and fresh air from each other. We need support, not prophesies of gloom that we're sure to fail. If I decided to ride Dick constantly about the money we've lost in the stock market in the past, I might shake some of his confidence in himself as a businessman and as a provider. I know that if I attacked him in a particular way, I could begin to make him timid and unsure of himself in future investments —and possibly in other things. If he wanted to constantly remind me of the time I got totally bombed at our own dinner party years ago and curled up and went to sleep (on top of everybody's coats and before serving dinner), he could. He could have used that little tidbit over and over to eventually destroy my confidence in myself as a hostess.

Instead he cared enough to want to restore my injured pride, and to lessen my disappointment with myself. He had no desire to tear me down further, which he could easily have done the next morning. I had embarrassed him in front of other people. But he wasn't concerned about them—only about me, and how I felt, and how he could help. That's the climate to grow in. No sermons, no lectures, no ridicule for human mistakes. Only support and understanding and a willingness to go on from today—not yesterday.

Your mate has the best opportunity to influence your feelings of worth and dignity. Years ago, I had a delightful but very timid neighbor. She seemed to have so much going for her that I couldn't understand why she was so shy and unsure of herself. As I got to know her husband Jack better, it became very apparent that he was the reason. A dominant, confident person, he did everything to keep Patsy from developing herself fully. They had been married about ten years, so the relationship and their roles were taken for granted. Nothing that Patsy did was quite right in his eyes; there was always the inference that he could have done it better. If she painted a room while he was on a business trip, he praised the job, and then immediately walked over to inspect the one corner where she had missed a spot.

He managed to take the wind out of her sails whenever she did anything on her own. He never let her shop for her own clothes; he insisted on accompanying her to make sure that she didn't buy something foolish. I almost cried one day when she came running over to show me a new spring coat that they had gotten the night before. I was excited for her until I noticed the pockets. They were still stitched down as they often are when coats come directly from the manufacturer. There was a pair of scissors on the kitchen table, and I offered to cut the threads. "Jack never lets me cut open the pocket slits. He says I'll only stuff them with Kleenex and junk, and soon the pockets will sag and ruin the appearance of the coat."

I was so stunned that I couldn't say anything. I finally understood why Patsy never did things on her own. She had never been allowed to. To Jack she was another child, who could never fully manage without supervision, who couldn't be completely trusted to make a wise decision. So she never made any. By belittling her and everything that she tried to do alone, he very effectively kept her on that level.

At the opposite end of the spectrum is a young couple we know who always try to make each other look good, and who so genuinely enjoy themselves, that it is a delight to be in their company. They are the only couple we know who don't interrupt each other when one is telling a story.

One night they came to our house after seeing a

play. They were bubbling with excitement and were eager to tell us about it. "You tell them," said Connie, who was obviously dying to tell us herself. "No, you tell them," insisted Ted. "You always do a better job at details." "No, you." "No, you." Back and forth for five minutes until Dick finally said, "If one of you doesn't tell us, I'm going to bed. Your nobility is too much to stand at this hour." They were so wound up that it took a half hour to tell the entire sory, but we all enjoyed it. There was nothing spectacular about the evening or the story itself, but Dick and I remember it because of their joyful camaraderie. They have been able to give each other a feeling of genuine worth and dignity, and as a consequence, do not have to compete for attention or for glory.

There is a vast difference between growing together and competing. In the early years of our marriage, Dick and I discovered that competing at the other person's expense wasn't much fun. Both of us have always been highly competitive, and we had to learn to do things together without encouraging rivalry.

Many years ago, Dick decided to take up shooting. He bought a gun and began some target practice on his own. Thinking it might be fun if we practiced together we borrowed another gun from a friend and set out one day, laden down with targets and tin cans. I had done some shooting years before, but I hadn't touched a gun for so long that I didn't think I'd be good anymore. So I never mentioned that fact to Dick. We set up the tin cans and we agreed to take turns shooting, three shots apiece. Dick took his three and missed two. My turn. The first can went flying into the air, and suddenly I remembered everything that I had learned as a child. I wanted to show off, so I sent the cans hopping and bounding through the air and over the ground as I emptied the entire clip.

After the last shot, I looked over at Dick. My flush of triumph quickly vanished when I saw his face. He looked crushed or furious or both. Not a word was said as he put his gun back in the case and walked toward the car. That was obviously the end of target practice as far as he was concerned. All the fun and excitement of having a good time together had disappeared instantly. Not only had I beaten him badly, which would have been fine under normal circumstances, but also I took advantage of him. I didn't tell him I had shot before. I used seven shots instead of three. I got carried away with myself and made him look like a fool.

It was years before either of us touched that gun again. Both of us learned a lot from that early incident, and we applied that knowledge to future competition. We would compete only if there was to be neither a winner nor a loser and if it didn't involve one's pride or self-respect. In good fun, we could compete in anything, but as soon as a feeling of intensity started to creep in, one of us was likely to get hurt. We didn't have the ability to make our partnership a rivalry and still live happily ever after.

Along with that realization came the ability to support and to help each other grow. We found that there were always going to be areas in which only one of us excelled. I can fix things better than Dick, but he can make better scrambled eggs than I. Because he's made me feel secure as a person, it doesn't matter to me who knows his eggs are better than mine.

Dick decided to take up water skiing last summer, much to everyone's surprise. The rest of the family had been accomplished skiers for several years and Dick had never shown much interest in trying it himself. For some men it might be an embarrassing experience to learn to ski before a critical audience of 8, 9, and 10-year-olds who are all proficient. The bigger and heavier you are when you begin, the more difficult it is. And during those early tries to get that big body out of the water, you're not your most graceful. It's not an experience or an audience that most adults would relish, but Dick wanted to try and felt no embarrassment, no hangup, no sense of competition. He didn't care if he ever became as good a skier as our youngest child, or if the neighbors massed on the docks to watch the big debacle. He was having fun and wanted to learn. And I wanted him to, hoping that he'd be good someday—as good or better than the rest of us. I couldn't help thinking, "We sure have come a long way with each other since that target-practice fiasco ten years ago." And I was glad.

By eliminating the intense sense of competition, we could enjoy and appreciate each other's achievements. Through our love, we had been able to convey to each other the feeling of being cherished despite our individual shortcomings.

Perhaps one of the best ways to build that cherished feeling is through open affection. Unfortunately, an honest display of feeling between two people who have been married for some time seems to be rare today. Did you ever notice that most married couples do not sit close to each other in the car? We don't show much affection in public after we're married; it suddenly becomes awkward and almost embarrassing. "Everybody knows we're married. We don't have to show it." Not to the outside world perhaps, but how about to each other?

What is it that makes young couples sit so close together and walk hand in hand down the street? They're in love, and they don't give a damn who else knows. That's a beautiful thing, isn't it? But what happens to that feeling? Do we no longer want to be as close as possible and to show each other that there isn't anyone in the world more important?

At what point do we move over toward the car door? Is it when the first baby comes, and the car seat goes between us? Long after Junior has grown big enough to move to the back seat, we stay on our separate sides. Why don't we ever move back? Don't we want to? Is it awkward now to move over and be close again? Is it that we don't need that outward proof of love in our lives anymore? After all, we make love every other night. Isn't that enough?

For Dick and me, affection and tenderness are a constant way of pumping life into our marriage. They don't signify passion, but rather care and love. They tell us over and over that we're not ever taken for granted.

Is there any man who would not enjoy being greeted at the door with a bear hug and a whisper, "I missed you today"? And wouldn't it be nice to have your wife snuggle close and put her head on your shoulder as you are driving home from a party? Are there any women so sophisticated that they would object to being tucked into bed early and fussed over when they have a cold? To have someone run to the drugstore unasked and bring back some magazines because they're going to be in bed tomorrow?

It takes so little time for me to squeeze Dick's hand, or for him to put an arm around my shoulder for a minute, or for him to rub my neck as he passes the chair. It takes so little effort to turn a peck into a real kiss, a "Hi" into a hug. Why do we take it for granted that affection isn't as necessary after we've been married for awhile? It's one of the simplest ways of saying, "I cherish you."

23.
Creative Living

BORING, STALE, DEADLY, dull, stagnant—these are words that we use to describe books, breads, ponds, and people. Occasionally, those same words can be applied to marriage. To assure that a relationship stays alive and vital, the two people concerned have to actively look for ways to keep themselves interesting and retain the electricity in their lives together.

Remember when you two began dating and were eager to share everything? You never wanted to go home no matter how late the hour, because you had a genuine desire to learn as much as you could about each other. Time flew by. You didn't feel tired nor were you ever bored with each other. And you never seemed to run out of things to discuss.

Those were the days when all of us were actively reaching out to know each other and to be close. Did we quit growing because it took away time from our babies and from our heavy work schedule? Did we stop trying to learn about each other because we thought we knew everything—or knew enough? When that day comes in a marriage, boredom sets in and your life together can become nothing more than a sad, lonely ritual. A prison for two people tied together by familiarity, children, and possessions.

Years ago an old friend of ours, an industrial psychologist, gave us some sound advice for living. He had his own theory for mental health and a creative lifestyle, which developed as a result of his work with people. "If each of us," he passed along, "could find one new physical interest and one new mental interest each year, we'd never grow stale. Why? Because when you find something that turns you on, it will trigger all kinds of changes in your life. Suddenly you have the time to do the project that stimulates you. But you're not actually finding that time, you're making it. When you're excited about something, you get so involved that you don't feel tired by 10:00 P.M. You didn't require all that sleep before, but you had bored yourself into inaction. A year is the approximate time it takes for the novelty of a new project to wear off. Then you need something fresh to get that adrenalin pumping again."

His hypothesis made a lot of sense to us at the time. We easily could remember reacting that way. Dick had gone from one stimulating project to another for years. He'd throw himself wholeheartedly into a new activity, thoroughly enjoying the time, the late hours, and the effort involved. By the end of a year, that particular project began to lose some of its appeal. Even though he often continued working on it for a few more years, that initial zest had disappeared. Something else seemed to come along to take its place. But when we took the time to think about it, something else never really "came along." Dick made it happen. Unconsciously, he sensed a gap beginning, and he began looking for a new involvement.

I recognized that the same thing had been happening to me. There was no logical or conscious pattern, but some new interest seemed to be awakened just as I was getting bored with a current one. The range was fantastic—archeology, guitar, Yoga, horses, ecology, art, Renaissance poetry. Each had absorbed me for some period of time, and I don't ever remember being tired or having difficulty finding the time to devote to each interest. The hours flew by because I was totally engrossed in something new.

Dick and I started thinking about our friends at that time. Most of those who were really stimulating had similar patterns in their lives. And whenever we got together, they always seemed to be excited about some new activity. They were fascinating people to be with because they were alert and wanted to share their enthusiasm.

Other friends remained comfortable to be with, but they were not stimulating. We would spend a leisurely evening talking about crabgrass and children, and go home content, but not very excited. At times it was great to relax and go to a movie together, or take off our shoes and laugh about high-school days, but more and more we found ourselves drawn to the other group because they were still growing.

As Dick and I considered our own lives during that period, we could see some definite patterns that we had developed, too. Some good, but some deadly. Why were there times when one of us fell asleep after dinner every night? Invariably, these would occur when nothing was happening, or when we were so stuffed with food that any effort to move after dinner was a chore. When were we irritable? When did we get on each other's nerves? When both of us were bored, or when one of us was absorbed in a project and the other was bored and starting to get that left-out and taken-for-granted feeling. When did our job or our role become an irritant or a frustration? When we had nothing else to stimulate us, and when we knew in advance that the day held nothing promising.

We decided that the next time those dull periods rolled around for either of us, we would creatively change our lifestyle, or we would avoid them completely by a change in habit patterns. The first thing we did was to slightly alter our dinner menu. I served more salads, more light foods, and not so many potatoes and heavy desserts. It was a small change, but it made a difference in that after-dinner energy and in our lovemaking.

Dick doesn't drink but I do. When I cut back on the before-dinner cocktail on week nights, I discovered that I was much more alert and energetic in the evening. If I wanted to relax before dinner, it seemed that a bath would serve the same purpose. By rearranging my schedule, I could have everything ready for dinner in advance and sneak in a half hour in the tub with a good book just before Dick came home. A glass of wine unwound me as well as a stronger drink.

On the nights when Dick came home exhausted, he tried taking a half-hour nap before dinner. That short sleep relaxed and revitalized him. After dinner, if either of us felt drowsy, we'd go immediately for a walk or for a bike ride. We had to keep moving, otherwise it was too hard to get out of that overstuffed chair in front of the television. After a walk, we both felt wide awake again and usually thought of a multitude of things that we'd rather do instead of watch TV.

One of the things that instantly comes to mind is making love. If you're not stuffed with food, half bombed, sleepy, or hypnotized by the Tuesday night movie, you're going to make love at an earlier hour and enjoy it more. The best aphrodisiacs in the world are common sense and desire.

Time and timing are just as important to creating an exciting daily life together as they are to establishing a good sex life. To grow and to keep a marriage from stagnating, we need time alone to follow our own interests. And we need time together to keep in touch as a couple, to share our thoughts and aspirations, and to learn about each other every day of our lives. As a couple we also need time away from the children, whether it be away from home or in the house. But how are we going to get that time together when our lives already seem full? Actually, we found that we wasted a great deal of time. We just had to go searching for it with the same incentive that we looked for project time.

We found that the television and the telephone cut into a substantial amount of our family time together in the evening. A tremendous number of calls seemed to be received at our house between the time Dick came home and the time the children went to bed. Not only were these taking away valuable time from the two of us, but also from the very few hours that Dick had to spend with the youngsters each day. We decided that we were allowing too many lengthy intrusions, legitimate or not. We both felt that we could probably recapture some of that time if we both made some changes. First, we agreed that there were to be no calls during the dinner hour. Whether it was my mother, someone calling long-distance, a client of Dick's, or one of the children's friends, we were going to say, "We're eating dinner now. Can we call you back in an hour?" Most people respond well to that reply and respect family time.

If the calls came later in the evening, we tried to keep them as short as possible. We had most of the daytime hours to discuss business with clients or chat with friends. If evening calls were necessary, as they often were, we weren't going to let them drag on for an hour. Besides, there is nothing more frustrating then receiving a call in the middle of a discussion. You have little incentive to resume a talk after a half-hour telephone conversation. Either you have forgotten what you were talking about, or the person left waiting has become involved in something else.

Another way that we found to recapture time, was to cut corners. For both of us, there were loads of jobs that we could do faster or less frequently, without causing any major changes in efficiency. If both of us stopped trying to be perfectionists or ceased trying to prove something, we could save minutes which we could give back to ourselves at the end of the day. The difference between a superior and a good job meant more hours together. Our home didn't have to have everything in place all the time. The carpet didn't have to be absolutely spotless every day. But first we had to get over that what-if-somebody-drops-in compulsion. We did that by deciding which was more important—us or the slight chance that Aunt Minnie might visit tonight. We won hands down over Aunt Minnie. It's even better to fill your house with candles. When someone drops in unexpectedly, turn off the lights and burn those candles. By candlelight nobody can see whether or not your house is clean.

After finding ways to free some of our time, we had to determine what to do with it. Use it for ourselves or for the children? Did they have a right to every free minute of ours until their bedtime? Did we have a right to any time for the two of us? In the past, we and many other friends had operated on the premise that family time together was short and therefore inviolate. When our children were very young, we seemed to wait until they were in bed before starting our projects or private conversations.

As our children got older and began to stay up later, that pattern no longer seemed sensible. Dick and I had practically no time left for ourselves. Did we have a right as parents to ask for some uninterrupted time together whenever we needed it? We thought that we did. So we explained to the children that once in a while it was necessary and good for us to have some privacy, too. We weren't ignoring them or relegating them to second place. But it was important that they know that occasionally Mom and Dad also had needs and problems. They seemed to accept this explanation with great understanding.

A device that we've initiated during the past year is quiet time. It doesn't actually provide us with free time, but it prevents some jangled nerves and makes

272

that period more pleasurable. We told the children that the last hour of the day before dinner was going to be a quiet one: This was the time that all the friends who normally congregated at our house after school were to go home. No more raucous hide-and-seek games through the kitchen while I was boiling spaghetti. Our children could play, read, do homework, or whatever they wished, but the house was going to be peaceful. Usually those sixty minutes are the worst of the day for women; they're frazzled, and their youngsters seem determined to be their noisiest and their most annoying. So Dick and I decided to turn that hour into one of the best of the day. It has worked out beautifully, and the children don't seem to mind. My nerves get a brief and pleasant respite, and consequently, I'm in a much better mood at dinner and throughout the rest of the evening. Dick comes home after his hectic day to a semipeaceful haven, and he has a chance to catch a breather himself.

I found a way to adjust to the fact that Dick is a night owl and I'm not. Our best time to be close, to talk, and to make love seemed to be late in the evening. However, I either got tired and flaked out on him, or stayed up and played crabby witch the next day. What were we going to do about this situation? First, that late-night time was valuable; it couldn't always be replaced by early evening time. If I was going to lose an hour's sleep each night adjusting to Dick's timetable, how could I pick up that time? I couldn't sleep late in the morning because there were children to get off to school. Could I take a half-hour nap in the afternoon? Yes, if I was willing to give up something else in my day. What was it worth to me to stay close to Dick by being able to talk with him for several hours at night? If I decided that the time with him was more important than reading a Shakespearean play or baking cookies, then I could easily have that quick nap.

Did I have to justify that nap to myself or to anyone else? At first, I did. Napping always connoted lazy women in my mind. But it soon became apparent that I was playing the conformity game. Was it really anybody else's business except ours if I chose to sleep in the afternoon so that I could stay up until 1:00 A.M. to talk with my husband? Of course not. Nor should I feel guilty about it. It was important to us and that's all that mattered.

If the problem of two different time schedules were reversed, I don't know how we would resolve it. A woman's day is more flexible because she's her own boss. Within resonable limits, a woman can set her own schedule. But what about a man? He certainly doesn't have that flexibility in his day.

We know a few men who are fortunate enough not to have a rigid time schedule at work. One of them loves to stay up late, but still needs his sleep. He manages to sleep late in the morning and catch up on the extra hour of his workday in the early evening when his wife is busy with other things. They still have the late evening hours together. Another friend occasionally sleeps for an hour in the early evening after his young children go to bed. He gets up refreshed and alert by nine.

Is there anything wrong with a lunch-hour nap for working men? Once a week or whenever necessary, you could brown-bag it to work, eat a quick sandwich, and close your office door for a refreshing forty-five minute snooze. You're catching up on your own time—not the company's and not the family's—and you'll probably put in a better afternoon's work as a result. Or take a walk during the lunch hour. It will help clear away the cobwebs and drowsiness which often result from a lack of exercise.

We may have to give up some comfortable habits in order to grow alone and as a couple. We may have to develop a lifestyle that's something different from our friends'. But isn't our continuing relationship the most important factor in our life? There are too many needs and variables in a marriage to establish a common norm for all people. What's best for us is the only valid question. Each lifestyle is hand tailored. Mutual creative thought comes first, and if love is already present, the effort is willingly made.

Someone defined real love with three questions: What are **you** willing to give? What are you willing to do? What are you willing to sacrifice? Dick and I believe that creative living for two people can be summarized by those very questions.

24.

Little Things—How We Show Love

WHEN WE CAST our bread upon the water, sometimes we do so with a cynical eye. It would be nice to reap it back a hundred fold, but often we end up with only a handful of soggy bread for our efforts. "Well," we sigh, "that's the way the world is today. Nobody appreciates anything, so why bother to try?" But marriage is different! When two people cast that bread, take the time and make the effort to give, the benefits are always returned. Looking for creative ways to give each other a boost is the best bread casting we've ever done. It's the difference between two people existing side by side in a house, and two people joyfully sharing a lifetime.

We've talked about our need for love, respect, dignity, and support. How can we creatively answer those needs? Without saying the words, we can show by our actions that we care and want to try. Small gestures change the humdrum of daily routine to the joy of living.

Dick often buys clothes for me, which is fantastic in itself. But the fun part is the way in which he gives them to me. He creates a little ceremony that includes the whole family. Mom is led to the rocking chair in the living room and told to close her eyes. The children gather around expectantly, checking to make sure that there is no peeking. One by one, Dick brings in the pieces of a new outfit and lays them out on the couch. A blouse. "Ohh-ahh!" from the gang. Then Mom gets to peek. Eyes closed. More exclamations while the pants are brought in and placed under the blouse. "Look again, Mom." The jacket follows, and then the remaining articles until the outfit is complete. "Try it on, Mom!" they cry, and nobody moves until the modeling show is complete. The gift alone would have been exciting, but it's infinitely more so with the whole family's involvement. After that ten-minute ritual, I not only feel well loved, I also feel like the Queen of Sheba, Elizabeth Taylor, and Princess Grace rolled into one.

Sometimes, horsing around can be a way to show love, too. The pinch on the fanny while riding on a crowded escalator invariably produces a shriek, and is a shared secret as we giggle and finish that ride, with everyone staring at the woman who cried out. It turns a routine shopping trip into a romp, with me trying to look decorous and cover my flanks at the same time.

The children often pick up the aura of games and teasing from their father. They are as open and high spirited with their affection as Dick. Once in a while, our oldest boy will come charging in from school, grab me at the sink, and bend me over backward, à la Charles Boyer. "Ah, chérie. I have missed you today. Smack, smack, smack!" At that point, we usually both collapse laughing.

Special occasions—anniversaries, Mother's Day, birthdays—involve the whole family and make me feel like a very special person. Dick once organized a surprise trip for Mother's Day. I was told to pack an overnight bag and not to ask questions. Conspiracy hung so heavy in the house for two days before that, I was certain our youngest would rupture a blood vessel from the sheer effort of trying to keep such a monumental secret. Everyone knew where we were going except me.

The day before Mother's Day, Mom and her suitcase were ceremoniously ushered to the car and whisked away for a delightful weekend at a lovely resort near town. All the little details that I normally would have attended to were done: the dog had a babysitter, the newspapers and mail were being gathered by neighbors. All I had to do was to relax and to enjoy myself for two days.

Dick makes me feel appreciated by remembering to say "Thank you," and reminding the children to do the same. "Thank you for a nice dinner . . . thank you for sewing my jacket . . . thank you for getting the library book back on time for me." Those are part of my job anyway, but that thank you is special.

Compliments are frequently given around our house. It's become a habit for us to pat one another on the back when we see something good. "Your hair looks nice," has a much more positive effect on a ten-year-old than, "I see you finally combed your hair." Her face lights up, "Do you really think so?" We all want and need that extra pat once in a while to keep us pleased with ourselves. We like to know that when we do something special it doesn't slip by unnoticed.

There are many little ways of saying, "I know what makes you tick, and I want to help you keep ticking," without saying the words. For some reason, it makes me happy to have mobiles and pieces of driftwood hanging everywhere from our kitchen ceiling. I guess it reminds me of the summer trees which I miss during the long winter. I'm sure it drives Dick crazy. Since he is taller than I, something jabs him in the head or pokes him in the eye whenever he tries to make a sandwich. Does he scream, "Take those damn things down before I blind myself"? No, he's learned to duck and weave through the kitchen like a prizefighter because he knows they give me pleasure.

Understanding works visibly in many small ways. Occasionally, if my art takes me out of town, Dick is just as willing to make dinner and take care of the children for me, as I am to handle some of his responsibilities when he's traveling. It is not only done cheerfully, but also with encouragement.

We try hard never to demean each other. We feel there's never any reason to say "Shut up" to someone whom you respect. That's how we feel about each other, and that's what we try to convey to our children. Like all youngsters, at times ours say angry things. But I've heard Dick stop one of them by saying, "Don't you ever speak to your mother that way again. You can argue with her and disagree with her if you like, but there's no excuse for doing it that way. She's not one of your friends on the playground. She deserves a little more respect than that."

Not surprisingly, the children have absorbed much of this attitude through the years. They fight and argue with us often. But they've never heard either Dick or me cut each other down, so they rarely do it themselves. Not too long ago, a group of fourth graders were having an argument in our daughter's bedroom, and I heard a small voice say with great authority, "Don't talk that way in our house, We never say shut up here." I was a little nonplussed but very glad. She was absorbing the idea that her friends are people with feelings.

Dick exhibits the same respect in many other ways in our home. He always backs me up on disciplinary matters. He assumes that I've made a fair assessment of the situation and reacted according to what I thought best. He refuses to undermine me by allowing the children to go over my head to him for a reversal or a reprieve. The same thing applies to the nagging and wheedling the youngsters are prone to do. "Get off your mother's back. If she said no, that's it."

That same respect is nourished by the spoken and unspoken feeling that I am the most important person in the world to Dick. He's often told the children that and has taken the time to explain why. In addition, he shows it daily.

Children interrupt constantly—that's a way of life. But many times Dick stops them with, "Not now. I'm talking to your mother." That approach is different from yelling, "If you run in here one more time during this conversation, I'm going to brain you." Either way they get the message, but Dick's response conveys another message, too. "Your mother is important to me.

278

It's just as important to hear what she has to say as it is to thank her for things that she does for us."

There are several ways to show respect for a person and for his or her ability. One is that of giving freedom to an individual. Dick respects my judgment, and I know that whatever I decide to do around the house is fine with him. It is not because he's weak, but rather that he believes I'm perfectly capable of making my own decisions. I have a separate account for running the house along with my other responsibilities. If, in my opinion, the couch needs to be re-covered, and we can afford to have it done, I make the necessary arrangements. Most of the time, Dick will know about it beforehand because I will have remembered to mention it, but if I don't or if he's out of town, I need not wait for his approval.

An incident comes to mind that really shocked me. We desperately needed new carpeting in our living room. A carpet salesman had come to the house with samples, and while I was looking them over, we began to talk about other things. He told me that he couldn't stand to have things out of place. Although his wife was a good housekeeper, there was one thing that she did which infuriated him. She couldn't remember to close the lids on the washer and drier after using them. "Whenever I go down to the basement to work," he fumed, "there are those two lids standing open, staring at me. And I blow my stack."

"Do you ever do the laundry?" I asked. Of course he didn't, that was his wife's job. He didn't let his wife leave the door to her washing machine open if she chose to. Yet he was sitting in our living room, expecting *me* to make a decision on carpeting that was going to cost us a fortune. The irony of the situation never occurred to him. It struck me, however, and I felt very happy to be Dick's wife and not his.

Many men think women are incapable of dealing with anything consequential. I have little tolerance for such men and fortunately, neither does Dick. There have been times that he's stepped in to defend my judgment with as much vigor as he would his own. Not long ago, I left my car to be repaired after getting a verbal estimate at a reputable place. Although the service manager couldn't give me an exact estimate, he said the final bill would be within a few dollars of the price he quoted. I told him to go ahead.

When I picked up the car, the bill was a hundred dollars higher than the estimate, but the service manager insisted that the amount was reasonable. Why hadn't he called for an approval of the added expense? The more I questioned, the angrier and the more insulting he became. Finally, I wrote a check for the amount of the original estimate and left. Two days later we got a bill for the remainder. Dick decided to call the man, who was very reasonable and polite to him over the phone. "You know how these dumb broads get things all screwed up," the service manager explained. "They never know which end is up when it comes to cars and figures. She just didn't understand."

Dick explained that "she" understood perfectly, and that not only was his wife completely correct in not paying the difference, but also she was not to be considered or called a "dumb broad." Dick demanded an apology for the comment and for the shabby treatment I received. The man told Dick to go to hell and said he'd be damned if he'd apologize to any dumb broad.

Dick very calmly called Ford's regional service manager and explained the situation. What did they suggest that he do? "Absolutely nothing." They were horrified. Within two more days we had an adjusted bill and a letter of apology from the company with an explanation. Evidently this was not the first time that our particular friend had tried to run through higher bills. Nor was it the first time that he had been abusive to customers. Ford informed us that the man had been fired.

Although I was sorry that the man had lost his job, I was glad that we hadn't been cheated and that Dick had supported me. I began wondering how many men would be willing to back up their wives' judgment. How many would have agreed with another man that women are "dumb broads?" A sizable number of men would have been content to have the bill adjusted and would have let the derogatory remark slip past. But not Dick. He thought that it was as important to straighten out as to get a proper bill.

There are many creative ways that a woman can state her special message to a man. They take little time and effort, and they are meaningful.

Hearing "I love you," is as important to Dick as it is to me. I often tuck a few scraps of paper into his suitcase when he has to travel: One note between two pairs of shorts might say, "Hi, I miss you." Another one rolled up in a pair of socks that may fall out on the morning of the fourth day might read, "I'm lonesome. Come home quickly." It takes two minutes to sneak them in, but I know it's nice to get dressed in the morning feeling that someone back home is thinking about you.

Sometimes I put a plastic bag of cookies into his suitcase. Did you ever get back to a hotel room at night and feel like a snack? You want something but it's too much trouble to put your clothes back on and go down to the lobby or the corner drugstore. The treat he finds is a reminder that he's been thought of, and shows my understanding that life on-the-road is not much fun.

Another small thing which expresses love and which Dick always notices, is that I change my clothes before he comes home from the office. If it's humanly possible, I try to schedule time for a quick change before dinner. A clean pair of slacks and fresh makeup are often enough. I think about Sarah and Sam—remember the lady with the rollers and the pink bathrobe? The image works in reverse. Dick and other working men leave offices peopled with well groomed women, and the contrast can be startling if you let him see you with the full battle regalia of the day clinging to your body—green strained spinach from the baby here, a little dog hair there, and a lot of loose ends and straggly hairs everywhere. You don't have to convince him you've had a tough day with those visible signs. He'll probably take your word for it without all the

281

props. Besides, I'd rather have a man who went through life appreciating me rather than feeling sorry for me.

Not only does changing at the end of the day boost your own pride and make you feel better, it also says to a man, "I changed for you." I think many men get the impression that they take second place when it comes to grooming. The only time that some women make an effort to look nice is when they expect guests or when they're going out. That habit tells a man "You're taken for granted. The impression that I make on other people is more important that the impression I make on you."

If a woman is lucky enough to have one of those rare men who enjoys buying clothes for her, she should realize that this is one way he can show that he cares. If you whisk his choice back to the store the next day for a different color or a different style you're saying, "The thought was nice but your taste is deplorable!" When that message eventually sinks in, he's going to do the only logical thing: stop buying clothes for you.

I think there's a better way to approach the problem. Over the years, I've tried to point out things that appeal to me when I'm with Dick. Window-shopping together after a movie at night, or pointing out what you think is an attractive outfit on another person are good ways to let a man know your tastes. If Dick buys the right article in the wrong size, I quietly take it back and change it for the same outfit in the correct size. Once I had to ask the store to have the manufacturer send out another dress from the factory because the store didn't have my size. Sometimes you can alter things yourself without having to change them.

But what do you do if he buys something that you really don't like? Why not level with him? Explain why it's wrong for you and ask if he'll accompany you to the store to exchange it. Together you can pick out something different. His ego is saved by your desire to have him participate in the choice, and you won't have to wear something that makes you feel uncomfortable.

There are still other ways that a woman can find to show her love for a man. Although most men claim to abhor mush, they do enjoy a little special attention. Ask a man if he would like to do something different for his birthday and he'll invariably answer, "It's just a birthday. Let's skip the whole thing." But do something special anyway, and usually you will have a beaming little boy on your hands.

Don't always wait for an occasion to fuss. I play geisha girl when Dick is sick or when he's overtired. I enjoy doing this, and it certainly seems to give him a boost.

People automatically think about making a special effort during times of triumph. But for a married couple, I believe it is more important to do something during the times of failure. Those are the occasions when Dick needs more attention and visible signs that I really care. I rack my brain to come up with new ideas to show him how much I care. It might be laying out his pipe and slippers, baking a batch of his favorite cookies, giving him a backrub or forcing him into a bubble bath to relax. Whatever I do, it usually helps. And so does making an extra effort to jazz up our sex life during that period. When you're trying to mend a man's wounded ego there isn't a better way to say, "I desire you, now more than ever."

Dick is a mail fiend. He loves to wait for and open the mail. Five days a week the mail comes while he's at the office. Unless a letter looks as though it should be attended to or is something of great interest to me, I leave it untouched, so that he has the pleasure of opening it himself. If I do open an invitation or a letter, when I'm finished I slip it back in its original envelope. I know this practice may sound strange, but it's another way that I can say, "I know you and I love you. Here's a little present."

Making Dick feel that he comes first in my life is the best way I know of telling him, "You're loved, understood, appreciated, respected." Many women give their husbands the impression that the children come first until they become adults. Time, effort, and attention go to the children while the husband is assigned to a back seat. His wife will catch up with his needs again someday, but in the meantime, he can fend for himself. That's a dangerous attitude. Every man has needs that must be filled. After twenty years, it may be too late. He's probably learned to fill them elsewhere. Relationships have to be on-going if they are to grow. You can't pick up after years of lapse and expect everything to be the way you want it.

There are times when a woman is torn between her husband's needs and her children's. We've faced many of those, and I try to remember that Dick needs me as much as our children. Sometimes, he has to get away and he wants and needs me with him. It may be difficult for me to leave the children because of some problem they are having at the moment. At other times, it may be annoying to have to hunt for a babysitter and organize the house so that we can get out of town. But I have to keep in mind that Dick is number one in my life and he needs me now. Am I going to say "No"? Or am I going to try to be to him what he tries to be to me? Dick usually senses my struggle and when I decide to go with him, the message is clear. "You're important; not twenty years from now but today."

The most meaningful way to show Dick that I understand and appreciate him is to make our house feel like a home. I know that he loves his frayed old rocking chair in the living room, even though it looks terrible to me. Is he entitled to a grubby favorite chair? That depends on whether it's more important for the house to be our home or to be a showcase. Our house is a home, and Dick is part of that home. If he drops the papers on the floor after he reads them, I can nag and demand that they be picked up right away. Or I can let him sit in his ragged rocker and read the papers the way he enjoys reading them. Letting him have his habits and idiosyncrasies is another way of saying, "I understand you." What if his den is strewn with stacks of papers, books, records, and half-finished articles? It is his den. If that's the way that he likes it, that's the way he should have it. I would not appreciate it if he told me to rearrange my kitchen to suit his taste. We all have some habits and tastes that differ from those of our mates. Sometimes accepting them is difficult to do if we don't keep in mind that we probably have a few which are similarly irritating. I don't want to be completely changed. Some of my bad habits are very comfortable to live with and so are Dick's. And learning to live with each other's shows understanding.

We found a trait very early in marriage that both of us had to accept. And this is the distraction level of a woman. Most women hear and sense things around the house that men don't notice. It's our domain. I can be in the living room and hear the broccoli boiling over on the kitchen stove. Dick doesn't hear a thing because he's not tuned in to my world in the same way. But what happens? He's in the middle of a sentence and looks up to find me gone. Different distractions may occur five times in one conversation. Women seem to be able to cope well, but it drives men wild! Their day isn't scattered and fragmented as ours; they don't live with one ear cocked toward the baby upstairs while they talk on the phone; and they don't understand why it's impossible to finish one conversation without their wives jumping up and down.

In order to resolve the problem, Dick and I had to understand both sides of the situation. He tried to be more understanding, and I attempted to look for ways to stay attentive. Sometimes I'd ask if we could wait until later to start what I knew would be a long discussion. "Bad timing. Let's not even try now." Other times when a conversation was already in progress, I'd explain why I was bouncing up and down. Maybe it meant five-minute breaks while I looked after the broccoli and the dog (and quietly took the phone off the hook). If I took the time to explain, there was no problem and no irritation.

In addition, I had to make a conscious effort to put Dick in the number one slot. It might mean that I didn't answer two phone calls, or that I refused to let the children interrupt until the conversation was finished. If talk seemed important at that moment, then I had to make the effort to stay put. Men are not dense. Those efforts never go unnoticed.

I can also let Dick know that he's appreciated and respected at home by praising him in front of our friends and his associates. No man likes to blow his own horn, but it's nice when somebody else does it for him. It's a good feeling to know that someone else is proud of you and pays attention to what you say. "She really was listening when I told her about the new plan I had for the production department."

If your man wants to take you along on a business trip, he is telling you, "I love you." For me, it also means that Dick wants me with him; he appreciates me enough to give me a break from the routine; and he understands my needs and knows that now would be a good time for it.

It also says a great deal to him when I do go along, and I do make an effort to remember that I'm on a vacation while he's on a business trip. I have to keep that in mind in order to refrain from demanding that he spend more time with me. I have to curb myself from complaining when his evenings may or may not be busy, with or without the inclusion of me. I have to show that I understand and appreciate what he's there for and that I am willing to support him in any way. Even dinner with Mrs. Gump!

It would be nice to help with clients if possible. It doesn't take too much extra time or effort to learn something about their city so that I can talk about it intelligently. Besides, people usually enjoy showing off their hometown. You might have to listen to an hour's praise of the new cultural center, but would you rather be home? No! And if I spend a night sincerely listening and participating, the Gumps are going to love me. So is Dick.

I try to be aware of what Dick's day entails on a business trip. It keeps me in better touch if I do have to spend time with the Gumps as well as affording me a clearer understanding of Dick's work. Why be a liability if you can be an asset? Moreover, it gives Dick the feeling that I really am interested—which I am.

Although it is very hard to do, I make an honest effort not to spend any more money than is necessary on a business trip. If I buy a new wardrobe for the trip to San Francisco, I feel as though I'm taking advantage of Dick. He was considerate enough to squeeze me in on this trip and that in itself is sufficient. Otherwise, your mate is going to think, "This trip is going to break me. It's the worst idea I ever had." The name of the game is not Take Me Along; it's Take Me Along, Again. The only way to get invited in the future is to show that you appreciate his thoughtfulness.

What we've attempted to do in this chapter is present some of the small things that make up our lifestyle. Most of them are actions rather than words. Love, appreciation, understanding, respect. Very seldom is it necessary for any of these words to be spoken aloud. It becomes apparent that each of us is interested in finding every possible way to make life better for the other. All those thoughtful minutes, those small gestures, and those pats make life together a joy to live.

25.
Please Touch

MOST PEOPLE HAVE a difficult time with the concept of touch. Beginning in early childhood we are taught to remain aloof; we are warned not to touch or allow ourselves to be touched by others. We're cautioned to say, "Excuse me," if we accidentally bump into someone. If we stand close to another person on a bus or at a store counter and our bodies touch, we quickly beg that individual's pardon. If we find ourselves in a crowded elevator, we try to keep our shoulders from touching the persons next to us. We are advised not to point at people because it's rude; not to let a person know we are looking at him because it would allow that individual access to us.

Recently, a friend told us about an incident he witnessed in our local supermarket that illustrates this conditioning very clearly. Two toddlers, strangers only moments before, were standing in an aisle hugging each other and enjoying their newfound friendship. Suddenly one of the busy mothers noticed, and jerking away her child, she whispered sternly, "You could get germs." There were probably more germs on the handle of the grocerycart than on the other child! But how very effectively that mother planted the seed of future noninvolvement in her son.

Years ago when our children were very small and Christmas was still a magical time, a group of my friends were discussing the various Santas who were installed in the local department stores and shopping centers. Where was the best place to take their children to see any of the Santas. She remarked, "You never know which of those old birds might have T.B.!"

In a similar fashion, we've been conditioned emotionally not to touch others. "Don't get involved. Don't reveal your inner thoughts to anyone because that person might recognize your weakness and use them to hurt you." We're afraid and we're embarrassed to put our arms around another human being in need because it's emotionally and physically awkward. We might embarrass him or ourselves. Or we might be rejected. Then what would we do?

I believe that we are becoming less comfortable with our own bodies and with others' as the world evolves. Today there are so many people and so little space, that a great number of us have become more withdrawn to cover our awkwardness. We have become frustrated because we feel it is safer to be untouchable mentally and physically, yet others continue to crowd in on us with their wants and their needs. Their bodies and voices are everywhere, and they are trying to touch us. But we don't want to be touched. We try to escape.

In the United States, we spend millions of dollars each year on tranquilizers and sedatives because we can't cope with the multitudes around us and the aloneness of our bodies and minds. Many people seem to be asking drugs to do what human nature should be doing—easing our troubled minds, soothing us so that we can sleep, and calming us when we are frightened or tense. Drugs will never fully resolve the problem for us. We turn to them as a substitute because we cannot turn to other people. We haven't learned how to be *in touch* with each other.

Consider the child's instinctive cry of need or of pain. By the time that child reaches manhood, he's no longer able to cry out, "I am hurt; I am lonely." Because his needs are locked inside him, a woman is prevented from responding with the natural and comforting gesture of touch. Maybe this is why many people are not very good lovers. Loving entails revealing all your fears, dreams, and weaknesses to another. And to make such disclosures is frightening for those of us who have been taught. "Don't touch; don't be close." Getting close to others physically and emotionally is probably the surest path to happiness, but many of us are not up to taking the risk. So we continue to grow out of touch with each other.

It must be possible to reverse this cycle of withdrawal if reaching out to touch others was a natural response in childhood. We may have to unlearn all the prior conditioning that has kept us apart from each other. Dick and I know that it's possible to reach out to another and have that person reach back. Without fear, in our own relationship, we have been able to penetrate each other with an emotional touch. We're inside one another as a life-giving inner touch, which is so strong a force that it can be felt in the same way as a physical touch is felt. And when we reach out to each other to touch with love, we are giving the very gift of life.

This concept of life-giving touch reveals itself as a dual support. We become healers of one another and creators of one another.

When we take on the role of healers to our loved ones, we're sensitized to recognize sickness as we have never done before. The lonely, the ridiculed, the frightened are in need of our healing touch as much as the person with influenza. Healing through love is primarily a sensitive touch. It can assume many forms: a glance, a tone of voice, a facial expression. Or it can be our presence even if we can say or do little to help another. Many times when I've been hurt or angry or troubled by my own problems, Dick has sat quietly with me, not talking. Just his presence was comforting.

As we learn each other's needs more deeply, this healing touch becomes a gift that we can give each other. A man who is experiencing a particularly trying period at his job, often needs his wife's touch in lovemaking more than when things are going well. In one major area of his life, his ego may be crumbling; he may be doubting his ability as a man and provider. She can soothe his ego and reflect his manliness back to him. By frequently initiating lovemaking, during what she senses to be a difficult time, she is in essence saying, "You are potent, you are needed, and you are desired." What greater gift can she give him than her healing touch?

Creative touch, on the other hand, is primarily a growing process. We never stop growing. We always need to be nourished. If the process of becoming (of reaching our full potential) is to continue, we have to be fed love, support, and freedom throughout our lives. Creative love between two people allows for a constant loosening of the bonds that tie us down or hold us back.

As we grow there will be times of pain, times of failure, and times of frightening change. When these occur, we need a creative touch to nourish and support us. A man may have an opportunity to advance his career if he moves to a new city. His wife's support at this point can be the encouragement that says, "Wherever we are together, our family can make a good life." Contrast this approach with what we frequently see happening. The wife throws up every obstacle to the move, bemoans the loss of her friends, and generally makes the poor man feel like a bastard for tearing the family away from the only place on earth where they could be happy.

A creative touch means freedom—to grow, to be allowed to become what you want. Once you have been unshackled, it's impossible to settle for a possessive or constricting type of love. Dick and I are very different from one another in almost every respect—personalities, interests, taste in music and movies. Most people would say we are a mismatched couple. And yet, our marriage is very solid and harmonious. Its success is based on freedom.

We started our relationship with a deep reciprocal love and the ability to communicate. Many couples have those same initial advantages, but flounder as they try to become carbon copies of one another in their interests, ideas, tastes, and activities. This is a natural tendency because they want to be together as much as possible. We tried, too, but soon accepted that we could never grind down all of our differences to similarities. Dick would never love listening to the Beatles blaring from the stereo, or be happy working with paints, palette, knives, and easels. Nor would I be comfortable deeply and actively involved in social and civic activities.

We both knew instinctively that some things cannot be made to happen, and so we did not force ourselves to find things to *do* together. Instead, we almost unconsciously established a lifestyle which allowed each one to do his own thing, but with one vital qualification—we maintained that touch of support. We encouraged and freed each other to do what we each did best, and retained the link of communication. Rather than finding ways of curtailing Dick's community activities, I let him grow and develop as far as he was able. Instead of stopping me from following my creative instincts, he encouraged and shared my enthusiasm, and he soothed my failures. That was and is what binds us together so tightly—the excitement of sharing the thoughts and feelings that make the other person tick.

Being freed by love to grow is an intoxicant. The more freedom you have, the more you want to grow. We have frequently been criticized for living this freedom. People don't understand that it is possible to love and let your loved one go at the same time. For us, it wouldn't be love without that; it would be confinement. Among our circle of friends, often we see one partner growing and the other resenting this growth as he or she is left behind. Because the latter cannot or will not share in the growth, he or she does everything possible to restrict it. To us, this is not creative, supportive love. It is selfish love, binding and shackling.

We have never played golf together, but we have spent countless hours while Dick probed, questioned, and tried to understand what I thought and felt about the kind of music I love, where it takes me, and what I become when I listen to it. We have never gone to the ballet together, but we've spent hours, talking on the telephone when we're far apart. I can honestly share and feel Dick's sense of accomplishment when a planned community project that means health, growth, and innovation becomes a reality. He knows as well as I can transmit it, what happens in my heart and soul when I sit on a mountaintop alone and watch a sunset. He will never feel the same things in the same way, but he knows what I feel as closely as if he were within me. In the truest sense, he has helped to create me as I am today, and I him. His touch has supported and nourished me in so many ways through the years as I have tested my wings and tried to fly. We two will continue to grow, because growth is natural, and we will remain free.

Perhaps the greatest task for those of us who love

is not to gather enough information to make us proficient in bed, but rather to discover and to remove those obstacles which prevent us from fully giving ourselves to another physically and mentally. We must reach the level where we can allow another to touch us in every aspect of our lives without fear. We need to be drawn out of ourselves more and more, to form a relationship of deepening mutual trust in which defenses can be peeled away because they are no longer needed. Once that trust has been established, we have the freedom to go outside of our own relationship and touch others in a healing or a creative way. A recent occurrence illustrates this freedom.

Dick and I have a male friend whom both of us love in every sense of the word. In the past year he has gone through a troubled and difficult time. He kept a great deal inside himself, but he reached a point where he needed a shoulder—a hand, a touch —some sign that he wasn't alone. One night, when the three of us were together, he suddenly began to cry. Immediately, I walked over and put my arms around him and held him tightly until the need passed. I did not pause to consider what he would think or what Dick, who was sitting in the room, would think. It never entered my mind that Dick would question my motives and feel jealousy, or that it would be an awkward situation. What hit me with greater impact later was that it wouldn't have mattered if Dick had not been there. I wouldn't have hesitated to do exactly as I had done if he had been 1000 miles away on a business trip. Why? Because Dick knows me fully, and he is intimately in my presence no matter how many feet or miles separate us, or whether another physical body comes between us temporarily. His inward touch is a part of me, no matter what the circumstances.

It made me think of something that Dick had said previously to the wife of one of his business associates. He was on a business trip without me, and he was being entertained by a small group of people. At the end of the evening, this woman said, "I really wish I could have gotten to meet Paula. It's too bad that she couldn't be with us." Dick simply answered, "But she was with us. She's with me wherever I go." The woman was stunned while he tried to explain. I'm sure she wondered for a moment if she had an ESP crackpot on her hands. We don't know if she ever understood what Dick was trying to say, but I knew immediately when he related the incident to me. We're a part of each other, somewhere deep inside where it can't be untangled. The touch is always present.

The strength of our relationship is built on mutual trust and mutual understanding, so that no explanations are necessary if either of us has to step beyond the small conventions of our society. The neighbors may lift their eyebrows when they see me with my arms around another man, but I know what I'm doing. More important, Dick knows what I'm doing. He supported me, nourished me, and freed me to grow. His touch has freed me to touch others without fear.

26.
Epilogue . . . June, 1976

In 1974, *Loving Free* became a best seller, startling everyone—most of all us. Its success had a devastating impact on our lives during the first year: individually, as a couple and as a family. It forced all six of us into a growth spurt that would have seemed impossible five years earlier. It changed our relationship with family members, friends and acquaintances. Some were enhanced; others were destroyed. The drastic difference between the local and the national reactions to *Loving Free* gave us the equivalent of an instant Ph.D in human nature. Success brings out the best and the worst in people.

We were totally unprepared. Overnight, we went from a family quietly going about its business, spilling milk and loving each other, to a family under a microscope. Suddenly, our business was everyone's business. There were widespread rumors that we were divorcing; that we made love in bathtubs filled with Jello (and that green was our favorite flavor); that our children were juvenile delinquents—or worse; that Dick's business was collapsing; that we wrote the book only for the money; that we were moving to Hollywood; that I was having an affair; he was having an affair; I was a lesbian; he was a homosexual and we had all been arrested on morals charges.

People evidently believed the rumors. A few children were forbidden to associate with ours. Two parents requested that their children be moved as far away from ours as possible in the classroom. (You can never tell what kind of contamination will occur in second grade!)

For months, a storm of controversy raged in our own community. Were the McDonalds perverted, crazy or what? "How could they do it? . . . Why would they do it? . . . And how come we never knew!" In the winter of 1974, *Loving Free* replaced Watergate as local cocktail party and bridge table conversation. There was a plague of anonymous and obscene phone calls. Unsigned letters arrived with clippings from the local papers: horns were drawn on our pictures; "fit for shit" scrawled across the copy. The McDonald family was villified, praised, fought over and generally talked to death—but never to our faces. For the first time in our lives, we knew what it felt like to be hated. Hatred is a difficult and unexpected emotion for an ex-prom queen and an ex-fraternity president to cope with. It scared the hell out of us.

If that was a shock, we were equally unprepared to be idealized . . . the perfect couple . . . the perfect family. Nationally, the reaction to *Loving Free* was exactly the opposite of our local reaction. Letters and phone calls poured in. "You've saved my marriage . . . You wrote the story of my life . . . I always thought I was the only one who had these problems . . . If I'd only had your book twenty years ago . . . You've touched me deeply . . . changed my life . . . Thanks." How does a person reconcile that with hate mail? Interspersed between the local heavy breathers, who clogged up our phone line for months, were the kind calls from Toronto, New York and Florida saying, "If you're ever in my city . . ."

With the exception of five suburban communities, *Loving Free* was being acclaimed by psychologists and marriage counselors across America and widely recommended in colleges and universities. But those five suburbs contained our friends and neighbors. Virginia Satir, one of the country's top family therapists wrote, "I would like to see this book in the hands of *all* therapists, family life educators, family members, school personnel, the clergy and all college and high school students." It was prohibited in our local high school, and a local Catholic college almost lost a department head in the war over whether to invite us to speak on campus. We, and the book, were both finally banned.

The reaction of the Catholic Church was equally inconsistent. On the same Sunday morning in two local churches, *Loving Free* was touched upon in the weekly sermons. One clergyman praised the book and urged that it be read. The other denounced it and warned his parishioners to avoid "that book." The National Catholic Reporter recommended *Loving Free* to all young married couples, and it is being widely used in other dioceses. In the diocese of Milwaukee, there has been only silence. Officially, the book does not exist here.

While the whispers were still circulating in Whitefish Bay about the perverts who lived down the block, we were being inundated with requests to speak, to appear on talk shows around the country . . . as instant experts on marriage. If you detect a case of galloping schizophrenia developing, you're so right. We clung to each other and wondered who we really were. We clung to our close friends and worried together about the kids. "Move," one of them said. "Get as far away from here as you can before they tear you to pieces." "No, dammit! We're not going to let them drive us out of here." Besides, where would we go? We careened through the ups and downs of each day and lay in bed at night wondering which side was right. Were the McDonalds perverts or saints? And could we survive the monster we had created?

We did. It's been two years since that unsettling first winter when our anonymity was lost. Time to let the dust settle and put things in perspective. Time enough to realize that we're neither saints, perverts, the perfect couple or anything more than we were before. A little different perhaps because we've all had to grow up some . . . in order to survive.

The most difficult transition was mine. Moving overnight from the role of artist and homemaker to signing autographs and giving speeches was not a comfortable change. Nor was being thought of as controversial. Baking 20,000 chocolate chip cookies is hardly preparation for living in a spotlight and being pointed at while shopping. Dick managed the initial success and controversy better than I did. The business world and politics had been a training ground for him that I had missed. He dragged me, kicking and screaming, through that period of change with a depth of patience that had never been tapped before. He pushed me onto stages and in front of microphones when my mouth was so dry from sheer terror that my tongue scraped. "You can do it," he kept saying, and I believed him.

We held on tightly to each other through the storm of admiration and hostility. The nitpicking that followed was almost harder to cope with. "Change your hair . . . It's too long . . . too short. . . . Your image is too mod . . . too stuffy . . . What you said was wonderful . . . boring . . . profound . . . trite . . . Come to our party . . . Drop dead!"

297

It's hard to keep your head straight when it's being bombarded from both sides, but it's infinitely easier for two people than for one. Being forced to question who we were, we painfully rediscovered we were only us. It was all we had that was real. Our own was the only authentic image we could project. We stopped listening to others and learned to work more closely. There were rocky times. There were new experiences to deal with like balancing two egos when sharing a microphone. We argued, criticized, complimented each other, talked each new experience through and eventually became a stronger team. At home and at work.

The kids helped to keep us on an even keel. If we hadn't maintained a normal family life, notoriety would surely have sunk us all. Success can be a confusing experience. It can do wicked things to your head . . . but not in a house full of teen-agers. Thank God for their perspective. Thank God they are rarely impressed by their own parents. I think the moment I realized how lucky we were was after our initial appearance on the *Phil Donahue Show*. It was our first nationwide television appearance and had been taped a week earlier. We had never had the opportunity to see a playback of ourselves before, and I was more nervous watching at home than I had been doing the show. The family sprawled all over the den, and for once, there was dead silence and no arguing during the commercials. When the program ended, Eric (then 14) stretched and said, "Well, you certainly wasted your time for an hour." My shoulders slumped. "Oh my God! Were we that bad?" "Naw, you were good, Mom, but I've been trying to get you to sew the new patches on my jeans for a week. You had a whole hour to do it while you were watching the show." That's perspective! Kids don't care how many copies of a book are sold as long as you don't run out of peanut butter.

How did the children themselves survive the notoriety? Everyone asks. They handled it far better than their parents did in the beginning. Youngsters don't allow much that occurs in the adult world to interfere with their lives. Nor do their friends. While the controversy tossed Dick and me back and forth, they played basketball. Those children who were forbidden to see ours, refused to let adult opinions destroy their friendships. They went underground but didn't abandon their friends. Notoriety? It lasts about a day on the playground. "Hey, I hear your mom and dad wrote a dirty book." "No, they wrote a book about marriage." "Oh . . . want to go to the Dairy Queen after school?" That was about it in their world. Because of what they saw happening in our world, though, all four drew closer together, sympathizing and helping us and each other when necessary. We relied on each other through the turmoil and learned a great deal in the process.

Our families were unanimously supportive: grandparents, parents, brothers and sisters. A few were shocked at first, but all backed us up, gave comfort when needed and never once said, "You shouldn't have done it." One of my favorite stories concerns the call to Dick's mother in Arizona after his parents read the manuscript for the first time. "Well," she said, "I must say you rattled my teeth a little with the sex section of the book, but I think I'm going to survive. Your father is still looking around for his teeth on the floor, but he'll find them eventually." He did and went on to become one of the biggest boosters of *Loving Free*.

Perhaps my 85-year-old grandmother best symbolizes the love, trust and pride evident throughout the family. When I called to tell her about the book, the loss of our anonymity and the local problems, she immediately wanted to read it for herself. I sent her a copy, Air Special, and waited, more than a little concerned about her possible reactions. A return call came two days later. "Paula," she said, "it's a beautiful book." "But Gramma, you just got it. Have you read it already?" "No, my glasses are broken, but I took a magnifying glass and read the whole front cover and the whole back cover. It's a beautiful book!" Her unquestioning support was typical of the entire family's.

Our friends were not as consistent. Community disapproval is one quick way to separate true friends from the horde of casual acquaintances most of us have. The handful of people who really care about you aren't easily swayed or threatened by what others may be thinking or saying. Sometimes our close friends were forced to fight for us because few people had the courage to attack us directly. For that we will always be grateful. One of the unexpected bonuses of writing *Loving Free* was discovering that we were almost completely correct in predicting who would stand by us and who would walk away. Only a few people surprised us.

The widespread rumors about our personal lives, especially those concerning our alleged divorce, shook even the staunchest of friends. Fortunately, most of them had the courage to question us directly and assure themselves that things were as they had always been. These close friends then took upon themselves the task of counteracting the "established facts." A few friends never asked. They passed on the gossip about our private lives and our children's supposed activities, embellishing each story in the process. I suppose it's only human nature to want to be "in the know," to be considered an authority, but it's always disappointing to be maligned by a friend of fifteen years. It's even more discouraging to see your children attacked without cause. Fortunately, the kids never heard much of what was said about them until later, and they were stronger then.

For that we owe a great debt of thanks to the teachers at their local grade school and high school. Some of them went out of their way to support the children, openly and directly during a difficult period. It was of no benefit to them to step into the middle of a fracas; they simply acted out of a genuine concern for fairness and the well being of four youngsters.

Within a few months, local reaction began to

polarize. The viciousness continued (and some still remains today), but supporters began to emerge too. One neighbor made calls to the PTA representatives of neighboring communities where we were scheduled to speak at a joint session. She tried to convince them to cancel our speech on the grounds that we were unfit parents. Other neighbors grew tired of the tirades and began to defend us. "Enough is enough. They couldn't possibly be capable of everything they've been accused of." The support grew stronger as the charges became wilder. Several neighbors later apologized for taking part in the gossip before reading the book and set out to correct any myths they had furthered.

A few interesting sidelights happened within the local business community. Dick has been a company president for many years. Naturally there was interest and speculation on the book and the controversy within his profession. One competitor took it upon himself to visit each of Dick's clients shortly after publication, blatantly hawking new business. His approach: "Surely you wouldn't want to ge associated with a man who wrote a dirty book." Not a single client flinched or changed allegiance. The rumor that we only wrote *Loving Free* for money had a more insidious effect though. Some clients, suppliers and even a few employees actually did believe that we had written the book because Dick's business was failing. Or that after writing it, Dick would soon leave the company for greener pastures or instant retirement. We still chuckle over the Hollywood contracts and the millions we've supposedly received. We stop chuckling when we recall the awkwardness, fear and concern that it caused within his own company for a time.

There have been many aspects of *Loving Free* to grow up to. With all that has occurred, good and bad, where are the McDonalds today? Just about where we were when you finished the final chapter a few minutes ago. A little wiser, a little stronger perhaps, and closer than ever. Are we the perfect family as some people have tried to portray us? Of course not. We're still the people next door. We haven't moved to Hollywood or into exile. We still drive a dented Volkswagen bus loaded with kids who drip Baskin-Robbins ice cream on the seats. The dog still attacks the garbage and eats houseplants at every opportunity. And at least two of the kids stage a rerun of World War II each lunch hour. "Who scratched my Elton John album? Mother, kill him!" (Donny and Marie Osmond, they're not.)

Dick has learned to put away his own shoes, but we still argue over getting the bills paid on time. I've learned that dustballs don't have a thing to do with my status as a good person, wife or mother. But I still compulsively wipe counters. He's learned to make his own chocolate chip cookies. Have we really changed in the past three years? No, but we have grown a few more steps together.

We've learned that it's impossible to live up to everyone's expectations of us. We've had to adjust to life within an uncomfortable spotlight. It's hard to scold your kids in the middle of Sears' paint department when five people are watching to see what you'll do. It's hard to have a normal disagreement at a party when you know people are waiting to pounce later. "See? I told you they weren't happy." But we are happy. That doesn't mean there are never arguments or that the children never get out of line.

Part of the growing up process has been learning to ignore our many images and remembering to be ourselves. It isn't always easy, but the learning process has been good for us. We understand each other at a deeper level. We're more excited than ever before about the vast possibilities we have together; marriage, family, friends and work. If *Loving Free* brought us a mixed bag of experiences, the scale has definitely tipped toward the positive side.

We've discovered that there's no end to the road ahead—for us or for anyone else. There are only different hills to climb each day, unexpected bends to round. We keep trying to make the road smooth, but it isn't always easy. Six of us work together at the smoothing process, though, and that makes all the difference.

Writing Free . . . About the Authors

Loving Free was originally published under the pseudonyms Jackie and Jeff Herrigan. Between publication of the hardcover edition and the first Ballantine Paperback edition in 1974, Paula and Dick McDonald were forced to discard their anonymous identities.

Dick is president of McDonald Davis & Associates, an advertising agency in Milwaukee. Paula, an artist, is president of PADE Productions, Inc., and is currently involved in writing full-time. Together they produce a nationally syndicated five-minute daily television and radio show on family living, and a thrice weekly syndicated newspaper column. Both enterprises use the title *Loving Free*.

The McDonalds appear regularly as guests on numerous radio and television talk shows across the nation and frequently address organizations, conventions and campus groups on the subject of communication in marriage. *Loving Free* has been widely praised by psychologists and marriage counselors for its common-sense approach to everyday problems. It is currently a required text at thirty-four universities and colleges.

Paula and Dick live in the Milwaukee suburb of Whitefish Bay with their four children: Eric 16, Kelly 15, Randy 14, and Mike 11.